Legalines

Editorial Advisors:
Gloria A. Aluise
Attorney at Law
David H. Barber
Attorney at Law
Robert A. Wyler
Attorney at Law

Authors:
Gloria A. Aluise
Attorney at Law
David H. Barber
Attorney at Law
Daniel O. Bernstine
Professor of Law
D. Steven Brewster
C.P.A.
Roy L. Brooks
Professor of Law
Frank L. Bruno
Attorney at Law
Scott M. Burbank
C.P.A.
Jonathan C. Carlson
Professor of Law
Charles N. Carnes
Professor of Law
Paul S. Dempsey
Professor of Law
Jerome A. Hoffman
Professor of Law
Mark R. Lee
Professor of Law
Jonathan Neville
Attorney at Law
Laurence C. Nolan
Professor of Law
Arpiar Saunders
Professor of Law
Robert A. Wyler
Attorney at Law

ANTITRUST

Adaptable to Fifth Edition of Areeda Casebook

By Jonathan Neville
Attorney at Law

THE barbri GROUP

HARCOURT BRACE LEGAL AND PROFESSIONAL PUBLICATIONS, INC.
EDITORIAL OFFICES: 111 W. Jackson Blvd., 7th Floor, Chicago, IL 60604

Legalines

REGIONAL OFFICES: Chicago, Dallas, Los Angeles, New York, Washington, D.C
Distributed by: **Harcourt Brace & Company** 6277 Sea Harbor Drive, Orlando, FL 32887 (800)787-8717

SERIES EDITOR
Deirdre E. Whelan, J.D.
Attorney at Law

PRODUCTION COORDINATOR
Sanetta Hister

FIRST PRINTING—1998

Printed in the United States of America.

SHORT SUMMARY OF CONTENTS

TABLE OF CONTENTS AND SHORT REVIEW OUTLINE

HALF PRICE BOOKS®

Half Price Books
1835 Forms Drive
Carrollton, TX 75006
OFS OrderID 39490745

Thank you for your order, Main Address!

Thank you for shopping with Half Price Books! Please contact Support@hpb.com. if you have any questions, comments or concerns about your order (113-7233375-2071466)

Visit our stores to sell your books, music, movies games for cash.

SKU	ISBN/UPC	Title & Author/Artist	Shelf ID	Qty	OrderSKU
S388937704	9780159004050	Legalines: Antitrust : Adaptable to Fifth ... Neville, Jonathan	20--16--5	1	

SHIPPED STANDARD TO:
Main Address
800 Avondale Ave
1033836-1-0028
Grandview Heights OH 43212
j1gg094j97htty5@marketplace.amazon.com

ORDER# **113-7233375-2071466**
AmazonMarketplaceUS

I. INTRODUCTION

A. COMPETITION AS AN ECONOMIC MODEL

1. **Introduction.** The antitrust laws are founded on the basic concept that competition is an appropriate means of social control. The primary statutes are the Sherman Act, the Clayton Act, the Robinson-Patman Act, and the Federal Trade Commission Act ("FTC Act"). As will be seen, these acts set forth legislative policies without much specificity. Judicial construction has been the primary means of implementing the statutory policies. To effectively deal with antitrust issues, however, a lawyer needs a fundamental understanding of economics.

2. **Basic Economic Concepts.** The objective of the antitrust laws is to control private economic power in order to protect competition. To understand why, it is helpful to acquire an elementary understanding of the price system and how it works in allocating available resources among competing uses.

   a. **Demand.**

      1) **Introduction.** "Demand" is an indication of the quantity of a particular good or service that buyers will purchase in a given time period at a particular price, all other factors remaining stable (*e.g.*, consumer tastes, prices of other goods, etc.).

      2) **The demand curve.** The following graph is known as a "demand curve." It indicates that generally the higher the price of a good, the less (in quantity) buyers are willing to purchase.

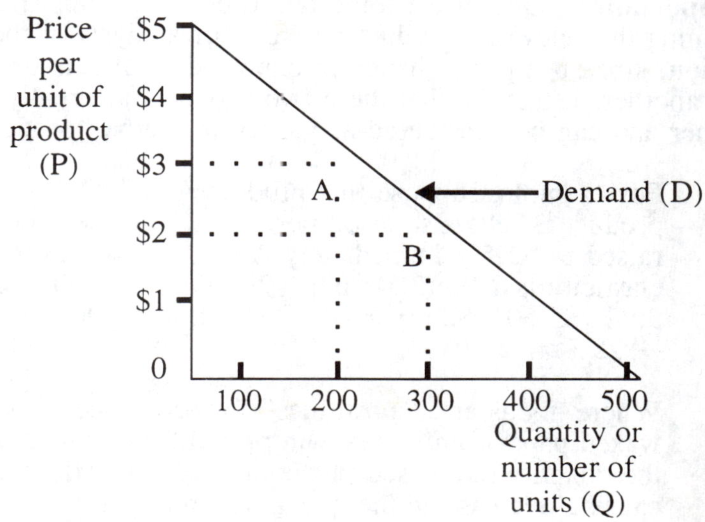

(Figure 1)

Note that at \$3 per unit, buyers will take 200 units; at \$2 per unit, they will take 300 units.

b. **Demand elasticity.**

1) **Definition.** Elasticity of demand is the percentage change in the quantity of goods taken, divided by the percentage change in the price of the goods.

2) **Purpose.** Elasticity of demand tells us what change in quantity purchased takes place when there is a change in the price.

So, for example, in the graph (*supra*), consider elasticity when the price moves from $3 per unit (point A) to $2 per unit (point B). Percentage change in quantity (300 - 200 = 100 ÷ 200 x 100% = 50%) divided by percentage change in price ($2 - $3 = -$1 ÷ $3 x 100% = -33 1/3%) = 50% ÷ -33 1/3% = -1.50. Thus, elasticity (which is negative in this case since price went down) equals -1.50.

3) **Determining factors.** One of the major factors that determines elasticity of demand is the availability of close substitutes. For example, if there are many close substitutes for product A, then there is more likely to be a large change in the quantity purchased if the price of A is raised (here demand is said to be very "elastic"). If, however, there are no close substitutes, then there may be little or no change in the quantity purchased even when the price of A is raised (and demand is said to be "inelastic").

c. **Cross-elasticity of demand.**

1) **Definition.** Cross-elasticity of demand is defined as the percentage change in the quantity of product A that is purchased, divided by the percentage change in the price of product B. Thus, cross-elasticity is designed to measure the interaction in the quantity purchased of two products when there is a price change in one of them.

2) **Importance.** One of the important uses of cross-elasticity is in determining the relevant "product market" for analysis of the effects on competition, since if a price change in one product affects the quantity purchased of another, it may be that these two products are really substitutes for each other and can be considered as part of the same "product market."

a) For example, suppose that product A sells 200 units at $2 per unit; product B sells also at $2 per unit. Suppose product B's price is raised to $2.50; immediately A's quantity goes to 300 units. Cross-elasticity is 2.00 (300 units - 200 units = 100 ÷ 200 units x 100% = 50%; $2.50 - $2.00 = $.50 ÷ $2.00 x 100% = 25%. Thus, 50% ÷ 25% = 2.00).

b) Where goods are "substitutes" for each other (*e.g.*, cellophane and waxed paper), an increase in price of one will cause an increase in the quantity purchased of the other good; a decrease in price will cause a decrease in the quantity purchased.

c) Where goods are "complementary" (such as tires and cars), then an increase in the price of one (cars) will cause a decrease in the quantity purchased of the other (tires); but a decrease in the price of one (cars) will cause an increase in the quantity purchased of the other (tires).

d. **Costs.**

1) **Opportunity costs.** When an economist speaks about "costs," he generally has in mind "opportunity" costs rather than historical accounting costs. Thus, for the economist, the cost of producing product A is the value of the goods (*e.g.*, product B) which the resources used in producing product A could have produced when put to their best alternative use. Thus, opportunity cost includes within it an element of what to the layperson would be "profit."

2) **Historical costs.** Most analysis done in the antitrust cases concerns "historical costs," or accounting costs. These are the costs that are familiar to the layperson.

3) **Fixed costs.** Assume that a manufacturer has a plant and is producing product A. Some of the costs of manufacturing may be called "fixed costs." These are the costs that do not vary over the short-run (*e.g.*, investment in equipment, plant, etc.).

   a) Thus, if fixed costs are $1,000 and 100 units are produced, then each unit has fixed costs of $10.

   b) But if the number of units goes up to 200, then the fixed costs per unit go down to $5.

4) **Variable costs.** Other costs vary with the number of units produced. For example, material costs go up as the number of units produced increases. Other elements included in variable costs are labor, power used, etc.

5) **Average costs.** Average cost is the total cost to produce a given quantity of product (which includes fixed costs and variable costs) divided by the number of units produced. Thus, if 100 units are produced, and fixed costs are $500 and variable costs are $500 (total costs being $1,000), then average costs are $10.

   a) **Average fixed costs.** Take total fixed costs and divide by the number of units produced. $500 – 100 units = $5 per unit.

   b) **Average variable costs.** Take total variable costs and divide by the number of units produced. $500 ÷ 100 units = $5 per unit.

   c) **Short-run average costs.** The average costs for producing a product vary with the level or quantity of output. The "short-run" is the period of time when the size of the plant stays the same. Thus, "short-run average costs" is the average cost curve for levels of production while the firm uses the same plant.

   The short-run average cost curve is generally a U-shaped curve. This represents the fact that it is generally inefficient to produce a small output in a large plant (due to the average fixed costs/unit). Therefore, increasing the quantity of output toward full plant capacity causes the average cost curve to fall. At some point, however, the curve begins to go up again (as the average cost per unit goes up). This is explained by the Principle of Diminishing Returns, which indicates that as one factor (size of the plant) is held constant, the productivity of the various inputs at some point begins to decrease, resulting in the average cost per unit beginning to increase at some level of production.

d) **Long-run average costs.** Over time, the firm may vary the size of its plant. Thus, the long-run average cost curve is the average costs for quantities of output over the long term, as the firm varies the size of its plant.

Generally the shape of the long-run average cost curve is also U-shaped. This indicates that the larger the size of the plants, the more efficient they are (due to economies of scale). After some point in size, however, the average costs bottom out and begin to climb, due to diseconomies of scale (*i.e.,* at some point the administrative problems, etc., of larger size begin to cut down on cost efficiency).

6) **Marginal costs.** Marginal cost is the incremental increase in cost due to the production of one more unit. For example, if it costs $100 to produce 50 units but only $101 to produce 51 units, then the marginal cost is $1.

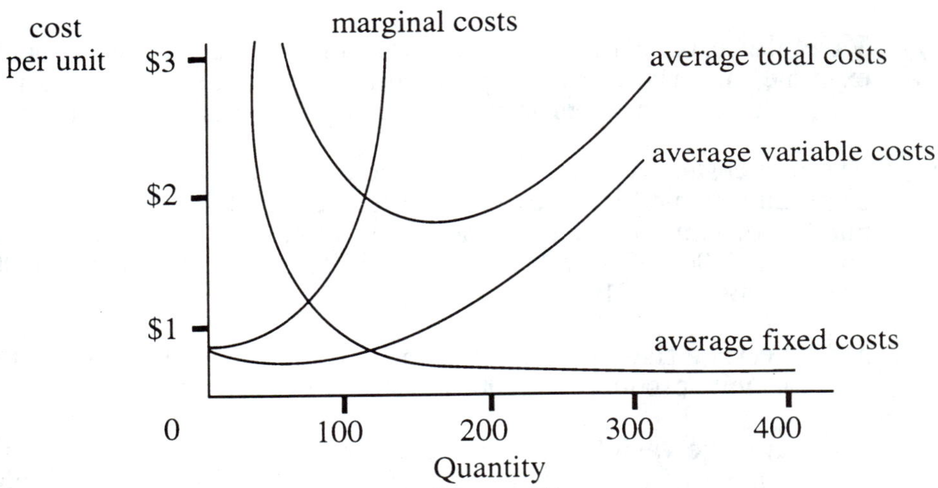

(Figure 2)

e. **Revenue concepts.**

1) **Total revenue.** Total revenue is equal to the price of the product times the number of units sold, assuming that all units are sold at the same price. So if the product price is $1 and 100 units are sold, there is total revenue of $100.

2) **Average revenue.** Average revenue is equal to total revenue divided by the number of units sold. Thus, average revenue equals price where all

units are sold at the same price per unit. For example, if there are 100 units sold and total revenue is $100, then average revenue equals $1. Note also that the average revenue curve is the same as the demand curve, since the demand curve tells how many units would be sold at any given price.

3) **Marginal revenue.** Marginal revenue is the change in total revenue for each unit change in output. Thus, if total revenue at 100 units is $200 (and average revenue is $2), but in order to sell more than 100 units the firm must drop its price to $1.99, then marginal revenue equals $.99 ($1.99 x 101 = $200.99 - $200.00 = $.99).

3. Market Structure.

a. **Introduction.** Much of the analysis in antitrust cases concerns the structure of the market, since the behavior of competitors in a market depends to a substantial degree on the market structure. "Structure" is primarily a function of the number of competitors in the market.

b. **Monopoly.** Monopoly exists where there is only one seller of a product. Several factors must be assessed to determine whether the condition of monopoly is anticompetitive (*i.e.*, one where the monopolist has control over price), such as the barriers to entry, whether there are substitutes for the product that meet the needs of most users, etc.

c. **Perfect competition.** A perfectly competitive market is one where there are many sellers, such that no single seller has control over the price of the product. For such a market to exist there must be no barriers to entry into the market, all sellers must be offering a uniform product, and all buyers and sellers in the market must have perfect knowledge of market conditions. The "perfect competition" model exists in relatively few situations, but it is helpful as a theoretical model in assessing the competitiveness of markets.

d. **Oligopoly.** This is a market with a small number of sellers; each contributes a significant amount of the quantity produced so that it can affect price. Note that firms in this type of market structure are very sensitive to what every other firm does.

4. The Price System.

a. **Function of the price system.** There are always more demands for economic goods than there is supply of those goods. In other words, we are constantly faced with the problem of limited or scarce resources. Thus, these resources must be allocated among competing uses. This is the function of the price system If demand for a product is great, then price goes up as consumers bid for the product. In turn, more resources are devoted to this product and away from other products that are desired to a lesser extent. Thus, the price system has allocated scarce resources among competing alternative uses.

b. **The effect of market structure on the functioning of the price system.**

1) **Perfect competition.** The theory is that under perfect competition there is an optimal allocation of resources.

a) Every firm in the market will attempt to maximize its profits by producing that quantity of goods so that marginal cost equals the marginal revenue received, but never to the point where marginal cost exceeds the marginal revenue.

b) And since in a perfectly competitive market, each firm can produce and sell as much product as it wants to, it will produce only to that point where marginal cost equals marginal revenue (or price).

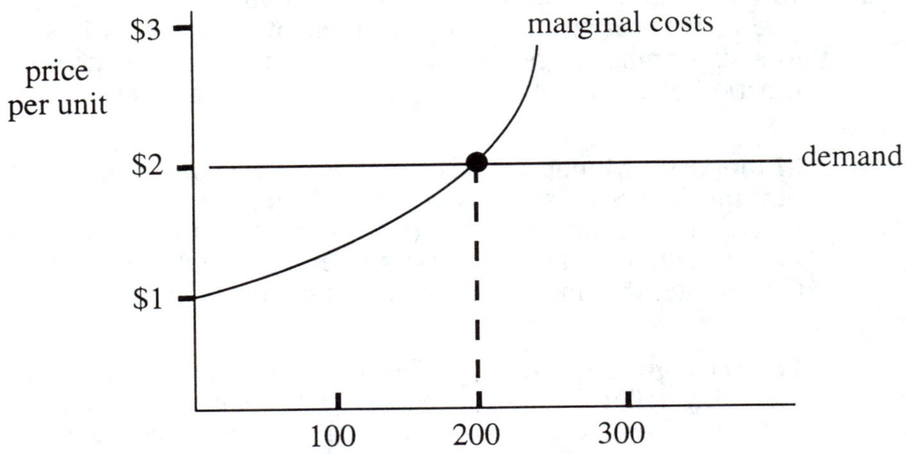

(Figure 3)

Thus, in Figure 3, the firm will produce 200 units since at that point marginal cost equals price and profit is maximized (*i.e.,* no more net revenue can be earned by selling even one more unit).

c) If firms in the market are making a "profit" (*i.e.,* if price is in excess of average cost), then other firms will enter the market due to the demand and begin to supply the demand. With increased supply, price will be driven downward to the point where price equals average cost. At this point, resources are being optimally allocated among competing uses (the price of the goods equals the marginal cost of producing them and no further resources will be committed to production of this product since the marginal cost of producing an additional unit would exceed the price received).

2) **Monopoly.** In a monopoly, resources are not optimally allocated since, at the price which the monopolist charges to receive unusual profits, more resources would normally flow into the production of the product if perfect competition existed.

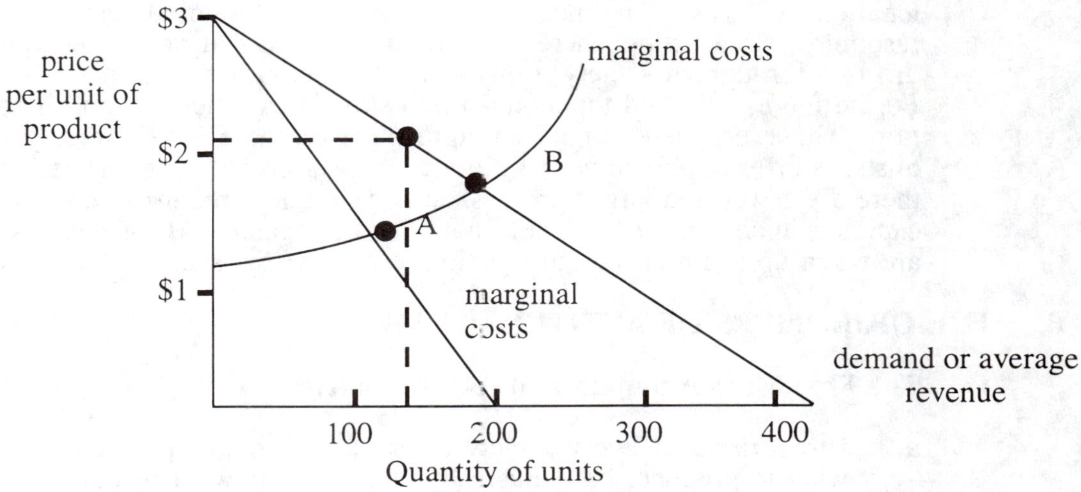

(Figure 4)

a) The more the monopolist sells (the greater the supply in the market), the lower the price that he receives. For this reason, marginal revenue is less than the price (average revenue). Thus, the monopolist could receive more revenue by selling more units of product, but the profits would be less because the price for all of the goods would be lowered.

b) Thus, the monopolist will produce to the point where marginal revenue equals marginal cost (point A) since this will maximize profits. Here, prices (set by the demand curve) will exceed marginal cost.

c) Society, on the other hand, would be better off if the firm would produce at the level of point B, since here marginal cost equals price or average revenue.

3) **Oligopoly.** Oligopoly is difficult to analyze since the behavior of each firm cannot be analyzed simply with regard to demand and firm costs. The behavior of all the other firms in the market must be considered as to what they would do if the firm changed its price or production.

a) In general, the belief is that oligopoly tends to result in a more restricted output than would exist in a perfectly competitive market.

b) It is also assumed that there is price rigidity in an oligopolistic market since the firms will tend to meet the price decreases of one firm. There is not the same tendency to meet price increases (unless there is a situation of "price leadership" by one firm in the industry or a uniform view of needing to increase prices due to increased costs).

c) Typically, oligopolists tend to compete on the basis of product differentiation (through product features, brand identification, etc.) rather than on the basis of price.

5. **Competition as an Ideal.** The model of perfect competition is cited as an ideal on the basis of the theory concerning the optimum allocation of resources. In addition, there is the political value that power remains diffused throughout society in many small units rather than in a few. Furthermore, it is said that competition stimulates efficiency and innovation. However, there is not total agreement on these issues among economists. For example, some believe that innovation is better fostered where there are fewer and larger units, since development requires enormous capital, which small firms could not afford to spend. All of these issues are taken up again at the introduction to each of the sections which follow.

B. THE OBJECTIVES OF ANTITRUST LAW

1. The Free Market System and Its Alternatives.

a. **Introduction.** Every society faces the "economic problem"; *i.e.,* what to produce, how much, by whom, using what resources, for whom, and for what reward? Economic theory is involved in attempting to answer these questions. Obviously, different models have been developed to answer these questions.

b. **The framework of the law.** Whatever model or system is adopted, the role of the law is to provide a framework in which private transactions can take place in accord with the values, decisions, and theories of the model.

c. **The free enterprise system.** The United States has adopted the so-called free enterprise or free-market system. This system relies principally on the interactions of individuals acting in their own self-interest, where prices set by supply and demand determine what is produced.

d. **The antitrust laws.** Every "society" or "government" interferes to some extent in the free play of market forces. The United States government is no exception. The antitrust laws provide the legal framework in which the United States economic model operates. They indicate when the free play of market forces will be interrupted in favor of other values.

e. **Antitrust conflicts with economic theory.** In some instances, antitrust laws agree with economic theory (*i.e.,* individual self-interest may take the form of restrictive arrangements which impede the operation of a free market and the antitrust laws intervene to reestablish a competitive market). In other instances, the antitrust laws may disagree with certain goals of the economists (*e.g.,* economies of scale may indicate that the most efficient producer would be a monopolist in a certain industry, but the antitrust laws in pursuit of other objectives may impede the ability of any firm to monopolize the market).

2. **The Main Objectives of Antitrust Law.** There are four main objectives of antitrust policy:

a. **Achieving desirable economic results.** These results are of four main kinds:

(i) Efficiency in the use of resources;

(ii) Progress, or the growth of total output and output per person;

(iii) Stability in output and employment; and

(iv) An equitable distribution of income.

Results (i) and (ii) may be affected by antitrust policy, while (iii) and (iv) are affected more by other factors.

b. **Promoting competition.** The relationship between fostering competition as an end in itself and economic performance is not clear. Market power here discussed has to do with purely business transactions (market relationships). The arguments for competition involve having decisions made by impersonal market forces and the existence of alternatives. Few markets in the United States are purely competitive in this sense.

c. **Fair conduct.** In antitrust, "unfairness" simply means that similarly situated parties are treated dissimilarly; also, unfairness is considered in relationship to the concept of market power and the objective of maintenance of competition.

d. **Limiting big business.** Another objective may be to limit the social and political power of big business and increase that of small business.

e. **Conclusion.** These policies are not always complementary. However, at the time the Sherman Act was passed, they may not have been seen to be conflicting (*i.e.*, the Act was aimed at breaking up the power of large trusts that were monopolizing and charging the public high prices and driving small businesses out of the market).

f. **Comment.** Antitrust law is difficult and confusing, largely because the decisions reflect disagreement over which of these objectives to affirm.

C. HISTORICAL BACKGROUND OF THE ANTITRUST LAWS

1. **Introduction.** The United States began as a nation of small farmers and shopkeepers. There was a distrust of largeness and concentrations of power. Yet by the end of the 1800s, the large corporation had become well-established. This transition frightened the populace, and when the common law and the law of the states seemed inadequate to deal with the large aggregations of power, federal laws were enacted. The history of antitrust may be divided into three phases:

a. **The founding period (1890 to 1914).** This was the era of the most vigorous enforcement and the highest public sentiment against big business.

b. **The period of neglect (1914 to 1937).**

c. **The period of revival (1937 to present).** Antitrust is sustained in this period by the same impulse that began it—a consensus that bigness should be checked. The economic issue is whether antitrust seriously interferes with the requirements of economic efficiency.

2. **The Antitrust Model of Competition.** It seems clear from case law that the antitrust model of "competition" is competition in some rough-and-ready, popular sense. It is not competition in the sense of the economist's theoretical models. Distrust of concentrated power has usually been the basis for the antitrust model; it is for this reason that enforcement is left to the courts and not to an administrative agency. If antitrust is close to any economic model, it is that of the market where perfect competition occurs: price competition among many competitors, with no restrictive agreements or practices among the competitors, and no power in any one competitor to determine price.

D. THE COMMON LAW BACKGROUND

1. **Introduction.** It is important to remember that the common law of trade regulation followed no consistent pattern; it changed back and forth in emphasis over time, and there were several conflicting lines of cases. Furthermore, many of the precedents cited by the founders of modern antitrust policy were in fact statutes and cases against certain restrictive practices that interfered with others who already had protected trade positions.

2. **Early Law on Monopolies.**

a. **Grants by the King.** Originally, a monopoly was a license or patent granted by the King that gave an individual the exclusive power to buy, sell, trade, or deal in a particular commodity.

b. **Guilds.** In addition, many towns in England had guilds set up by the local artisans to protect their home markets from outsiders.

c. **Precedent against monopolies.**

1) **Case law.** The first case which can be cited in the common law against monopolies is *Darcy v. Allin*, 77 Eng. Rep. 1260 (K.B. 1603). Here, the court held that a patent granted by Queen Elizabeth giving the plaintiff the sole right to manufacture and import playing cards was a monopoly and void. The action was defended by members of the local guilds (themselves monopolies). The rationale of the decision was that the monopoly granted by the Queen interfered with others already carrying on their trades.

2) **Statutory law.** The Statute of Monopolies was passed in 1623. It voided all monopolies granted by the King. However, the local guilds and monopolies granted by Parliament remained untouched.

3. **Contracts in Restraint of Trade.**

a. **Covenant not to engage in a trade.** In *Dyer's Case*, 2 Hen. V. (Eng. 1415), the plaintiff sued the defendant on a note; the defendant argued that his contract with the plaintiff provided that if he refrained from practicing his trade in the town for six months, the debt would be forgiven. He had so refrained. The court held that a contract in which one party covenants not to engage in a lawful trade is void.

b. **Starting a competing business.** In the *Schoolmaster Case*, 11 Hen. IV (Eng. 1410), the plaintiff ran a grammar school in the town; the defendant started a new school, and consequently the plaintiff could not charge as much as before, so the plaintiff sued. The court held that there was no cause of action.

c. **Covenants not to compete.**

1) **Introduction.** The law against restraints of trade continued to develop in the area of covenants not to compete, basically involving two areas:

a) Covenants given pursuant to the sale of a business; and

b) Covenants given by an employee to an employer pursuant to an employment relationship.

2) **The rule of reason.** Eventually, the courts developed a "rule of reason" under which such restraints of trade could be upheld if they were "reasonable." The factors considered:

a) **Restraint must be ancillary.** The courts held that the restraint had to be ancillary to some lawful transaction, such as the sale of a business (where the seller agreed not to compete with the buyer). "Naked" restraints of trade were presumed illegal.

b) **Limited.** The restraint had to be limited and not total. Typical limitations included time, scope of prohibited activity, and locality.

c) **Reasonable effect.** Furthermore, the courts required that the restraint be "reasonable." That is, looking at its effect, it must not pose an unreasonable threat to the public interest.

d. **Modern common law.**

1) **Restatement (Second) of Contracts sections 513 through 515.** The Restatement essentially adopts the "rule of reason."

a) A contract is in "restraint of trade" when its performance would limit competition in any business, or restrict the promisor in the exercise of a gainful occupation. [Restatement (Second) of Contracts §513]

b) But contracts in restraint of trade are not illegal per se. They are illegal only if they are "unreasonable." [Restatement (Second) of Contracts §514]

c) The factors to be considered in determining "reasonableness" are as follows:

(i) Is the restraint greater than required for the protection of the person on whose behalf it is imposed?

(ii) Does it impose an undue hardship on the person restricted?

(iii) Does it tend to create, or have the purpose of creating, a monopoly, controlling prices, or artificially limiting production?

(iv) Does it unreasonably restrict the alienation or use of property?

(v) Does it contain a promise to refrain from competition and yet is not ancillary to sale of a business or an employment contract?

[Restatement (Second) of Contracts §515]

2) **The law in different jurisdictions.** While the Restatement may be said to be the law in most jurisdictions, there are many states which have taken differing positions. For example, California has made covenants by employees not to compete or accept competitive employment illegal, whether reasonable or not.

4. Combinations and Conspiracies in Restraint of Trade.

a. **Definition of combination.** Concerted action among competitors which tends to restrain trade or create a monopoly is a "combination."

b. **Factors considered in analyzing combinations.** At common law, the following factors were considered in determining the legal effect of various types of combinations:

1) **Nature of the market.** The nature of the market in which the combination occurs, whether for services or commodities.

2) **Business relations.** The prior business relations between those that are part of the combination.

a) Were they competitors? How?

b) Did they operate in the same geographical area?

3) **The object of the combination.** Was it to share market information? To fix prices?

4) **The form of the combination.** Formal contract? Informal agreement? Trade association? Cross-licensing of patents? Merger?

5) **Other factors.**

a) Degree of control the combination had over the industry; strength relative to nonmembers.

b) Conditions in industry prior to the combination.

c) Methods used to establish the combination.

d) Effect of the combination on competition, prices, etc.

e) Treatment of the public by the combination.

c. **Conspiracy.** Some actions at common law were brought under a theory of "conspiracy." A conspiracy exists when two or more persons combine for an objective which is contrary to the public interest or which violates some law. "Combinations" and "conspiracies" will be compared *infra.*

E. THE LEGISLATIVE HISTORY OF THE SHERMAN ACT

1. Basic Provisions of the Sherman Act.

a. **Section 1—restraints of trade.** "Every contract, combination in the form of trust or otherwise, or conspiracy, in restraint of trade or commerce among the several states, or with foreign nations, is hereby declared to be illegal."

b. **Section 2—monopolization.** "Every person who shall monopolize, or attempt to monopolize, or combine or conspire with any other person or persons, to monopolize any part of the trade or commerce among the several states, or with foreign nations, shall be deemed guilty of a misdemeanor, and, on conviction thereof, shall be punished by fine not exceeding fifty thousand dollars, or by imprisonment not exceeding one year, or by both said punishments, in the discretion of the court."

2. **Background on the Act.** It seems clear that the Sherman Act was passed in response to public feeling against the trusts (*e.g.*, Standard Oil). Hatred of monopoly was a long in-grained attitude of most Americans; there had even been strong support for a provision in the Bill of Rights outlawing monopolies. In the 1880s, the trusts grew quickly and were blamed for many abuses.

Opinion differed on how to deal with the trusts. Economists generally felt that both competition and combination should be part of the economy. Lawyers generally felt that the common law permitted combination in some instances and prevented it in others. It was thus the common point of wanting to eliminate the "excesses" that allowed opposing viewpoints to get together. A federal solution was required since the states did not have the needed power to regulate interstate commerce.

As to the exact meaning or intention of the Act, this may be impossible to fully sort out. The following indications seem relevant:

a. Most of the members of Congress were proponents of a "private enterprise system" based on the principle of "full and free competition."

b. Most thought that the common law supported such a system.

c. They had little understanding of the economic theory underlying such a system, the implications of economic theory, or the conflicts of economic theory with their own common understanding.

d. They believed that the ultimate beneficiary of the theory they supported was the consumer. But they also believed that they were protecting the small business owner from the ruthless practices of large, predatory trusts.

e. The most specific instances they had in mind against which the Act legislated were trusts which possessed market power akin to monopolies and used such power to control prices, divide markets, and drive competitors out of business.

f. There is evidence that there was expectation that the courts would change and enlarge upon the original meaning of the Act as the conditions of the economic environment changed.

F. THE INSTITUTIONAL FRAMEWORK OF THE ANTITRUST LAWS

1. **Principal Antitrust Statutes.** At present, the following are the main sources of federal antitrust law:

a. **The Sherman Act.**

1) **Restraints of trade.** Section 1 makes unlawful "every contract, combination . . . or conspiracy in restraint of trade" in interstate or foreign commerce.

2) **Monopolizing.** Section 2 makes monopolizing, attempting to monopolize, or combining to monopolize unlawful.

3) **Enforcement.** The Sherman Act is enforced by the Antitrust Division of the Justice Department and also in actions by private parties. There are also criminal penalties, injunctions, and damage actions.

b. **The Clayton Act.**

1) **Price discrimination.** Section 2 prohibits price discrimination between different purchasers where the effect thereof is to

substantially lessen competition or to tend to create a monopoly in any line of commerce.

2) **Restrictive arrangements.** Section 3 prohibits sales on condition that the buyer not deal with competitors of the seller (*i.e.,* tie-in sales, exclusive dealing arrangements, and requirements contracts) where the effect may be to lessen competition substantially or to tend to create a monopoly in any line of commerce.

3) **Mergers and acquisitions.** Section 7 prohibits mergers where the effect may be to lessen competition substantially or to tend to create a monopoly in any line of commerce in any section of the country.

4) **Interlocking directorates.** Section 8 prohibits any person from being a director of two or more competing corporations, any one of which has capital in excess of $1 million.

5) **Enforcement.** The Clayton Act is enforced by the Antitrust Division of the Justice Department, the Federal Trade Commission, and by private parties. There are no criminal sanctions for violation.

c. **Federal Trade Commission Act.**

1) **Unfair methods of competition.** Section 5(a) prohibits unfair methods of competition in commerce and unfair or deceptive acts or practices in commerce.

2) **The Federal Trade Commission.** The Act created the Federal Trade Commission ("FTC"), an administrative agency.

a) **Enforcement of the Act.** The FTC has exclusive authority to enforce section 5 of the Act.

b) **Other antitrust laws.** In addition, the FTC has concurrent powers to enforce the Clayton Act (with the Justice Department and the courts). The FTC is not responsible for enforcing the Sherman Act, but the courts have held that section 5 is broad enough to cover any acts that might be found to be illegal under this Act as well.

c) **Other responsibilities.** In addition to its antitrust duties, the FTC is charged with enforcement of a number of other important areas: labeling, packaging, deceptive advertising, etc.

d. **Amendments to the basic antitrust laws.** There have been a number of important amendments to the basic antitrust laws.

1) **Robinson-Patman Act.** This act amended section 2 of the Clayton Act on price discrimination.

2) **Resale price maintenance.** The Miller-Tydings Act of 1937 amended section 1 of the Sherman Act to exempt from the antitrust laws resale price maintenance agreements between a manufacturer and his dealers, if such agreements were valid under state law. The McGuire Act of 1952 amend-

ed section 5(a) of the FTC Act to permit the states to enforce resale price agreements against both signers and nonsigners of such agreements.

e. **Specific industries.** There are a number of industries which have statutes which affect competition in the industry, and agencies which enforce these statutes. Some contain exemptions from the general antitrust laws; *e.g.*, the Federal Aviation Act (the FAA controls competition over air routes) and the Federal Communications Act (the FCC regulates competition for radio and television outlets).

2. **Jurisdiction Requirements of the Antitrust Laws.**

a. **The "interstate commerce" requirement.**

1) **The Sherman Act.** Sections 1 and 2 cover restraints of commerce among the several states or with foreign nations, and monopolizing any part of commerce among the several states or with foreign nations.

a) **Historical background.** In *United States v. E.C. Knight Co.*, 156 U.S. 1 (1896), the Court held that the manufacture and production of goods was not "interstate commerce," even though the goods might be destined for shipment in interstate commerce.

b) **Modern law.** Subsequent decisions have indicated that where some activity has a "substantial economic effect" on interstate commerce (although it occurs in intrastate commerce), the jurisdictional requirements have been met.

(1) **De minimis exception.** There appears, however, to be a de minimis exception. That is, where the effect on interstate commerce is insubstantial, there may be no jurisdiction under the Sherman Act.

(2) **Effect of the restraint.** There is an unsettled issue as to whether the restraint itself must affect interstate commerce, or whether it is sufficient if some of defendant's activities affect interstate commerce (*e.g.*, the local branch office of a national company engages in local antitrust violations).

2) **The Clayton Act.** The original jurisdictional language of the Clayton Act was narrower than the Sherman Act. It applied only to ***corporations directly engaged in interstate commerce***. However, in the Antitrust Procedural Improvements Act of 1980, Congress expanded the Clayton Act to apply to ***persons*** engaged in commerce ***or in any activity affecting commerce***.

3) **The Robinson-Patman Act.** There are specific jurisdictional requirements in this Act indicating that the discriminating seller must be engaged in interstate commerce and at least one of the two sales on which the claim of discrimination is based must be across state lines.

4) **The Federal Trade Commission Act.** The language of the FTC Act is similar to that of the Clayton Act.

b. **Foreign commerce.**

1) **Statutory coverage.** International law recognizes that conduct outside a country may be subject to the laws of the country. Thus, it has been held that the Sherman Act applies to extraterritorial activities where: (i) the intent of the parties is to affect commerce in the United States, and (ii) the conduct actually does cause effects in the United States.

2) **Conflict with foreign law.** Application of United States law to firms doing international business can create conflicts with the policies of foreign governments. Hence, in some situations it is necessary to accommodate these sources of conflict.

a) Thus, where the defendant's foreign activities are required by foreign law, this activity will not be condemned by United States antitrust law.

b) And unless there is a clear congressional direction to the contrary, the antitrust laws will not be applied where they conflict with settled principles of international law.

3. **Remedies Available Under the Antitrust Statutes.**

a. **Criminal penalties.**

1) **Statutory provisions.** There are limited criminal penalties provided for.

a) **The Sherman Act.** Violations of sections 1 and 2 are crimes. Individuals can be fined up to $100,000 and imprisoned up to three years. Corporations can be fined up to $1 million.

b) **The Robinson-Patman Act.** Section 3 of this Act provides for criminal penalties in the case of certain intentional price discrimination violations.

2) **Corporations.** Officers and others responsible for criminal antitrust violations by corporations may also be found guilty of crimes (punishable by a $5,000 fine and imprisonment of up to one year).

3) **Enforcement.** The Antitrust Division is responsible for undertaking criminal prosecutions.

a) **Discovery.** The Antitrust Civil Process Act authorizes the Justice Department to issue discovery demands to any person who possesses material relevant to an antitrust investigation, prior to the institution of any civil or criminal proceeding.

b) **Indictment.** Normally, criminal charges are instigated through the grand jury process.

b. **Equitable relief.** The government and private parties can obtain injunctive relief to prevent and restrain antitrust violations. [See Sherman Act §4; Clayton Act §§15, 16]

1) **Remedies available to the government.** The scope of equitable remedies available to the government is extremely broad. For example:

a) **Restraints.** Acts or conduct can be restrained.

b) **Divide or dispose of assets.** A company can be required to divide or dispose of certain lines of business, assets, etc.

c) **Granting licenses.** A company can be required to grant patent licenses to potential competitors.

2) **Private parties.** There is some question as to whether the remedies available to private parties are as broad as those granted to the government. For example, divestiture may not be available to private parties.

3) **Consent decrees.** The government will often agree with a private party defendant to a "consent decree," which is a settlement of an antitrust action where the defendant acknowledges the violation and accepts the determined remedy (without court trial).

a) **Court supervision.** The court must agree to the decree.

b) **Motivation for consent decrees.** Such consent decrees are very important, since a judgment against a defendant may be used as prima facie evidence against the defendant in private litigation, whereas a consent decree cannot be so used.

4) **Intervention.** Private parties may seek to intervene in government antitrust suits. Federal Rule of Civil Procedure 24 allows intervention on two bases: of right, and with permission.

a) **General rule.** Generally, the courts have denied parties the right to intervene.

b) **Exceptional situations.** In exceptional situations, the United States Supreme Court has allowed nonparties to intervene. For example, in *Cascade Natural Gas Corp. v. El Paso Natural Gas Co.*, 386 U.S. 129 (1967), the government suit charged that the defendant's acquisition of a pipeline company was an attempt to strangle competition in the sale of natural gas in California. The State of California and the Southern California Edison Co. (the state's largest industrial user) were allowed to intervene "as a matter of right" in the case.

c) **The Federal Trade Commission.** In FTC cases, intervention is purely discretionary with the FTC.

c. **Private actions for damages.**

1) **Treble damages.** Section 4 of the Clayton Act provides that "any person . . . injured in his business or property by reason of anything forbidden in

the antitrust laws (*i.e.*, for a violation of either the Sherman Act or Clayton Act) . . . may recover threefold the damages by him sustained, and the cost of suit, including a reasonable attorney's fee."

2) **Prima facie case.** Section 5(a) of the Clayton Act provides: "A final judgment or decree heretofore or hereafter rendered in any civil or criminal proceeding brought by or on behalf of the United States under the antitrust laws to the effect that the defendant has violated said laws shall be prima facie evidence against such defendant in any action or proceeding brought by any other party against such defendant under said laws . . . as to all matters respecting which said judgment or decree shall be an estoppel between the parties thereto; provided, that this section shall not apply to consent judgments or decrees entered before any testimony is taken."

   a) Criminal or civil judgments of fine or injunction brought by the government qualify under this section. Actions brought by the government for damages do not.

   b) Nolo contendere pleas do not qualify, and the courts are split over guilty pleas.

   c) FTC decrees do qualify.

3) **Injury to business or property.** A plaintiff can recover lost profits, increased costs incurred, or decrease in value of property due to antitrust violations.

   a) **Actual business.** The injury must be to an actual business. However, a plaintiff may show that he was actually prepared to go into business. A mere intent to do so is not enough.

   b) **Standing limitation.** There have been limitations placed on who can sue. (*See* the discussion of "proximate cause," *infra.*) For example, a shareholder of an injured company cannot sue as an individual shareholder in his own capacity for loss in the value of his stock in the injured company.

4) **Certainty of damages.** The plaintiff must prove that there have been actual damages. Beyond that, the courts have been willing to estimate the amount of damages on a "reasonable basis" even where uncertainty exists as to the exact amount.

5) **Proximate cause.** There is a proximate cause requirement; *i.e.*, the injury to the plaintiff must be the direct result of the defendant's action. So, for example, the lessor with a percentage lease was not permitted to sue for injury to a lessee which reduced the lessee's business and the rent paid. [Hoopes v. Union Oil, 374 F.2d 480 (9th Cir. 1967)]

6) **Antitrust injury.** Plaintiffs must not only prove causation; they must also prove an antitrust injury, meaning an injury of the type the antitrust laws were intended to prevent. [Brunswick Corp. v. Pueblo Bowl-O-Mat, 429 U.S. 477 (1977)] This requirement applies to equity suits also; *e.g.*, a suit for an injunction. [Cargill v. Monfort, 479 U.S. 104 (1986)]

7) **Defenses.**

a) **The "passing on" defense.** The defense that the plaintiff passed on his increased costs to his customers is theoretically available to the defendant accused of an antitrust violation. However, in practice this defense is not available, since the United States Supreme Court has indicated that the defendant must show that the plaintiff raised his price in response to and in the amount of the overcharge and also that the plaintiff's margin of profit and total sales did not decline. [Hanover Shoe, Inc. v. United Shoe Machinery Corp., 392 U.S. 481 (1968)]

b) **Unclean hands.** Earlier decisions allowed the defense that the plaintiff had participated in the same antitrust violation or some other antitrust violation; a more recent decision, however, held that a franchisee involved in the antitrust violation of the franchisor could sue the franchisor. [Perma Life Mufflers, Inc. v. International Parts Corp., 392 U.S. 134 (1968)] Where the plaintiff is involved but had the power to resist the involvement in the violation, the result may be different.

c) **Statute of limitations.** There is a four-year statute of limitations on private damage actions. [Clayton Act §4B]

(1) **Commencement of period.** The period normally commences from the date damage is suffered. There is an exception made in situations where the defendant fraudulently conceals the facts of the violation; in this case the statute begins to run when the facts are discovered.

(2) **Tolling of the statute.** When the government brings a suit, the statute is tolled.

d) **Public injury.** The older cases indicated that an action could be brought only where the injury to plaintiff could also be shown to have injured the public generally. This is probably no longer a requirement.

d. **Cease and desist orders by the FTC.** The FTC can issue cease and desist orders against violations of sections 2, 3, 7, and 8 of the Clayton Act or section 5 of the FTC Act (which might include violations of the Sherman Act). Such orders are reviewable by the United States Courts of Appeals.

4. **Exemptions from the Antitrust Laws.**

a. **Introduction.** There are numerous exemptions from the general antitrust laws. In most instances, these exemptions are very narrowly construed.

b. **Government-owned enterprises.** One instance of exemption exists where the government owns an enterprise, such as the Post Office.

c. **Agricultural organizations.** Section 6 of the Clayton Act provides that "Nothing contained in the antitrust laws shall be construed to forbid the existence and operation of . . . agricultural, or horticultural organizations, instituted for purposes of mutual help and not having capital stock or conducted for profit, or to forbid or restrain individual members of such organizations from lawfully carrying out the legitimate objects thereof; nor shall such organizations or the members thereof be held or construed to be illegal combinations or conspiracies in restraint of trade under the antitrust laws." The Capper-Volstead Act extends this exemption to capital stock agricultural cooperatives also.

d. **Regulated industries.** There are a number of "regulated industries" that have exemptions from the antitrust laws.

1) **Air carriers.** The Civil Aeronautics Board ("CAB") is given extensive regulatory powers under the Federal Aviation Act over foreign and domestic airlines, including the power to regulate methods of competition, to set rates, etc. By implication, approved agreements or transactions subject to CAB authority are exempt from the antitrust laws.

2) **Interstate rail, motor, or water carriers.**

a) **The Interstate Commerce Commission.** The Interstate Commerce Commission ("ICC") has extensive powers under the Interstate Commerce Act over motor, rail, and ship common carriers in interstate and foreign commerce. Many agreements and transactions which affect competition (*e.g.*, mergers, rates, etc.) are subject to ICC approval and, if approved, are in general exempt from the antitrust laws.

b) **The Federal Maritime Commission.** The Shipping Act of 1916 gives the Federal Maritime Commission ("FMC") the power to approve agreements between water carriers relating to rates, etc. These agreements are exempt from the antitrust laws, at least where they require the ongoing supervision of the FMC.

e. **Export trade associations.**

1) **The Webb-Pomerene Act.** This Act exempts from the Sherman Act those agreements or acts done in the course of export trade by an association of producers formed solely for the purpose of engaging in export trade. However, such activities are not exempt if they have the effect of restraining trade within the United States, or if they artificially or intentionally enhance or depress prices in the United States.

2) **Purpose of the Act.** The purpose of the Act was to allow American competitors to group together in order to compete with foreign cartels in the world market. That purpose became largely obsolete when foreign cartels disappeared and American firms began to dominate international trade. Also, it is impossible in reality for a group of producers with any degree of market power to agree on the amount they will export without affecting the level of domestic supply and the level of domestic prices. Hence, it is rare when such activities are exempt.

f. **Insurance.** The McCarran-Ferguson Act provides that federal antitrust laws are applicable to the insurance business, but only to the extent that the business is not regulated by state law. However, state law cannot render legal any act or agreement to boycott, coerce, or intimidate. The United States Supreme Court has indicated that it will give a very narrow interpretation to the definition of "insurance" activities which are exempt from federal regulation due to state regulation.

g. **Bank mergers.**

1) **Introduction.** Bank mergers are exempt from section 1 of the Sherman Act and section 7 of the Clayton Act by special legislation. [12 U.S.C. §1828(c)]

2) **Approval of the regulatory unit.** Merging banks must obtain the approval of regulating government authorities. Such authorities must obtain a report of the Attorney General as to the anticompetitive effects of such a merger. The Attorney General can attack the merger within 30 days after the approval.

3) **Standard for approval.** The United States Supreme Court has held that if the merger is shown by the Attorney General to have an anticompetitive effect, the parties must show that there is no other alternative to the merger in order to meet the needs of the community to be served, or the merger will be enjoined. [United States v. Third National Bank, 390 U.S. 171 (1968)]

h. **Labor unions.**

1) **Introduction.** As a general rule, the activities of labor unions in pursuing the welfare of their members are exempt. This results from the policy of favoring collective bargaining expressed in the National Labor Relations Act.

2) **Exceptions.** However, there are many exceptions to the general rule of exemption.

a) For example, a union-employer agreement must protect a legitimate interest of labor union members for the exemption to apply. This issue is often raised in situations where the discretion of the employer to deal with third parties is limited by the union agreement.

b) Also, a union cannot agree with one set of employers to impose a certain wage scale on its employees and another wage scale on another set of similarly situated employees. [United Mine Workers v. Pennington, 381 U.S. 657 (1965)]

G. PATENTS

1. **Introduction.** Although the patent system is considered at length *infra*, the issues arise in numerous cases. It is important to understand the basic concepts.

2. **Sources of Patent Law.** The Constitution, Article 1, section 8, clause 8, gives Congress power to "promote the progress of science and useful arts,

by securing for limited times to authors and inventors the exclusive right to their respective writings and discoveries." Patents of inventions are governed by the Patent Code. [35 U.S.C. §154] The exclusivity period is 17 years.

3. **Economics.** Because a patent confers a monopoly, the patented invention is theoretically overpriced and underutilized. There are other disadvantages as well, but these are theoretically outweighed by three factors: (i) patents provide an incentive for creative invention and discovery; (ii) full disclosure of the process or product is a condition for issuance of a patent; and (iii) patents protect the natural property interests inventors have in their ideas.

4. **Requirements.** To be patented, three requirements must be satisfied: (i) utility; (ii) novelty; and (iii) invention. Of these, invention is the most frequently litigated. It requires that the patented process or item not be "obvious" to one skilled in the art.

5. **Antitrust Law.** Because they confer a monopoly, patents are frequently challenged in the courts. In such challenges, the courts apply the legal tests to the facts independent of the Patent Office's determinations.

II. HORIZONTAL RESTRAINTS OF TRADE: COLLABORATION AMONG COMPETITORS

A. EARLY DEVELOPMENT OF THE RULE OF REASON: PER SE ILLEGALITY OF PRICE FIXING

1. **Introduction.** A "cartel" is an association of companies that cooperate to eliminate competition among themselves by fixing prices, allocating production or territories, etc. In other words, horizontal restraints on competition are those arranged as agreements or conspiracies between competing firms at the same level (*e.g.,* competing manufacturers, distributors, etc.).

2. **Background on Cartels.**

   a. **Factors required for an effective cartel.** It is not as simple as one might think to organize an effective cartel. Consideration must be given to the following factors:

      1) Number of firms to be involved.

      2) Elasticity of demand for the product.

      3) Preventing or restricting entry into the industry by other firms.

      4) Policing the agreement so that there are no defectors.

      5) Determining the appropriate production amounts, prices to be charged, etc.

      6) Adjusting to market changes, such as demand, etc.

   b. **Purpose of cartels.** Cartels are run by businesses for one purpose—to eliminate competition and thus to make more profit than would otherwise be the case. Arguments that prices charged in a cartelized industry are not unreasonable should be considered with caution.

      1) Cartels distort resource allocation by attempting to prevent the entry of the maximum amount of resources that would ordinarily be in an industry.

      2) Even though earnings of cartel members are not high, this is not a good argument for supporting the cartel because:

         a) There may be inefficiencies of management.

         b) Earnings may be higher than with competition.

         c) Data on return on investment are deceptive.

3. **Development of the "Per Se" Rule on Price Fixing.**

a. **Introduction.** The courts indicate that it is only "unreasonable horizontal restraints" that violate the antitrust laws. Beginning with *United States v. Addyston Pipe & Steel Co.*, *infra*, the Court indicated that if the restraint involved was a "direct" restraint (*i.e.,* not ancillary), the restraint was illegal. It made no difference whether competition remained, what the purpose of the restraint was, etc. The holding in this case is the precursor of the rule that horizontal price fixing agreements are per se unreasonable restraints.

b. **Per se rules.** Application of the per se rule makes the ultimate issue in a case one of fact. For example, price fixing is no longer an "ancillary" restraint of trade; there is no longer any question of degree or intent to be decided. Questions about the harm it might do are answered in a general presumption that it harms competition. Thus, horizontal price fixing is per se illegal.

   1) **Rules of evidence.** Per se rules are rules of evidence. If the prosecution proves that price fixing has occurred (a fact question), then the presumption takes effect and judgment must follow.

   2) **Practices not per se illegal.** If the courts agree that a practice is not per se illegal, they are saying that they must judge the actual effect on competition in each instance because there may be some instances where such a practice has little or no inhibitory effect.

   3) **Limitations on per se rules.** It is dangerous to call anything per se illegal. For example, to say that "price fixing" is per se illegal is to say that in every instance where it is proved it is illegal. However, there is nearly always an exception where the courts will not want to find something illegal which has been labeled per se illegal. [*See* Chicago Board of Trade v. United States, *infra*]

c. **Early cases.**

   1) **Sherman Act makes illegal "all contracts in restraint of trade"--United States v. Trans-Missouri Freight Association,** 166 U.S. 290 (1897).

United States v. Trans-Missouri Freight Association

      a) **Facts.** The United States (P) brought a suit in equity under section 1 of the Sherman Act to dissolve the Trans-Missouri Freight Association (D), an association of 18 railroads whose lines ran from the Mississippi River to the West Coast, controlling most of the freight in this area. D set rates, rules, etc., and imposed penalties for violations. P claimed that this conduct constituted restraint of trade. D argued that section 1 prohibited only those restraints that had been held unlawful at common law. The court of appeals had dismissed the complaint, and P appeals.

      b) **Issue.** Does the Sherman Act prohibit only those restraints of trade that were prohibited at common law?

      c) **Held.** No. Judgment reversed.

         (1) The Sherman Act says that "all contracts in restraint of trade" are unlawful. It is unnecessary to decide whether this particular restraint was valid at common law.

United States v. Joint Traffic Association

2) **Ancillary restraints upheld--United States v. Joint Traffic Association,** 171 U.S. 505 (1898).

a) **Facts.** The Joint Traffic Association (D) was an association of railroads operating between Chicago and Atlanta. The railroads had combined to regulate rates. The United States (P) sued under section 1 of the Sherman Act, charging that the rate fixing was a restraint on competition. D argued that rate fixing was needed in order to avoid ruinous competition, and that unless such competition was halted, eventually the consumer would pay even higher prices.

b) **Issue.** Is an agreement between competing railroads to fix freight rates a violation of section 1 of the Sherman Act?

c) **Held.** Yes.

(1) An agreement to fix prices in interstate commerce among competitors is prima facie illegal under the Sherman Act.

(2) It does not make any difference whether free competition raises or lowers prices. The test is whether such a price fixing agreement among competitors has a direct and immediate effect of restraining competition.

(3) There are some restraints that are indirect (*e.g.,* formation of a partnership, the appointment by two independent agents of a common sales agent, etc.). These restraints are "ancillary" and acceptable. But the restraint here was not one of these.

d) **Comment.** The Court in this case adopted a "rule of reason" to evaluate horizontal restraints.

United States v. Addyston Pipe & Steel Co.

d. **Purpose or intent of restraint--United States v. Addyston Pipe & Steel Co.,** 85 F. 271 (6th Cir. 1898), *aff'd,* 175 U.S. 211 (1899).

1) **Facts.** Addyston Pipe and Steel Company and five other companies (Ds) manufactured and sold iron pipe in the central and southern states. Ds had entered into a two-year agreement to divide the sales territory and fix prices. Certain cities were assigned to members and rates were set; in other areas, a secret auction was held and the winner paid the association a bonus amount; in the "free territory," members could sell without restriction because there was substantial outside competition in this territory. Members had 220,000 tons of capacity. Nonmembers in the restricted territory had 170,000 tons of capacity and in the free territory 348,000 tons of capacity. There was a significant price advantage in the restricted territory over outsiders due to freight costs. This theoretically set the maximum price that could be charged. The United States (P) brought suit in equity under section 1 of the Sherman Act against Ds. Ds claimed that their object was to prevent ruinous competition; that only reasonable prices were charged; that competition from nonmembers remained; and that the prices charged in the free territory were always less because they sold at a loss to keep their plants going.

2) **Issue.** Is a horizontal agreement among competitors to allocate territories and fix prices an unlawful restraint of trade under section 1 of the Sherman Act?

3) **Held.** Yes. Judgment for P.

a) Whatever is unlawful at common law is unlawful here. Common law permitted only reasonable "ancillary" restraints.

b) The restraints in this case were for the sole purpose and object of restraining competition. In this situation it makes no difference how reasonable the prices were, how much competition there was, or what the necessity was of preventing financial distress.

c) In addition, on the facts, members in their reserved territories really had no competition.

e. **Price fixing and the rule of reason--Chicago Board of Trade v. United States,** 246 U.S. 231 (1918). Chicago Board of Trade v. United States

1) **Facts.** Most grain trading in the United States is done through the Chicago Board of Trade (D). The three basic types of trading are: (i) spot sales (sales for immediate delivery); (ii) future sales (sales made for delivery at a future time); and (iii) sales "to arrive" (sales to be delivered when the grain arrives in Chicago). Spot and future sales are made during D's regular sessions, but sales "to arrive" are made only after the close of D's regular sessions in special sessions termed the "Call." D adopted a Call rule whereby sales "to arrive" could not be made at any price other than the closing bid at each day's Call. The United States (P) sought an injunction against enforcement of the Call rule. D claimed that the rule was not intended to prevent competition or control prices, but to give members limited hours of business and to break up a specific monopoly held by Chicago warehousemen. The trial court struck the allegations regarding the purpose for the rule and enjoined its enforcement. D appeals.

2) **Issue.** May restraints on trade which may have anticompetitive effects be permitted if they are reasonable (*i.e.,* have some economic benefit)?

3) **Held.** Yes. Judgment reversed.

a) P claims that any agreement that fixes prices is an illegal restraint of trade, but every agreement or regulation restrains competition. The true test is whether the restraint imposed merely regulates and thereby promotes competition, or actually suppresses or destroys competition. This test requires consideration of several factors:

(1) The facts peculiar to the business to which the restraint is applied;

(2) Its condition before and after the restraint was imposed; and

(3) The nature of the restraint, its scope, and its effect, actual or probable, as well as the reason for which it was adopted.

b) In this case, the nature of the rule was to require members who wanted to buy grain "to arrive" to decide before the close of the Call how much they wanted to pay. The rule encouraged them to attend the Call, where they could affect the final bid as necessary.

c) The scope of the rule was limited to contracts for grain "to arrive." This was a small part of the total market, and the restriction applied for only a small part of the business day. Every board of trade imposes some restraints upon the conduct of business by its members, and those imposed by D here, intended to shorten the working day, are not significant.

d) The rule had a minimal effect on general market prices and the volume of trade shipped to Chicago. At the same time, it had several benefits, including (i) creating a public market for grain "to arrive"; (ii) bringing buyers and sellers together during the Call; (iii) increasing participation by country dealers in the market, thus improving competition; and (iv) making it possible for grain merchants to trade on a smaller margin, making the Chicago market more efficient.

4) **Comment.** This case is difficult to reconcile with succeeding cases, although it remains good law. It may mean:

a) If the court can clearly see that the effect on competition is de minimus, it will not invalidate a price-fixing agreement.

b) The case may be analogous to those upholding "ancillary" restraints that are not unreasonable. This is essentially a "purpose" argument. The problem is that every agreement to fix prices can be characterized as having other legitimate purposes.

c) The case may be read to mean that agreements between competitors, even if they affect prices, may be legal if they improve the functioning of a competitive market.

United States v. Trenton Potteries Co.

f. **Per se unreasonableness of price fixing--United States v. Trenton Potteries Co.,** 273 U.S. 392 (1927).

1) **Facts.** Trenton Potteries Company and other individuals and corporations (Ds), which together controlled 82% of the business of manufacturing and distributing vitreous pottery (bathroom fixtures) in the United States, formed a trade association through which they fixed prices and limited sales to a select list of jobbers. Ds were tried for Sherman Act violations. At the trial, the judge withdrew from the jury the consideration of the reasonableness of the restraints. The court of appeals reversed that ruling, and the United States (P) appeals.

2) **Issue.** Are all horizontal price fixing agreements per se illegal?

3) **Held.** Yes. Judgment reversed.

a) The *Standard Oil* and *American Tobacco Co.* cases, *infra*, held that only unreasonable restraints upon interstate commerce are prohibited by the Sherman Act. This does not mean that a price-fixing scheme is permitted as long as the prices are reasonable.

b) The reasonableness of restraints of commerce must be determined in light of the basic assumption of the Sherman Act, which is that the public interest is best protected from the evils of monopoly and price control by the maintenance of competition. However, the purpose and result of every price-fixing agreement is to eliminate one form of competition. A power to fix prices includes the power to control the market and fix unreasonable prices.

c) A test making the difference between legal and illegal conduct depend on whether prices are reasonable could not be enforced because economic conditions that affect the reasonableness of a price vary from day to day. The Sherman Act is not only a prohibition against the infliction of a particular type of public injury; it is also a limitation of rights that may be pushed to evil consequences. For these reasons, price fixing is prohibited by the Sherman Act, regardless of the reasonableness of the prices agreed upon.

d) Ds claim that *Chicago Board of Trade, supra,* permits reasonable price controls. That case, however, dealt with a regulation of a board of trade, and was limited to a small market and only a portion of the business day. That case does not permit a price agreement among competitors in an open market.

4) **Comment.** In *Appalachian Coals v. United States*, 288 U.S. 344 (1933), the Court upheld an organization of regional coal producers who designated the organization as their exclusive sales agent. The organization was created to deal with the depressed condition of the coal industry in Appalachia. The Court noted that the organization did not have power to fix prices because other producers also sold in the region. This case arose during the Depression, however, and has not had any significant progeny.

g. **Reaffirmation of *Trenton*--United States v. Socony-Vacuum Oil Co.,** 310 U.S. 150 (1940).

United States v. Socony-Vacuum Oil Co.

1) **Facts.** Socony-Vacuum Oil Company and other large integrated oil companies (Ds) sold large amounts of gasoline to jobbers who in turn supplied service stations. The prices were based on the spot market price for gasoline. The states in the region tried to restrict production, but much oil was illegally produced. When sold, this illegal oil drove prices down considerably. As a result, independent refiners who relied on legal oil had to sell their gasoline as fast as it was produced at distress prices. Ds agreed among themselves to buy the distress gasoline from specified refiners at market prices. The result was to eliminate distress gasoline as a market factor and raise prices to jobbers and retailers. Ds were charged with violation of the Sherman Act. The trial court instructed the jury that price fixing was a per se violation of the Sherman Act, regardless of the reasonableness of the prices, but that a criminal conviction could result only if the jury found, beyond a reasonable doubt, that the price increase was caused by the combination and not exclusively by other factors. The

court of appeals reversed and ordered a new trial, holding that the combination was not per se and that the jury should determine whether the activities promoted rather than impaired free competition. The United States appeals.

2) **Issue.** Do the motives or purposes of a horizontal price fixing combination of competitors make any difference?

3) **Held.** No. Price fixing is illegal per se.

a) It is clear under *Trenton Potteries*, *supra*, that an agreement to fix prices, made by competitors who control a substantial part of an industry, is an unreasonable restraint of trade regardless of good intentions or the reasonableness of the prices. By whatever means used to accomplish it, price fixing is illegal per se.

b) Ds claim that *Appalachian Coals* and *Chicago Board of Trade*, *supra*, provide defenses. *Appalachian Coals* did not involve a plan to fix prices, and any effect on prices the plan may have had was incidental and conjectural, since the plan had not yet operated. The district court retained jurisdiction should the actual operation of the plan prove an undue restraint on interstate commerce. Ds' plan here had the intent and effect of raising prices. The *Chicago Board of Trade* case did not involve price manipulation and had neither the purpose nor effect of raising prices; it was merely a rule regulating the period of price-making.

c) Ds also claim that *Trenton Potteries* involved the substitution of an agreed-on price for a competitive price by parties who had the power and purpose to suppress the play of competition, while Ds themselves bought the distress oil at market prices; and the only effect of the practice was to eliminate a competitive evil. Furthermore, Ds claim they lacked the power to set arbitrary noncompetitive prices. However, there was evidence that Ds intended to raise prices and actually succeeded in doing so. It is sufficient that Ds' buying programs resulted in a price increase that would not have otherwise happened. It does not matter that spot market sales were still governed by some competition; the scheme clearly curtailed competition.

d) Elimination of competitive evils is not a defense to Sherman Act violations; if it was, the Act would become meaningless. The Act is not limited to the removal of monopoly power, but applies to any combination that tampers with price structures. Even though Ds lacked the power to control the market, by stabilizing prices they tampered with price structures. Prices need not be rigid and uniform to be fixed. Even though the prices Ds paid did fluctuate, they were fixed because they were agreed upon.

4) **Comment.** The opinion seems to create a requirement about the actual effect on prices and a requirement that a substantial amount of commerce be involved. However, in a famous footnote, Justice Douglas indicated that an illegal conspiracy could exist even though the combination did not commit any overt act, had no actual power to affect prices, and the amount of commerce involved was immaterial.

B. MODERN APPROACH TO DETERMINING WHETHER RESTRAINTS ARE REASONABLE

1. **Introduction.** Although the *Socony* opinion, *supra*, apparently held that any agreement among competitors that has any effect on price is illegal, the opinion did not overrule the rule of reason established by *Standard Oil*, *infra*. Thus, some restraints may be upheld so long as they are "reasonable." In evaluating particular conduct, the first determination should be whether the conduct fixes prices and is per se illegal. If there are mitigating factors that bring the conduct within the rule of reason, the next determination is which party bears the burden of proof and persuasion.

2. **Competitive Restraints Other than Price Fixing.** Competitors may agree to practices other than outright price fixing that have similar effects. Some of these alternatives may be even more effective in giving competing firms control over their prices than direct price fixing. With price fixing, no one firm is guaranteed of gaining market share, but under other arrangements, market share may be specifically allocated among the competitors.

    a. **Production limitations.** Competitors may agree to divide the market based on production limitations, such as by restricting the hours of plant operation, or by channeling business through a common sales agent. This practice is typified by the OPEC oil cartel.

    b. **Division of sales territory.** Competitors may agree to divide the market by geographic region, giving exclusive rights to specified territories.

    c. **Division of market by class of customer.** Competitors may agree to divide the market by type of customer.

    d. **Effects of anticompetitive agreements.** The adverse effects that such anticompetitive agreements may have include: (i) limiting expansion of firms otherwise capable of expanding; (ii) protecting the least efficient producers; (iii) conferring price control to participating firms; and (iv) limiting new methods and products developed by one firm to that firm's market.

3. **Territorial Divisions--United States v. Topco Associates,** 405 U.S. 596 (1972). **United States v. Topco Associates**

    a. **Facts.** Twenty-five small to medium sized food chains formed a cooperative buying association, Topco Associates, Inc. (D), that had suppliers manufacture Topco label brands for the members. Combined sales of D's members totaled $2.3 billion, larger than all but three national grocery chains. Each member had from 1.5% to 16% of the market in its area, comparable to the national chains; the Topco labels amounted to about 10% of the members' sales. D's rules provided that each member had a near veto over new members joining, thus protecting each member's competitive geographic market. The rules also provided that no member could sell Topco brands except in the area where it was licensed by D, and most licenses were exclusive. D's permission was required before a member could sell Topco labels wholesale. Such permission had been applied for by some members, but was never granted by D. The United States (P) sued to enjoin D's operation. The trial court found that although the agreement prevented competition in Topco brands, it improved competition generally by permitting the members to compete more effectively. P appeals.

b. **Issue.** May relatively small competitors join in a cooperative venture to better compete with larger competitors if their cooperation involves territorial allocations?

c. **Held.** No. Judgment reversed.

1) Agreements among competitors at the same market level to allocate territories in order to minimize competition is a classic per se violation of the Sherman Act. Horizontal territorial limitations have consistently been held illegal as restraints of trade with no purpose other than limiting competition.

2) The courts cannot weigh the effects of destroying competition in one sector of the economy against the benefits of improving competition in another. Such a balancing must be made by Congress. The courts are not in a position to evaluate the merits of complex competing interests and the data that would be used to support various positions.

d. **Dissent** (Burger, C.J.). The Court has never before held that market-sharing agreements are per se illegal. This plan promotes competition. There should be no per se rule in situations where there is no price fixing, where only trademarked products are involved, and there is no monopoly or near-monopoly in the products involved.

e. **Remand.** On remand, the trial court permitted D to continue granting areas of "primary responsibility" to members and allowed "pass-overs" whereby a member selling Topco products outside its area of primary responsibility had to pay a pro rata share of the primary territory member's advertising and other promotional expenses.

Broadcast Music v. Columbia Broadcasting System

4. **Separate Product Doctrine--Broadcast Music v. Columbia Broadcasting System,** 441 U.S. 1 (1979).

a. **Facts.** Broadcast Music, Inc. ("BMI") and the American Society of Composers, Authors, and Publishers ("ASCAP") (Ds) were organized as "clearinghouses" for copyright owners and users to solve practical problems associated with the licensing of music. Copyright owners grant Ds nonexclusive rights to license nondramatic performances of their works, and Ds issue licenses and then distribute appropriate royalties to the owners. Ds use blanket licenses, which permit the licensees to use any works owned by Ds' members. The Columbia Broadcasting System (P) filed suit alleging that Ds are unlawful monopolies and that the blanket license is illegal price fixing, an unlawful tying arrangement, a concerted refusal to deal, and a misuse of copyrights. The district court dismissed the complaint on grounds that direct negotiation with individual copyright owners is available and feasible. The court of appeals held that the blanket licenses were a form of price fixing and were illegal per se. Ds appeal.

b. **Issue.** Should the courts consider the practical realities of an industry in determining whether a particular practice falls within the per se rule?

c. **Held.** Yes. Judgment reversed and case remanded.

1) It is only after considerable experience with certain business relationships that courts classify them as per se violations. This case marks the first time this practice has been examined by this Court. ASCAP operates under a consent decree formulated to ensure competitive freedom, and there are indications that these practices may have redeeming competitive virtues.

2) The blanket license performs a useful, even necessary service in avoiding thousands of individual negotiations. The blanket license is actually a different product from the individual compositions. It gives licensees rights and flexibility they could not acquire by contacting each individual composer. Thus, Ds are not really joint sales agencies offering the goods of many sellers in combination, but are separate sellers of blanket licenses. Ds' practice is not a per se violation and should be examined under the rule of reason.

5. **Maximum Price Fixing by Physicians--Arizona v. Maricopa County Medical Society,** 457 U.S. 332 (1982).

Arizona v. Maricopa County Medical Society

a. **Facts.** About 70% of the physicians in Maricopa County were members of the Maricopa County Medical Society (D). D provided peer review services, was authorized to draw checks on insurance company accounts to pay physicians for services provided to insured persons, and established a schedule of maximum fees for participating doctors to charge insured patients. D used relative values of various medical services and conversion factors for the various medical specialties to determine the fees that could be charged. D's board of trustees would formulate the fee schedule and the membership would approve it by voting. Physicians were free to charge insured patients lower fees, and could charge uninsured patients any fee. Arizona (P) brought suit, claiming that the effect of the practice was to stabilize fees at a high level, which in turn increased insurance premiums. D claimed that the fee limit actually made insurance less expensive and saved patients and insurers money. P moved for summary judgment. The court of appeals held that a full trial on the merits was necessary, and the Supreme Court granted certiorari.

b. **Issue.** Is an agreement among physicians to establish maximum fees a per se violation of the Sherman Act?

c. **Held.** Yes. Judgment reversed.

1) Prior cases have established that horizontal agreements to fix maximum prices are on the same legal footing as agreements to fix minimum or uniform prices. The per se rule reflects faith in price competition as a market force. By establishing a maximum price, D has provided the same economic rewards to all physicians, regardless of skill, experience, training, or innovative or special services. It could also degenerate into an agreement to fix uniform prices.

2) It is irrelevant that physicians are professionals. The agreement is not based on public service or ethical requirements.

3) Although the Court has not previously applied the per se rule to the health care industry, there is no requirement that the Court have antitrust experience in a particular industry before applying the per se rule. The per se rule is intended to avoid unnecessary litigation.

4) D claims that its activity has procompetitive justifications. However, the anticompetitive potential inherent in all price-fixing agreements justifies the facial invalidation despite allegations of procompetitive justifications because such claims are so unlikely to prove significant. Even if a maximum fee schedule has real economic advantages, there is no reason why the physicians themselves must set the fees.

5) D also claims that its practice is merely literal price fixing such as was involved in *Broadcast Music*, *supra*. That case involved a product, the blanket license, that was entirely different from what one composer could provide. Although the composers delegated to BMI the power to fix the price for the blanket license, this merely reflected the fact that the price had to be established somehow. It did not limit the power of individual composers to set a price for their individual works. In this case, however, all of D's members competed among themselves for patients. They did not sell any different product through their association; they simply sold medical services. This is unlike a situation in which doctors in a clinic agree to prices to be charged by the clinic for complete medical coverage.

National Society of Professional Engineers v. United States

6. **Canon of Ethics--National Society of Professional Engineers v. United States,** 435 U.S. 679 (1978).

a. **Facts.** The National Society of Professional Engineers (D) adopted a canon of ethics which prohibited competitive bidding by its members. The United States (P) charged that this canon violated section 1 of the Sherman Act as an interference with the price structure of engineering fees. D admitted the alleged facts but claimed that the canon was reasonable because competition among professional engineers was contrary to the public interest in safe designs and structures. The district court held the canon per se illegal, so that the validity of D's reasonableness argument was irrelevant. The court of appeals affirmed, and the Supreme Court granted certiorari.

b. **Issue.** May the courts consider noneconomic factors in determining whether a particular restraint of trade is reasonable?

c. **Held.** No. Judgment affirmed.

1) The rule of reason does not open antitrust analysis to any arguments that may fall within the realm of reason. The only inquiry mandated by the rule of reason is whether the challenged agreement is one that promotes competition or one that suppresses competition.

2) The Sherman Act reflects a legislative judgment that ultimately competition will produce not only lower prices, but also better goods

and services. The statutory policy precludes inquiry into whether competition is good or bad. Because D's canon is anticompetitive, it cannot be upheld.

d. **Concurrence** (Blackmun, Rehnquist, JJ.). D's canon is overbroad and therefore illegal, but there may be ethical rules that have a more than de minimus anticompetitive effect and yet are important in a profession's proper ordering.

7. **Horizontal Restraints Necessary--National Collegiate Athletic Association (NCAA) v. Board of Regents,** 468 U.S. 85 (1984).

National Collegiate Athletic Association (NCAA) v. Board of Regents

a. **Facts.** The National Collegiate Athletic Association (D) adopted a plan for the televising of football games involving its members. The purported objective of the plan was to minimize the adverse effects of live television upon football game attendance. Under the plan, ABC and CBS were permitted to telecast 14 games each. Each network was permitted to select games they desired to televise. Once a first choice for any given date was made, that network had the exclusive right to submit a bid at a fixed price; the schools involved could not sell the TV rights to another network. The plan also created appearance requirements and limitations. The Board of Regents of the University of Oklahoma (P) and other universities formed the College Football Association ("CFA") to negotiate television appearances for football games outside of D's plan. D announced it would discipline any of its members that participated in the CFA arrangement. In response, P sued. The trial court found that D's plan had significant anticompetitive effects, including restricting the number of games televised and thus raising the price networks paid for rights. The court held D's plan a violation of the Sherman Act, and the Supreme Court granted certiorari.

b. **Issue.** Is a plan by an organization of colleges to restrict negotiations between TV networks and member colleges for televising football games a per se violation of the Sherman Act?

c. **Held.** No. Judgment affirmed under the rule of reason.

1) Ordinarily, horizontal price fixing and output limitation are deemed illegal per se. The per se rule does not apply in this case, however, because the industry involved—college football games—requires horizontal restraints on competition in order to exist. The various colleges must agree to certain ground rules, including the rules of the game itself and player eligibility, in order to preserve the character and quality of the product. D is vital in this process as the means for obtaining the necessary mutual agreement. The rule of reason must be used to assess the competitive significance of the challenged restraint.

2) The trial court found that D's plan, by restraining price and output, had a significant anticompetitive effect. But for the plan, many more games would be televised, and at lower prices to the networks. The plan eliminates competitors from the market. D clearly has market power sufficient to cause these effects.

3) D claims that its plan is a joint venture such as BMI and ASCAP in *Broadcast Music*, *supra*. While a joint venture that creates a new product may be permitted, D's plan does not create a new product; it merely provides for the sale of individual games in a noncompetitive market. The plan has no pro-competitive efficiencies and is not necessary to enable D to penetrate the TV market. D's product is already unique.

4) D's plan does not protect live attendance because the televised games are shown at the same time as other games are being played. D's protection justification is actually a scheme to protect noncompetitive ticket sales by limiting output of more popular televised games—a typical monopolist tactic.

5) The restraints on TV rights are not similar to the other mutual agreements that make college football possible. The plan does not serve to equalize competition; it merely limits one of many sources of revenue. D's other rules are clearly sufficient to preserve competitive balance and preserve amateurism. Thus, the plan cannot stand under the rule of reason.

8. **Joint Ventures.** Many things can be accomplished through a joint venture that might not be accomplished by a single firm, such as the combination of technology that neither firm possesses by itself. However, such combinations also have anticompetitive possibilities. As in many other areas of antitrust analysis, the issue is: Under what circumstances will a joint venture be legitimate?

a. **Legitimacy of objectives.** A joint venture may have desirable or undesirable objectives having various probabilities of success and different levels of significance.

b. **Significance of restraint.** To the extent that the joint venture restrains trade, the restraint may be more or less likely, more or less significant in quality, and more or less significant in magnitude.

c. **Various dimensions.** A joint venture may involve many dimensions, each having different objectives and degrees of restraint. In the *NCAA* case, *supra*, the dimensions relating to player eligibility and game rules were permissible, while those pertaining to TV rights were not.

d. **The National Cooperative Research Act of 1984.** Congress enacted a statute to facilitate joint research and development. [15 U.S.C. §4301] The Act applies the rule of reason to joint research and development ventures, and provides for only actual, not treble, damages if a venture filed with the FTC and Justice Department proves illegal.

C. THE AGREEMENT REQUIREMENT

1. **Introduction.** The cases studied so far involved undisputed agreements among companies and persons. The focus was on the nature of the illegal conduct itself. The Sherman Act requirement of a contract, combination,

or conspiracy can itself present difficult problems of proof as conspiring companies learn to avoid express agreements. In some situations, a conspiracy may be inferred based on the parties' conduct. In other situations, separate companies may act in concert based on knowledge of each other's behavior but without an actual agreement. Such activity is possible where the parties share an oligopoly.

2. Oligopoly, Price Leadership, and Conscious Parallelism.

a. **Economic theory.** Economic theory is not clear-cut in this area, but the following observations are characteristic of oligopolistic industries:

1) The more competitive a market, the more difficult to maintain collusive behavior; markets with few firms are able to achieve effects equivalent to overt collusive monopolistic behavior.

2) In oligopolistic industries, the combined decisions of the firms may approximate the profit-maximizing decisions of a monopolist.

3) There is no natural erosion of concentration in an industry over time; erosion requires positive antitrust action.

4) Some studies suggest that profits over long periods in highly concentrated industries are higher than in nonconcentrated industries.

5) Firm sizes in most concentrated industries have reached beyond the point necessary to achieve the best economies of scale.

6) Highly concentrated industries never move in perfect unison, however, since individual firms have individual characteristics (*e.g.*, costs, capacity, etc.).

7) Empirical facts suggest that of the several strategies open to firms in concentrated industries, normally the strategy selected is to cooperate in an informal way.

8) Barriers to entry are a significant factor in what happens in a concentrated industry.

9) In a concentrated industry price may be higher than otherwise, but profits are not always higher.

10) There is some evidence that government intervention is a major source of monopoly power (*e.g.*, regulation raising cost of doing business, eroding ease of entry into business, etc.).

3. Tacit and Inferred Express Agreements.

a. **Proof of agreement or conspiracy.** It is clear that an agreement or conspiracy in restraint of trade can be proved by circumstantial evidence. It is also theoretically clear that the existence of such an agreement cannot be proved simply by showing that the effects usually associated with such an agreement have occurred (*i.e.*, uniform prices over several years, etc.). In reality, however, this type of evidence is submitted and inferences are drawn therefrom. The issue is always whether the evidence justifies the inferences.

Thus, the underlying issue is what, at the minimum, constitutes a "meeting of the minds" which must be directly or circumstantially proved? What degree of mutual knowledge, confidence, and/or awareness among competing entrepreneurs amounts to a common understanding?

Interstate Circuit v. United States

b. **Conspiracy established from conduct--Interstate Circuit v. United States,** 306 U.S. 208 (1939).

1) **Facts.** A company with two subsidiaries, including Interstate Circuit (D), in the movie exhibition business owned all first-run theaters in six major Texas cities and many subsequent-run theaters. As a condition of D's continued exhibition of their films in its first-run theaters, D demanded that eight distribution companies (controlling 75% of all first class feature films) require subsequent-run theaters in these cities to charge higher admissions, and not to run films shown in first-run theaters in double bills when they exhibited them in the subsequent runs. The letter making the demands was sent to all eight distributors, with all eight names on it; meetings were held with the exhibitor and the distributors; all distributors adopted the proposal and acted on it (two incorporated the restrictions in their exhibition contracts). The United States (P) charged a conspiracy in restraint of trade among the distributors and between the distributors and the exhibitors, and sought an injunction. The trial court inferred from this evidence that the parties did agree with each other to carry out the contracts, which were illegal. D appeals.

2) **Issue.** May the courts infer an agreement or conspiracy from the fact that the parties knew that concerted action was contemplated when they adhered to the scheme?

3) **Held.** Yes. Judgment affirmed.

a) There is no direct evidence of the conspiracy, but it may be inferred from the conduct of the distributors.

b) The inference comes from: (i) the nature of the proposals (which would raise prices and be more profitable to all parties); (ii) the unanimity of action (all were aware of the plan and the need for all to cooperate if it was to work); (iii) the fact that the plan was a radical departure from past ways of doing business; and (iv) the fact that defendants did not call as witnesses any of their superior officials who were involved in negotiating the agreement.

4) **Comment.** This is the leading case on "conscious parallelism." Consciously parallel action that is interdependent may provide the basis for inferring agreement. Here, there was no explanation for a firm entering into the contract independently; its success depended on the participation of all parties.

c. **Independent but uniform action--Theatre Enterprises v. Paramount Film Distributing Corp.,** 346 U.S. 537 (1954).

Theatre Enterprises v. Paramount Film Distributing Corp.

1) **Facts.** Theatre Enterprises (P) is a theater owner in the suburbs of Baltimore. P tried to get first-run films from Paramount (D) and other major distributors but was refused, since all first-run films were given to downtown Baltimore theaters. P could only show the films it obtained after the downtown theaters had shown them. The distributors all stated economic reasons for their decisions, the main reason being that P's suburban theater drew less than one-tenth as many patrons as the downtown theaters. There was no evidence of agreement between the distributors. A jury found for D, and the court of appeals affirmed. P appeals.

2) **Issue.** Does proof of parallel business behavior, by itself, conclusively establish an agreement?

3) **Held.** No. Judgment affirmed.

a) Proof of conscious parallel business behavior does not conclusively prove agreement or conspiracy. Although Ds acted uniformly, each acted in response to individual business judgment. The doctrine of conscious parallelism has not replaced the conspiracy requirement of the Sherman Act.

b) P's evidence was insufficient to support a directed verdict, and the jury found for Ds. This verdict is not clearly erroneous.

4) **Comment.** The business reasons cited by the defendants made a lot of sense. Their action was not interdependent like the action involved in *Interstate Circuit, supra*.

d. **Course of dealing--American Tobacco Co. v. United States,** 328 U.S. 781 (1946).

American Tobacco Co. v. United States

1) **Facts.** American Tobacco Company, Liggett & Myers, and R. J. Reynolds (Ds) together produced 90% of the total United States cigarette production. Their price lists were virtually identical for several years and actually identical after that. Despite falling raw material and manufacturing costs, Reynolds raised the list price of its cigarettes from $6.40 to $6.85 per thousand. The same day, American and Liggett also raised their prices the identical amount. As explanations, they claimed that Reynolds' price increase would permit it to increase its advertising, and they had to keep up. The result was a decline in volume of sales but greatly increased profits. The United States (P) prosecuted Ds for violating the Sherman Act. The jury convicted Ds, and the Supreme Court granted certiorari.

2) **Issue.** May a conspiracy under the Sherman Act be shown by a uniform course of dealing among competitors?

3) **Held.** Yes. Judgment affirmed.

a) The Sherman Act does not focus on the form of the combination or the particular means used, but on the result achieved. Even innocent acts may be performed to give effect to a conspiracy and thereby fall within the Act.

b) A formal agreement is not necessary to constitute an unlawful conspiracy. The necessary combination may be found in a course of dealing as well as in an exchange of words. As long as the jury can legitimately find, based on evidence of the circumstances, that the conspirators had a unity of purpose or a common design and understanding, or a meeting of minds in an unlawful arrangement, their conclusion that a conspiracy exists is justified.

4) **Comment.** These cases demonstrate that similar actions taken by competitors—conscious parallelism—may give rise to an inference of conspiracy that may be rebutted by proof of legitimate business decisions made by each company independently. The reasons put forward by the tobacco companies were not credible, while the reasons given by the theater operators in *Theatre Enterprises*, *supra*, were. Two additional cases give further insight.

a) In *First National Bank of Arizona v. Cities Service Co.*, 391 U.S. 253 (1968), Cities Service Company broke off all dealings with an oil broker who represented the nationalized Anglo-Iranian Oil Company. Other companies had allegedly conspired to prevent the broker from selling the oil, and Cities Service allegedly joined this conspiracy. Cities Services won a summary judgment based on its explanation that had it purchased the oil, it would have faced considerable litigation and boycotts.

b) In *Ambrook Enterprises v. Time*, 612 F.2d 604 (2d Cir. 1979), Ambrook Enterprises challenged the print media practice of giving a 15% advertising discount to advertising agencies but not to advertisers who do not use ad agencies. The trial court gave summary judgment because there was insufficient evidence of a conspiracy. The court of appeals reversed, holding that a jury could infer that the discount was the result of an agreement among and between the media and advertising agencies. Critical to its holding was the absence of any legitimate business reason for the discount other than habit and fear of reprisal from ad agencies.

4. Intra-Enterprise Conspiracy.

a. **Introduction.** Business organizations are generally considered single entities, so that concerted action among a corporation and its officers or employees, or among persons within a single organization, are not considered to fall within section 1 of the Sherman Act. However, commonly owned corporations, such as parent and subsidiaries, may be treated as separate for purposes of section 1. Traditionally, this notion has been called the "intra-enterprise conspiracy" doctrine. It stemmed from *United States v. Yellow Cab Co.*, *infra*, which involved actions taken by the owner of several formerly independent taxicab companies. In that case, the Court noted that the common ownership of the various corporations did not make their conspiracy immune from the Sherman Act. The doctrine was also followed in *Kiefer-Stewart Co. v. Joseph E. Seagram & Sons, Inc.*, 340 U.S. 211 (1951).

b. **Parent-subsidiary rule--Copperweld Corp. v. Independence Tube Corp.,** 467 U.S. 752 (1984).

Copperweld Corp. v. Independence Tube Corp.

1) **Facts.** Copperweld Corporation (D) bought Regal Tube Company ("Regal") from Lear Siegler, Inc. ("Lear") and transferred its assets to a new wholly owned subsidiary. Regal had been an unincorporated division of Lear. Lear agreed not to compete with Regal for five years after the sale. However, an officer of Lear formed Independence Tube Corporation (P) to compete with Regal. P ordered a tubing mill from Yoder Company. D notified Yoder that it would do what it had to to enforce D's noncompetition agreement with Lear. Yoder voided P's purchase order. P sued, claiming that D and Regal conspired to violate section 1 of the Sherman Act. The jury found for P and awarded treble damages, and the court of appeals affirmed. The Supreme Court granted certiorari.

2) **Issue.** May a parent and its wholly owned subsidiary conspire within the meaning of section 1 of the Sherman Act?

3) **Held.** No. Judgment reversed.

a) *Yellow Cab*, *infra*, involved a pattern of acquisitions made pursuant to an anticompetitive purpose; the intra-enterprise doctrine was not a basis for the decision. *Kiefer-Stewart*, *supra*, did rely on the intra-enterprise doctrine, but the conspiracy involved others rather than just the related company. All other cases invoking the doctrine did not rely on the doctrine alone.

b) The difference between section 1 and section 2 is that the former requires a combination between separate entities, while section 2 applies only to monopoly action and may include unilateral activity. Concerted behavior is treated more strictly than unilateral behavior because it presents greater anticompetitive risk.

c) Section 1 clearly does not apply to coordinated conduct among officers or employees of the same company, which is actually necessary for the company to compete effectively. The same principle applies to coordinated conduct of a corporation and an unincorporated division, which offers organizational efficiencies. For the same reason, the coordinated activity of a parent and its wholly owned subsidiary must be treated as that of a single enterprise under section 1.

d) A parent and subsidiary always have a unity of purpose or a common design. There is no basis for finding an "agreement" between the parent and subsidiary, since they always act together. The intra-enterprise doctrine is based on form, not reality. Antitrust liability should not depend on whether a corporate subunit is an unincorporated division or a wholly owned subsidiary. The only effect of the doctrine is to encourage formation of unincorporated divisions instead of a subsidiary, which has no antitrust benefits.

e) The gap left in the Sherman Act—permitting a single firm to act anticompetitively as long as it does not threaten monopoly—is a policy choice made by Congress. It represents the difficulty and competitive disincentive of subjecting a single firm's every action to judicial scrutiny for reasonableness. Section 1 of the Sherman Act and section 7 of the Clayton Act regulate a corporation's initial acquisition of control, and section 2 of the Sherman Act and section 5 of the FTC Act govern corporate activity thereafter. The intra-enterprise doctrine adds nothing to these.

D. TRADE ASSOCIATIONS AND DATA DISSEMINATION

1. **The Role of Trade Associations.** Trade associations perform a number of functions, many of which seem clearly to assist association members and have no anticompetitive effect. Other functions clearly have an anticompetitive effect. But there are a large number of functions in the middle area which could have anticompetitive effects, depending on the circumstances.

   a. **Legitimate activities.** The following activities probably (at least in most cases) do not have anticompetitive effects: cooperative industrial research, market surveys, developing new uses for products, operation of employment bureaus, collective bargaining, mutual insurance, commercial arbitration services, joint advertising concerning the industry, and joint legislative efforts.

   b. **Questionable activities.** The following activities may or may not have anticompetitive effects:

      1) **Cost accounting.** Standard forms, procedures for computing costs, uniform mark-ups, publishing average costs for the industry, including a profit factor in average costs, efforts to enforce uniform prices, etc.

      2) **Statistical activities.** Production statistics (volume, sales, backlog, inventories, idle capacity, etc.).

      3) **Price reporting.**

      4) **Product standardization.** Efforts to create quality standards, common credit terms, standardized contracts, discounts, allowances, freight, etc.

      5) **Credit bureaus.** Sharing information from bad credit risks, attempting to establish common credit policies, etc.

2. **Characterizing the Activity.**

   a. **Introduction.** Again the problem is determining whether there is an agreement or conspiracy to fix prices or divide markets, and again the difficult cases are those where there is no express agreement but the courts must characterize arrangements by drawing inferences from the facts as to the probable effects of the arrangements. Factors considered are functions or activities, actual effects (price uniformity, etc.), and sanctions or enforcement practices.

American Column & Lumber Co. v. United States

1) **Agreements to exchange information--American Column & Lumber Co. v. United States,** 257 U.S. 377 (1921).

   a) **Facts.** This case involved an association of 400 firms manufacturing hardwood (D) that adopted an "open competition" plan, the express purpose of which was stated to be that "knowledge regarding prices actually made is all that is necessary to keep prices at reasonably stable and normal levels." Participation in the plan was optional, but in practice, 90% of member firms, accounting for one-third of the national output of hardwood, took part. Members were required to give D daily reports of sales and deliveries (with copies of invoices), monthly reports of production and stocks, and monthly reports on prices. D collated material and sent out weekly and monthly reports. In addition, there were regular monthly meetings, and territories were broken up and members therein met weekly. Future estimates of production were asked for. At the meetings, the attempt was made to arrive at "policies" which were strongly urged on members. No specific agreement to restrict output and set prices existed. The United States (P) challenged the plan. The district court found for P, and D appeals.

   b) **Issue.** May an agreement among competitors to exchange specific information about their business, including prices, through a trade association constitute a violation of section 1 of the Sherman Act?

   c) **Held.** Yes. Judgment affirmed.

      (1) Agreement is found in the tendency of intelligent people to follow a common course based on elaborate distribution of information and the restraint of business honor and social penalties.

      (2) Furthermore, the facts show an actual adverse effect on interstate commerce in that the association developed a policy and members adhered to it in an anticompetitive manner (in the early months of 1919 there was a policy to restrict production; later the policy was to raise prices, which the firms did).

      (3) The conduct involved clearly is not that of competitors.

   d) **Dissent** (Brandeis, McKenna, JJ.). Information sharing will tend to equalize prices, but there is no coercion involved. There is no unreasonable restraint involved in sharing information, even in great detail. It was a purely voluntary system, and no prices were actually set. All information was made available to the public.

   e) **Comment.** In *United States v. American Linseed Oil Co.*, 262 U.S. 371 (1923), the facts were similar to *American Column*, except here there were only 12 firms controlling a very large part of the industry and, in addition to the reports and meetings, there were penalties assessed for nonattendance and for violation of the agreement. The court found a violation.

Maple Flooring Manufacturers' Association v. United States

2) **No actual agreement--Maple Flooring Manufacturers' Association v. United States,** 268 U.S. 563 (1925).

a) **Facts.** The Maple Flooring Manufacturers' Association (D) computed average costs from information of the individual firms; distributed a freight book showing rates from a central point to thousands of locations; gathered and distributed information on past prices, stock on hand, etc.; and held meetings to discuss conditions in the industry. There was an express finding that prices were not discussed at these meetings. Also, no identification of individual sellers and buyers was made. The district court found a violation of the Sherman Act, and D appeals.

b) **Issue.** Does dissemination of business information alone violate the Sherman Act?

c) **Held.** No. Judgment reversed.

(1) The ultimate result of the association may be to stabilize prices, but this is not in itself unlawful.

(2) There is no evidence of concerted action or actual agreement.

(3) It was also shown that prices were not uniform among members and that they were generally lower than for nonmember competitors in the industry.

d) **Comment.** Much of the information exchanged in *American Column*, *supra*, could only have had an anticompetitive effect, while the information exchanged in *Maple Flooring* was more general.

United States v. Container Corp. of America

3) **Exchange of price information--United States v. Container Corp. of America,** 393 U.S. 333 (1969).

a) **Facts.** Eighteen of 51 manufacturers of corrugated containers in the Southeast (Ds), controlling 90% of production, informally agreed to share price information on products (without adhering to a price schedule) and to exchange information concerning specific sales or quotations to identified customers. Demand in the industry had been growing and was inelastic. The number of competitors was growing since entry into the industry was easy, there was overcapacity, and prices were falling; the product was undifferentiated. Price competition could have the effect of changing market shares of the competing companies. The district court dismissed the complaint, and the United States appeals.

b) **Issue.** Does the legality of data dissemination vary with the characteristics of the industry involved?

c) **Held.** Yes. Judgment reversed.

(1) Exchange of price information seemed to have the effect of stabilizing prices, since defendants seemed to match the prices of their competitors.

(2) Here, the industry is dominated by relatively few sellers, the product is fungible, and competition is over price. In this situation, the exchange worked to prevent competition.

d) **Concurrence** (Fortas, J.). I agree with the result. However, the exchange of price information among sellers is not a per se violation.

e) **Dissent** (Marshall, Harlan, Stewart, JJ.).

(1) Ds only amount to 18 of 51 producers; entry is easy. This is not sufficiently oligopolistic such that an extreme danger exists from price information sharing. The government must prove intent to fix prices or that the defendant's conduct had this actual effect. Evidence submitted is insufficient.

(2) There is deterrence to maintaining prices because of the large number of competitors.

(3) Evidence is that Ds used the price information as they pleased and that the information was actually employed to engage in price competition.

(4) Ds have shown a downward trend in prices, price variations among themselves, and shifting of accounts.

(5) The government has not shown profit levels of defendants or price levels; it relies on the theoretical argument that even though there is overcapacity, unusually high profits exist, and that prices would have fallen faster except for the sharing of price information.

f) **Comment.** This case illustrates the difficulty with per se rules. Most of the members of the Court seem to be saying that the problem is to "characterize" something as "price fixing." Of course it is illegal if it is price fixing, but there are many situations where conduct might be for other worthwhile purposes. Thus, we have a fact question and a proof problem in each instance. The evidence submitted must go to (i) intent or purpose or (ii) necessary or probable effect on prices.

b. Summary comments.

1) The rationale for permitting the exchange of information is that many types of industry-wide information are helpful in planning for efficient operation.

2) Since a rule of reason is employed, the issue is whether the information collected and distributed is no more anticompetitive than necessary to accomplish the legitimate objectives. This is a fact question.

3) Industry structure and market share represented by the association may make a difference in the outcome.

a) The government will be anxious to prevent an industry from becoming in effect an "oligopoly." That is, where most of an industry is represented in an association, information sharing may in effect help this industry to become an oligopoly.

b) Query the situation where an oligopolistic industry has an association. Does it make any difference in this situation what the association is like as long as it stops short of actual agreement to fix prices? In other words, does it make it any worse that an association exists when, in an oligopoly, firms follow each other's prices anyway?

FTC v. Cement Institute

c. **Delivered price systems--FTC v. Cement Institute,** 333 U.S. 683 (1948).

1) **Facts.** The government brought an action against the Cement Institute, member firms, and individuals associated with the Institute. Seventy-four firms belong, and 10 of these firms control over 50% of the mills in the United States. They have used a multiple base point delivered price system (*i.e.,* the country is cut up into zones; prices charged by all producers in each zone are based on mill prices at a base mill and freight charges from that mill to the point of sale, no matter where the seller and buyer are) so that for years all sales of cement were at the same price and bids on jobs were exactly the same from all firms. The Institute was shown to have engaged in an active campaign to maintain the pricing system (firing uncooperative employees, selling cement in a price cutter's territory at prices so low that the firm had to capitulate, distributing freight rate books, etc.). The FTC, under section 5 of the FTC Act, issued a cease and desist order, which was vacated by the court of appeals. The FTC appeals.

2) **Issue.** May parallel business behavior violate section 5 of the FTC Act even if it does not violate the Sherman Act?

3) **Held.** Yes. FTC decision affirmed.

a) The base point system was conducive to price parallelism and could destroy competition. It therefore was an "unfair method of competition" under section 5.

E. CONCERTED REFUSALS TO DEAL

1. Collective Exclusive-Dealing Agreements.

a. **Introduction.** The aim of exclusionary agreements is to preempt a market completely for some participating group. One means of doing this is for a single firm or a group of firms to control sources of supply of vital material, or by tapping essential channels of distribution exclusively to themselves. Often this is done by firms at different market levels (*e.g.,* manufacturers and wholesalers making an agreement whereby no nonparticipating wholesaler will be supplied and the wholesalers will sell for no other manufacturers).

b. **The general rule.** Collective agreements whereby only firms within the participating group can obtain supplies or favorable terms of trade (discounts, etc.) are unreasonable restraints of trade. It makes no difference that the amount of trade restrained is negligible.

2. **Collective Boycott Agreements.**

a. **Introduction.** Competitors may also be excluded from a market by the positive action of a dominant group (*e.g.*, by blacklisting or boycotting). Where large groups of firms are involved, as with exclusive-dealing agreements, a successful boycott often requires groups at different levels of the market to combine (*e.g.*, retailers and their suppliers).

b. **Inferred conspiracy--Eastern States Retail Lumber Dealers' Association v. United States,** 234 U.S. 600 (1914).

Eastern States Retail Lumber Dealers' Association v. United States

1) **Facts.** Retail Lumber Dealers' Association (D) circulated among its members a list of wholesalers who sold to retail customers. The effect was that members of the Association withheld their patronage from the identified wholesalers.

2) **Issue.** Is a practice which has the effect of enforcing an informal boycott against disapproved dealers illegal if its purpose is to lessen competition?

3) **Held.** Yes. This is unlawful concerted refusal to deal.

a) An individual firm may refuse to deal, but where there is a group conspiracy or agreement it may be unlawful. Here the unlawful conspiracy is proved by circumstantial evidence; information circulated was designed to prevent retailers from dealing with wholesalers who sold to retailers. It had this effect in numerous instances.

c. **Refusal to deal for valid business reasons--Cement Manufacturers Protective Association v. United States,** 268 U.S. 588 (1925).

Cement Manufacturers Protective Association v. United States

1) **Facts.** Members of the Cement Manufacturers Protective Association (D) submitted monthly reports on production, shipments, and stocks. A freight book, involving a basing point system, was distributed; periodic meetings were held, but prices were not discussed. Extensive credit information was exchanged, but nothing about credit policies. Information about specific contracts was also exchanged and checkers were employed to determine the exact amounts needed on specific jobs. This was done to remedy the problem of buyers ordering in advance their requirements from several firms and having excess cement in rising markets but canceling their orders in a declining price market.

2) **Issue.** May competitors exchange information about specific deals to protect against fraud?

3) **Held.** Yes. No violation of the Sherman Act. There was no agreement to act in a uniform way, and the information helped the members avoid buyer fraud.

4) **Comment.** The main difference between this case and *Eastern States*, *supra*, is the purpose for the cooperation.

Fashion Originators' Guild of America v. FTC

d. **Group boycott per se illegal--Fashion Originators' Guild of America v. FTC,** 312 U.S. 457 (1941).

1) **Facts.** Members of a textile manufacturers' association and members of a garment manufacturers' association joined together in the Fashion Originators' Guild (D). They agreed that they would not sell to retailers who sold "copies" of original designs of the members of D. D controlled a significant percentage of the garment business. D enforced the arrangement by patrolling the retail stores, and fined members that violated its rules. In addition, D had other restrictive rules: no retail advertising, regulation of discounts, prohibition of selling garments to retailers in homes, etc. The FTC found a violation under section 5 of the Sherman Act.

2) **Issue.** May competitors associate and agree among themselves to refuse to deal with buyers who participate in possibly tortious conduct with respect to members of the association?

3) **Held.** No. Findings affirmed.

a) Group boycott is per se illegal. Competition is unreasonably restrained by limitations on outlets to which manufacturers can sell and limitations on sources from which retailers can buy.

b) It makes no difference that the purpose of the boycott is to regulate practices that may be a tort under state law (*i.e.,* pirating designs).

Klor's v. Broadway-Hale Stores

e. **Public injury not required--Klor's v. Broadway-Hale Stores,** 359 U.S. 207 (1959).

1) **Facts.** Klor's (P) operated a small retail store in San Francisco, selling appliances. Broadway-Hale Stores (D) operated one of its chain stores next door, selling the same brands of appliances. D and 10 national manufacturers of appliances agreed that the manufacturers would not sell to Klor's or would sell only for higher prices. There were other competitors in the vicinity, so there was no showing that the public was injured by this group boycott. P sued D under the Sherman Act. The district court found that the dispute was purely private and dismissed the complaint. The court of appeals affirmed for lack of a public injury, and P appeals.

2) **Issue.** May a combination of manufacturers, distributors, and one retailer boycott one particular retailer as long as no injury to the general public results?

3) **Held.** Yes. Judgment reversed.

a) Group boycotts, or concerted refusals by traders to deal with other traders, are forbidden by the Sherman Act because by their very nature they are unduly restrictive. It does not matter that the boycott may lower prices or temporarily stimulate competition.

b) P has alleged a boycott that excludes P from the market. The boycott interferes with the natural flow of interstate commerce and has a monopolistic tendency.

c) The fact that P's elimination does not significantly impact the economy is irrelevant. A monopoly may flourish through elimination of small businessmen.

4) **Comment.** Some lower courts have resisted the full implications of the per se rule in *Klor's*. Also, the United States Supreme Court has indicated that the *Klor's* rule does not necessarily have the same application in situations involving organizations which are organized for other than commercial purposes (*e.g.,* it may not apply in situations where the boycott is used to coerce others to adopt certain conduct for reasons that do not directly apply to market considerations).

3. **Bottleneck Agreements.**

a. **Introduction.** Sometimes a single firm has sufficient command over some essential commodity or facility in its industry to be able to impede new entrants into the industry. Alternatively, a group of firms may together control such essential commodities or facilities and agree among themselves not to share them with others.

b. **General rule.** The Sherman Act requires that where facilities cannot practically be duplicated by would-be competitors, those in possession of them must allow them to be shared on fair terms.

c. **Access to news--Associated Press v. United States,** 326 U.S. 1 (1945).

Associated Press v. United States

1) **Facts.** Twelve hundred newspapers subscribed to Associated Press (D). According to the bylaws, members agreed to be bound by its rules and violations were enforced by heavy fines. No member could sell news from its own area to nonmembers, nor make news supplied by D available to nonmembers in advance of publication. An existing member could prevent competing members from joining D. The United States brought an action under sections 1 and 2 of the Sherman Act. The district court found the bylaws illegal, and D appeals.

2) **Issue.** May independent businesses become associates in a common plan which hampers business rivals' opportunities to buy or sell the things in which the groups compete?

3) **Held.** No. Judgment affirmed.

a) D limited opportunity for any newspaper to enter competition where there was already a member of D.

b) Independent businesses have become associates in a common plan to reduce competition. This is an unreasonable combination which might be used to achieve victory over nonmember firms.

c) It makes no difference that there are other news services; members control 96% circulation of morning papers. But even if nonmembers can still compete, this is a violation.

d) It is not required that the product or service be indispensable in order to compete.

e) The association may continue, but membership cannot be unreasonably restricted.

Northwest Wholesale Stationers v. Pacific Stationery & Printing Co.

d. **Exclusion from cooperative wholesale distributor--Northwest Wholesale Stationers v. Pacific Stationery & Printing Co.,** 472 U.S. 284 (1985).

1) **Facts.** Pacific Stationery & Printing Company (P), which was engaged in both retail and wholesale sales of office supplies, was a member of Northwest Wholesale Stationers (D), a cooperative that acted as a wholesaler for its nearly 100 office supply retailer members. D adopted a rule that prohibited members from engaging in both retail and wholesale, but it permitted P to continue as a member. P's owners sold the stock, and the new owners did not notify D. Subsequently, D expelled P without notice. P sued, claiming that the expulsion was a group boycott. D's wholesale operation sold to all retailers, whether members or not, but it distributed its profits through a rebate to members based on their purchases. P claimed that its expulsion limited its competitive position. The trial court granted summary judgment for D, finding no anticompetitive effect. The court of appeals reversed, holding that the expulsion was an anticompetitive concerted refusal to deal with P. Although section 4 of the Robinson-Patman Act permits price discrimination resulting from an expulsion brought about through self-regulation, the court held that under *Silver v. New York Stock Exchange*, 373 U.S. 341 (1963), D had a duty to provide procedural safeguards to claim the protection of Robinson-Patman. D appeals.

2) **Issue.** Does the per se rule apply to a cooperative wholesaler's exclusion of one of its members, absent a showing that the wholesaler had market power or unique access to a business element necessary for effective competition?

3) **Held.** No. Judgment reversed.

a) Concerted refusals to deal or group boycotts have long been held to be per se violations of the Sherman Act. The court of appeals, however, held that D could find relief in the Robinson-Patman Act, and then relied on *Silver* to require D to provide adequate procedural safeguards.

b) The Robinson-Patman Act is different from the Securities Exchange Act under which *Silver* was decided. Section 4 of the Robinson-Patman Act is merely an immunity from the price discrimination prohibitions of the Act itself; it is not a broad mandate for industry self-regulation. In addition, procedural protection cannot save a concerted activity that amounts to a per se violation of the Sherman Act.

c) Group boycotts that are per se illegal generally consist of joint efforts by firms to disadvantage competitors by denying, or persuading or coercing others to deny, relationships the competitors need in the competitive struggle. However, not every cooperative activity involving a restraint or exclusion is illegal. It depends on whether the particular form of concerted activity characteristically is likely to result in predominantly anticompetitive effects.

d) D's activity was intended to increase economic efficiency and make the market more competitive by giving the retailers cost savings and inventory; it was not likely to result in anticompetitive effects. P does not challenge D's existence, but only P's exclusion from D. But D has to have some rules to govern its membership. The expulsion was not likely to result in predominantly anticompetitive effects because there was no showing that D possesses market power or exclusive access to an element essential to effective competition; therefore, the per se rule does not apply. On remand, the court of appeals must evaluate the trial court's rule of reason analysis.

e. **Concerted refusal to provide information--FTC v. Indiana Federation of Dentists,** 476 U.S. 447 (1986).

FTC v. Indiana Federation of Dentists

1) **Facts.** As a means of containing the cost of dental treatment, insurers required dentists to submit dental x-rays with insurance claim forms to permit review of the diagnosis and treatment. The Indiana Dental Association succeeded in getting its members to refuse to submit the x-rays, but the FTC (P) ordered it to cease these efforts. In response, the Indiana Federation of Dentists (D) was formed to continue resistance to the x-ray submission requirements of insurers. In certain cities, D persuaded the majority of dentists to refuse to submit x-rays. P found that D's practice violated section 5 of the FTC Act. The court of appeals vacated the order as not being supported by substantial evidence, and P appeals.

2) **Issue.** Is it a violation of section 5 of the FTC Act for professionals to agree among themselves not to provide information required by insurers to monitor the quality of care?

3) **Held.** Yes. Judgment reversed.

a) P found that in the absence of concerted behavior, individual dentists would have had incentives to comply with the insurers' request to respond to competition. The effect of D's activity was to deny the information the customers requested in the form they requested it, forcing them to choose between forgoing the information or acquiring it through more expensive means. D restrained competition among dentists with respect to cooperation with insurers.

b) Because D's activity consists of a concerted refusal to deal on particular terms with insured patients, it resembles a group boycott. Group boycotts have been deemed unlawful per se, but that approach has been limited to cases involving the use of market power to discourage suppliers or customers from doing business with a competitor. That is not the case here. Thus, the rule of reason should apply.

c) D's refusal to compete with respect to the services provided to customers has much the same effect as a refusal to compete with respect to price; it impairs the market's ability to ensure that goods and services are provided at a price approximating the marginal cost of providing them. Under the rule of reason, the restraining cannot be upheld unless it has some countervailing procompetitive virtue. D's policy lacks such a virtue.

d) D claims that because P did not make specific findings about the definition of the relevant market, it could not properly conclude that D unreasonably restrained trade. However, P made findings that D's activity actually did have an adverse effect on competition in two specific cities, so there was no need for further proof of market power. Nor was P required to prove that D's activity made dental services more costly; the withholding of information desired to evaluate the cost-effectiveness of a particular purchase of services is likely to disrupt the proper functioning of the price-setting market mechanism.

e) D also claims that the x-rays, by themselves, provide inadequate information to diagnose dental problems, so that if insurers rely on the x-rays, they may decline to pay for needed treatment to the detriment of the patients. This argument is really a claim that customer access to this information will lead them to make unwise or dangerous choices.

F. DEALINGS WITH GOVERNMENT

1. **Introduction.** Firms may get together to seek favorable government actions, including legislation, regulations, and other rulings. Although such combinations may be formed for anticompetitive objectives, there is an interest in access to government that outweighs the Sherman Act in many cases.

Eastern Railroad Presidents Conference v. Noerr Motor Freight

2. **Lobbying--Eastern Railroad Presidents Conference v. Noerr Motor Freight,** 365 U.S. 127 (1961).

a. **Facts.** Noerr Motor Freight Company and 40 other Pennsylvania truck operators and their trade association (Ps) sued 24 eastern railroads, the Eastern Railroad Presidents Conference, and its advertising firm (Ds). Ps charged restraint of trade by an advertising and lobbying effort conducted by the ad firm without disclosing that its client was the railroads, to get tighter enforcement of laws of the motor carriers and new restrictive and taxing legislation passed. Ds cross-claim against the motor carriers on the same charges. No legislation was actually passed, but Ds did get the governor to veto legislation favorable to Ps. Ps also charged that the campaign damaged their reputation with consumers and caused a loss of profits. The trial court found that Ds' publicity campaign violated the Sherman Act. The court of appeals affirmed, and Ds appeal.

b. **Issue.** Does the Sherman Act prohibit competitors from joining together for lobbying activities undertaken for anticompetitive purposes?

c. **Held.** No. Judgment reversed.

1) No violation of the antitrust laws can be based on a mere attempt to influence legislation or enforcement of the laws. This is true even where the legislative effort is an attempt to get the government to pass legislation which would restrain trade or create a monopoly. To hold otherwise might threaten the legislative process and offend constitutional rights.

2) It makes no difference what Ds' intent or purpose was in seeking the legislation.

3) Ds need not have disclosed that they were the source of the advertising.

4) Efforts to influence legislation will always have an incidental effect on the public.

5) There may be some situations where a publicity campaign is a mere "sham" to cover what is nothing more than an attempt to interfere directly with the business relationships of a competitor. In this case, the antitrust laws might apply.

3. **Limitation on Lobbying--California Motor Transport Co. v. Trucking Unlimited,** 404 U.S. 508 (1972).

California Motor Transport Co. v. Trucking Unlimited

a. **Facts.** California Motor Transport Company and other highway carriers (Ps) sued Trucking Unlimited and other carriers (Ds) under section 4 of the Clayton Act. Ds went to administrative (state and federal) hearings when Ps were seeking new routes, etc., and resisted favorable ruling on the applications. Ps alleged that Ds did this without probable cause and regardless of the merits, solely to put Ps out of business. The trial court granted Ds' motion to dismiss, citing *Noerr*, *supra*. The court of appeals reversed, and the Supreme Court granted certiorari.

b. **Issue.** May competitors combine to institute and prolong legal proceedings for the sole purpose of preventing would-be competitors from entering a market?

c. **Held.** No. Judgment affirmed and case remanded for trial.

1) There is a constitutional right to make appearances before administrative agencies. However, *Noerr* recognized that certain combinations may be mere shams to protect direct interference with competitors.

2) In this case, Ds went beyond exercise of their constitutional rights and sought to bar competitors from meaningful access to adjudicatory

tribunals. Thus, exercise of their constitutional rights was a "sham" to cover anticompetitive intent and purpose.

d. **Comment.** How can *Noerr* be distinguished from *California Motor Transport*? Clearly, intent and purpose are important, and the intent is determined from the facts. In *Noerr*, there was no actual effect (*i.e.*, no legislation was passed) and the Court probably trusted the openness and difficulty of influencing the legislature more than it did the power of private parties to influence administrative tribunals.

Professional Real Estate Investors v. Columbia Pictures Industries

4. **"Sham" Exception to *Noerr* Immunity--Professional Real Estate Investors v. Columbia Pictures Industries,** 508 U.S. 49 (1993).

a. **Facts.** Professional Real Estate Investors (D) owned a hotel and rented videodisc movies to its guests for in-room viewing. Columbia Pictures Industries (P) and other motion picture studios had licensed a cable system operator to offer pay-per-view movies to hotel guests. P sued for copyright infringement. D counterclaimed on the ground that P's suit was merely a sham to exclude a competitor and thus was not protected under *Noerr*, *supra*. The courts held for D on P's claim, but dismissed D's counterclaim on the ground that because P had probable cause to bring its original claim, it could not be considered a sham. The Supreme Court granted certiorari.

b. **Issue.** Does *Noerr* immunity apply to litigation so long as the litigation is not objectively baseless?

c. **Held.** Yes. Judgment affirmed.

1) *Noerr* immunity does not apply to "sham" activities because the Sherman Act should apply when petitioning activity "ostensibly directed toward influencing governmental action, is a mere sham to cover . . . an attempt to interfere directly with the business relationships of a competitor."

2) D argues that litigation may be "sham" merely because the litigant is not motivated by a subjective expectation of success. However, *Noerr* immunity applies regardless of intent or purpose. Anticompetitive intent or purpose, by itself, cannot transform otherwise legitimate activity into a sham.

3) The better rule is that an objectively reasonable effort to litigate cannot be a sham regardless of subjective intent. To constitute a "sham," a lawsuit must be "objectively baseless in the sense that no reasonable litigant could realistically expect success on the merits." If it is objectively meritless, the court must then determine whether the baseless lawsuit conceals "an attempt to interfere directly with the business relationships of a competitor" by using governmental process instead of the outcome of that process as an anticompetitive weapon.

4) A lawsuit cannot be deemed objectively baseless if there was probable cause to institute legal proceedings. This requires merely a reasonable belief that there is a chance that a claim may be held valid upon adjudication.

5) In this case, the courts correctly found that P had probable cause to sue D for copyright infringement. There had been a split among the circuits regarding the applicability of copyright law to on-site private screening such as D offered in its hotel rooms.

d. **Concurrence** (Stevens, O'Connor, JJ.). A lawsuit might be objectively unreasonable even if success could be expected if that success would be insignificant.

e. **Comment.** Once the two elements of sham are shown, the plaintiff still must prove a substantive antitrust violation.

5. **Immunity for Municipality's Anticompetitive Ordinances Prompted by Competitor--City of Columbia v. Omni Outdoor Advertising,** 499 U.S. 365 (1991). City of Columbia v. Omni Outdoor Advertising

a. **Facts.** Omni Outdoor Advertising (P) began erecting billboards in a market dominated by Columbia Outdoor Advertising ("COA"). COA's owners had cozy relationships with city officials in the City of Columbia (D). COA persuaded D's officials to enact zoning ordinances that limited construction of new billboards. P sued D under the Sherman Act, claiming that it had formed an anticompetitive conspiracy. The jury awarded damages to P, but the district court granted judgment n.o.v. to D on the ground that D's adoption of zoning ordinances was outside the scope of the Sherman Act. The court of appeals reversed, holding that D's participation in a conspiracy voided its *Parker v. Brown*, 317 U.S. 341 (1943), immunity. The Supreme Court granted certiorari.

b. **Issue.** Is a city subject to federal antitrust liability if it adopts anticompetitive ordinances at the prompting of one competitor who directly benefits from the ordinances?

c. **Held.** No. Judgment reversed.

1) In *Parker v. Brown*, the Court held that principles of federalism and state sovereignty make the Sherman Act inapplicable to anticompetitive restraints adopted by states as an "act of government." The *Parker* immunity has also been extended to municipal anticompetitive actions taken pursuant to state policy.

2) D was prima facie entitled to *Parker* immunity because its billboard ordinance was an authorized implementation of state zoning statutes, and suppression of competition is a foreseeable result of zoning regulations.

3) The court of appeals should not have applied a "conspiracy" exception to the *Parker* immunity. Such a conspiracy exception would effectively eliminate *Parker* immunity because public officials are supposed to respond to the demands of their constituents. Public input on policymaking cannot be considered "conspiracy" under the antitrust laws, nor can "conspiracy" be limited to cases of bribery or other corruption, because the Sherman Act targets trade restraints, not political activity.

4) COA's efforts to have D pass the zoning ordinance are immune from liability under *Noerr*, *supra*. The "sham" exception to *Noerr* does not apply here because COA did not use the governmental process itself as an anticompetitive weapon. It was the final result that was anticompetitive. The "conspiracy" exception should not apply to *Noerr* immunity for the same reason it does not apply to *Parker* immunity.

d. **Dissent** (Stevens, White, Marshall, JJ.). D should not be immune where its authority to enact zoning ordinances was intended to promote public health and safety, not to protect favored citizens from competition. The conspiracy should also have eliminated COA's *Noerr* immunity.

e. **Comment.** The Court noted that the situation in which the state acts as a market participant may be a possible exception to the rule that state action is exempt from antitrust liability.

Allied Tube & Conduit Corp. v. Indian Head

6. **No Immunity for Controlling Private Trade Association's Action--Allied Tube & Conduit Corp. v. Indian Head,** 486 U.S. 492 (1988).

a. **Facts.** The National Fire Protection Association ("NFPA") was a private organization of industry, labor, insurers, firefighters, and other interested parties. One of NFPA's purposes was to establish product standards and codes for fire protection, including the National Electrical Code. The Code was widely adopted by state and local governments and was used by insurance underwriters, electrical inspectors, and contractors as a standard for covered products. The Code permitted the use of steel conduit such as the product manufactured by Allied Tube and Conduit Corporation and other manufacturers (Ds). Indian Head (P), a manufacturer of plastic conduit, made a proposal to NFPA to extend Code approval to plastic conduit. The matter was set for a vote by NFPA's members. Prior to the meeting, Ds agreed to defeat P's proposal by packing the meeting with new members of NFPA who would vote against it. Ds paid all the expenses and closely coordinated the vote to defeat P's proposal. P sued, claiming that Ds had unreasonably restrained trade in the electrical conduit market. The jury found for P, but the district court granted judgment n.o.v. by applying *Noerr* immunity (*supra*). The court of appeals reversed, and the Supreme Court granted certiorari.

b. **Issue.** Does *Noerr* immunity apply to coordinated efforts to persuade an influential but private trade organization?

c. **Held.** No. Judgment affirmed.

1) *Noerr* gives antitrust immunity to those who urge a governmental action, even though the action results in an anticompetitive restraint. This case, however, involves the standard-setting process of a private association. NFPA's members have horizontal and vertical business relations and economic incentives to restrain competition. The fact that legislatures routinely adopt the Code does not make NFPA a legislative body. *Noerr* immunity cannot apply to efforts to influence private bodies such as NFPA, which are not accountable to the public and have no official authority.

2) Ds claim that influencing NFPA is the best way to influence legislation regulating electrical conduit. While this may be true, *Noerr* does not immunize every concerted activity intended to influence governmental action. Otherwise, actions such as boycotts intended to influence governmental action would also be immune. The availability of *Noerr* immunity depends not only on the impact of the anticompetitive activity, but also on its conduct and the nature of the activity.

3) Rounding up supporters in a public election setting, which is a valid activity, is not comparable to rounding up economically interested persons to set private standards. The context and nature of Ds' activity make it the type of commercial activity that has traditionally had its validity determined by the antitrust laws themselves. Private standard-setting by associations such as NFPA is permitted under the antitrust laws only with the understanding that it will be conducted in a fair manner offering procompetitive benefits.

4) Ds did not merely seek to persuade an independent decisionmaker, but orchestrated the actual exercise of NFPA's decisionmaking authority.

5) The context and nature of Ds' activity should be characterized as commercial activity with a political impact, not as political activity.

6) Ds are free to take advantage of the NFPA forum by presenting its facts and arguments, so long as the decisionmaking process remains nonpartisan. What Ds cannot do is bias the process by stacking NFPA with decisionmakers sharing Ds' economic interest in restraining competition.

d. **Dissent** (White, O'Connor, JJ.). The majority's consideration of the "context and nature" of Ds' activity has not provided adequate guidance. To the extent that Ds' activities "exceeded the bounds of propriety," they should be considered "sham" and therefore lose *Noerr* immunity.

7. **Politically Motivated Economic Boycotts--Missouri v. National Organization for Women,** 620 F.2d 1301 (8th Cir. 1980), *cert. denied*, 449 U.S. 842 (1980).

Missouri v. National Organization for Women

a. **Facts.** The National Organization for Women (D), in an effort to promote passage of the Equal Rights Amendment, organized a convention boycott against all states that had not ratified the amendment. Missouri (P) was one of the target states. Because P was losing convention revenues, it sought an injunction against D's boycott. The district court found that D's boycott was politically oriented, and did not have any type of anticompetitive purpose. Because the boycott was noneconomic, the court denied the injunction. P appeals.

b. **Issue.** Is a boycott undertaken for political purposes outside the coverage of the Sherman Act even if it has an economic impact on the target of the boycott?

c. **Held.** Yes. Judgment affirmed.

1) The Sherman Act was apparently aimed at competitors in commerce, not at noncompetitors motivated by political objectives. In *Noerr*, *supra*, the Supreme Court stated that mere attempts to influence the passage of laws cannot be the basis for a violation of the Act.

2) *Noerr* involved legislation that affected the parties commercially. By contrast, D is promoting social or political legislation and has no profit motivation. It is only P that is concerned about the financial repercussion of the boycott. The fact that the boycott has a commercial impact does not eclipse the fact that it is political activity.

3) P claims that because this is an actual boycott, it is more than the mere attempt involved in *Noerr*. But even *Noerr* recognized that solicitation of government action could not violate the Sherman Act because of: (i) the dissimilarity between agreements to jointly seek legislation and agreements clearly covered by the Act; (ii) the inability of the government to deny people the right to freely inform the government of their wishes; and (iii) the significant constitutional questions that would arise if the Act could be used to hinder political activity.

FTC v. Superior Court Trial Lawyers Association

8. No Immunity for Economic Boycott with Political Elements--FTC v. Superior Court Trial Lawyers Association, 493 U.S. 411 (1990).

a. **Facts.** Members of the Superior Court Trial Lawyers Association (Ds) regularly acted as court-appointed counsel for indigent criminal defendants in the District of Columbia. To force the District to raise their fees, Ds agreed to stop providing representation until the District took action. The District eventually gave in. The FTC (P) then sued Ds under the FTC Act, alleging that Ds had entered into a conspiracy to fix prices and to conduct a boycott. P ruled that the boycott was illegal per se and entered an order prohibiting Ds from engaging in such boycotts in the future. The court of appeals vacated P's order on the ground that the boycott was a political message protected by the First Amendment; as such, the governmental interest in prohibiting boycotts is not sufficient to justify a restriction unless P could prove that Ds had market power. The Supreme Court granted certiorari.

b. **Issue.** Is an economically motivated boycott immune from antitrust laws if it is partly intended as a political statement?

c. **Held.** No. Judgment reversed.

1) Ds' boycott was clearly a horizontal arrangement among competitors in violation of the antitrust laws. Ds' social justifications for the boycott do not make the restraint of trade any less unlawful. *Noerr*, *supra*, does not extend to horizontal boycotts designed to exact higher prices from the government, even if they are genuinely intended to influence the government.

2) In *NAACP v. Claiborne Hardware Co.*, 458 U.S. 886 (1982), the Court held that the First Amendment prevented a state from prohibiting a politically motivated civil rights boycott. But unlike the boycott

in *Claiborne Hardware*, Ds' boycott was used to gain economic advantage for its participants.

3) The court of appeals, relying on *United States v. O'Brien*, 391 U.S. 367 (1968), created a new exception for boycotts having an expressive component. This approach is incorrect because it exaggerates the significance of the "expressive component" in Ds' boycott; every concerted refusal to do business with a potential customer or supplier has such a component.

4) The court of appeals approach also minimizes the importance of the per se antitrust rules. Per se rules are justified in part by administrative convenience. They also reflect a long-standing judgment that every horizontal price-fixing arrangement among competitors poses a threat to the free market even if the participants do not have power to control market prices.

d. **Dissent in part** (Brennan, Marshall, JJ.). "In any particular case, it may be difficult to determine whether political or economic power was brought to bear on the government." The approach taken by the court of appeals is an appropriate way to deal with this issue.

III. PROBLEMS WITH PATENTS

A. ANTITRUST LAW CONFLICT WITH THE PATENT SYSTEM

1. **Introduction.** The patent system creates a source of tension with the antitrust laws. This is true since (i) the holder of a patent is in a position of monopoly and (ii) certain kinds of restrictive agreements made by the patent holder (such as an exclusive license to make and sell the patented product in a defined territory) may be no more than the legitimate exercise of rights inseparable from the grant of the patent, although if the patent were not present, the agreement would violate the antitrust laws.

   Thus, the rights of patent holders must be accommodated with the public policies inherent in the antitrust laws. That such an accommodation is necessary is evident from the fact that the granting of a patent may in effect give control to the patentee of an entire industry, possibly one of a critical nature to society as a whole.

2. **An Analysis of the Benefits and Costs of the Patent System.**

   a. **Introduction.** The rationale for the patent system is that it promotes the development of new products and processes. The cost is that it gives monopoly power to the person holding the patent.

   b. **Objective.** The objective is to create a system that encourages the maximum development of useful new products but at the same time limits the costs of giving monopolies.

   c. **Alternative systems.** It seems clear that a great many inventions would occur without patent protection. The following conditions normally exist with larger corporate entities. Patent protection may be needed to encourage the smaller company or the individual inventor.

      1) **Time lags in imitation.** Developments occur in secret. It takes time to learn of and imitate a new development. In many instances, this is enough time for the originator to recoup his investment plus a profit.

      2) **Advantages to competitive leadership.** There are numerous advantages to being first, even without patent protection (*e.g.*, enhancing company image or getting an initial share of the market).

      3) **Nonpatent barriers to competition.** Lack of production facilities, managerial experience, and distribution channels often prohibit entry of competitors. Also, where the industry is concentrated, firms will normally pursue a pricing policy that allows the originator to recoup his investment and make a substantial profit.

   d. **Situations where patents assist development.**

1) **Perfect competition.** Where imitation is easy and development might not otherwise occur.

2) **Poor cost benefit ratio.** Where the cost of development is high and the potential benefits are low in comparison.

3) **Radically new developments.** Where inventions are off the beaten track from established technology and exploitation requires setting up entirely new production and distribution capabilities.

e. **Monopoly power.** The extent of monopoly power given depends on several factors.

1) **Substitutes.** The availability of substitutes is an important factor.

2) **Elasticity of demand.** The more inelastic demand is, the more monopoly power is available.

3) **Surrounding patents.** It is possible to patent a whole field by securing enough patents to "fence in" the technology.

4) **Improvement patents.** It is also possible to extend the life of the monopoly by continually developing new improvements.

3. The Patent Act and Its Requirements.

a. **Purpose.** *Motion Picture Patents Co. v. Universal Film Manufacturing Co.*, *infra*, stated that the purpose of the Patent Act was not to make people rich, but to stimulate the progress of science and the useful arts.

b. **Rights granted.** *Bauer & Cie v. O'Donnell*, 229 U.S. 1 (1913), held that the patent law gave the inventor the exclusive right to make, use, and vend his invention for the term of years stated, and the exclusive right to transfer the title for a consideration to others. Section 261 of the Patent Act states that the patentee may grant an exclusive right to the whole or any specified part of the United States.

c. **Standards for granting a patent.** The Patent Act gives standards for granting a patent: section 101 ("new and useful process, etc."), section 102 ("novelty"), and section 103 ("patent may not be obtained . . . if the differences between the subject matter . . . and prior art are such that the subject matter . . . would have been obvious at the time the invention was made to a person having ordinary skill in the art to which said subject matter pertains").

d. **Cannot patent an idea.** In *Gottschaulk v. Benson*, 409 U.S. 63 (1972), the patent office rejected a patent application involving claims to a method of programming any type of general purpose digital computer to convert binary-coded-decimal numerals into pure binary numerals, since the claims were not limited to any particular art or technology, machine, or end use. The Supreme Court sustained the patent office on grounds that it cannot issue a patent for an idea or for a scientific truth, mathematical expression, principle, etc.

e. **Patents procured by fraud.** If a patent is issued by fraud, a plaintiff affected thereby may bring a treble damages action under section 4 of the Clayton Act. Such an action may be sustained either under the Sherman Act or section 5 of the FTC Act.

f. **Acquisition of patents by purchase.** It is possible that the acquisition of patent rights by a company could lead to a charge of antitrust violations. It depends on the company's intent or purpose in the purchase, whether the patents were purchased from a competitor or noncompetitor, etc.

g. **Nonuse of patent.** In *Special Equipment Co. v. Coe*, 324 U.S. 370 (1945), the Court stated that in granting a patent it made no difference whether the grantee ever intended to make use of the patented invention. There was a dissent, arguing that the policy of the Patent Act was violated if it could not be shown that the patentee intended to develop the invention. Note that if the purpose of nonuse is to restrain competition, the result may be different.

B. PRICE RESTRICTED LICENSES

1. Rationale for Limiting Patent Rights.

a. **Introduction.** Patent holders have attempted to restrain competition in every way conceivable under the umbrella of patent rights. For example, cartels have been formed and patent agreements and cross-licenses entered into where the firms normally would compete with each other since they really had "substitute" products.

b. **Complementary and dependent products.** The argument is often made that where firms have complementary patented products (*i.e.,* neither can produce efficiently without the other) or dependent products (*i.e.,* one cannot be made without the other), it is important economically to allow restrictive cross-licensing. But it has also been argued that an alternative policy would require compulsory licensing in this situation.

c. **Rationale for limitations on patents.** Every patent will necessarily restrict the output of surrounding goods and services. Thus, the general rule should be that a patentee is entitled to extract monopoly income by reducing utilization of his invention, even if other goods and services are also restricted, provided that in each case, the restriction to the invention is confined as narrowly and specifically as technology and the practicalities of administration will permit.

1) The idea of a patent is that the patentee will get a reward directly proportional to the usefulness of the invention. Normally, this reward is to come from manufacture and sale, or licensing others for a royalty. Presumably, in a license the licensee in arm's length bargaining will pay what the patent is worth.

2) The problem in licenses is that the patentee and the licensees often agree on many other things that are in their competitive

interest but which are not limited to returning the invention's utility to the patentee.

3) For example, if a patentee gives a license to a licensee to manufacture a product where the patent is merely one of the inputs, and the parties agree to a fixed price for the unpatented end product, this may be unduly anticompetitive. In effect, this unpatented end product becomes a monopoly product (there is no competition between the patentee and the licensee), and the parties divide monopoly profits according to their share of the market. If the price-fixing were not allowed, then the patentee would be limited to a royalty on his patent, which would add to the patentee's competitive edge (*i.e.*, the licensee would have the additional product cost of the royalty), and this return would be the direct, legitimate worth of the patent.

4) Note that if the antitrust law were otherwise than as suggested here, there would be more motivation for licensing than for the patentee doing the manufacture and sale itself (since the patentee-licensee could make more broadly anticompetitive agreements than the anti-competitive effects of the patent in the hands of the patentee).

2. Price Fixing and Market Division in Patent Licenses.

a. Horizontal price fixing of patented products.

1) **Introduction.** The first issue is how far the patent holder may go in fixing the price at which the patented product may be sold by licensees.

2) **Where the license covers manufacture and sale of the patented product.**

a) **Introduction.** The simple case concerns the situation where the patentee grants a license to another to manufacture and sell its patented product, exacting as a condition of the license that the licensee charge a set price for the product.

b) **Not an unreasonable restraint--United States v. General Electric Co.,** 272 U.S. 476 (1926).

United States v. General Electric Co.

(1) **Facts.** General Electric (D) had a patent on electric lamps; it granted a license to Westinghouse, indicating that the product had to be sold at the same price that D was charging and distributed through the same means (D had devised an "agency" distribution system, divided into retail and industrial user markets aimed at retail price maintenance, which it wanted to maintain—hence the price restrictions on Westinghouse).

(2) **Issue.** May a patentee, by agreement, restrict the price for which a licensee can sell the patented product?

(3) **Held.** Yes.

(a) The license does not violate the antitrust laws and it is not an unreasonable restraint.

(b) Part of the right of a patentee is to acquire profit by setting the price at which the product is sold.

(c) It is reasonable for the patent holder to restrict the price at which a licensee may sell the product in order to protect the profit which the patentee will make.

(4) Comment. What motivation is there for General Electric to grant such a license? A possibility would be to avoid dispute with Westinghouse as to the validity of the patent and to prevent Westinghouse from coming up with a substitute product.

c) *General Electric* holding reaffirmed. In *United States v. Huck Manufacturing Co.*, 382 U.S. 197 (1965), the Court affirmed the *General Electric* doctrine. The government made the argument that the competitive effects in each situation should be assessed in determining whether to permit such licenses. For example, it may be that competitors selling substitute products might be the licensees, agreeing not to promote the substitute product but instead to divide a monopolistic market with the patentee.

d) Comment. Where there is a factual question as to whether the patentee actually controls the product by patent, an agreement between otherwise possibly competing firms will be illegal (as where the other firm has a patent on a competing product, or could possibly successfully test the validity of the patentee's patent). The courts may articulate this result by saying that the parties have an "intent" or "purpose" to restrain trade, rather than to accommodate the legitimate rights of a patentee.

3) Where the license covers part of a product.

a) In *United States v. General Electric Co.*, 80 F. Supp. 989 (S.D.N.Y. 1948), the court held that a license violated the antitrust laws. General Electric had a patent covering various hard-metal compositions used in the manufacture of tools and dies. It had given licenses to use the patents, conditioned on licensees charging a fixed price for their products.

b) In *Cummer Graham Co. v. Straight Side Basket Corp.*, 142 F.2d 646 (5th Cir. 1944), the court held that a license by the manufacturer of a patented machine, to use the machine in the manufacture of an unpatented product, did not allow the patentee to fix the price of the licensee's product.

4) Cross-licensing agreements.

a) Introduction. Typically what happens is that one manufacturer gets a patent and others discover improvements. Then these firms need each other's technology in order to manufacture at the state of the art. This situation leads to cross-licensing, so that all firms can produce the improved product.

b) Antitrust policy. On the one hand, it may appear that price fixing in this circumstance is nothing more than the right of the patent holders to secure the optimum return from their inventions. The danger is that such cross-licensing could lead to total suppression of price competition in an industry or a substantial part thereof; also, firms with independent but competing techniques might combine in order to avoid competition. Finally, it is arguable that a fair return is given to each patent holder if royalties are paid to each patent holder based on the relative importance of the patent to the end product.

For these reasons, the general rule of the courts is that antitrust law prohibits price stipulations in patent licenses whenever patents of different ownership are combined in the manufacture of goods.

c) **Illegality found--United States v. Line Material Co.,** 333 U.S. 287 (1948). United States v. Line Material Co.

(1) **Facts.** Southern States Equipment ("S.S.") owned the basic patent on a type of fuse; Line Material Company (D) got an improvement patent, subservient to the S.S. patent. It took both patents to make a commercially successful product. A cross-license provided that S.S. was to manufacture and sell at prices set by Line; Line was to grant sublicenses (which it did) to both patents, setting selling prices. Cross-license and sublicenses accounted for 40% of the market in this type of device. The arrangement was upheld by the trial court.

(2) **Issue.** May owners of two patents cross-license the patents and fix the prices to be charged by themselves and their licensees for the respective products?

(3) **Held.** No. Violation of section 1 of the Sherman Act.

(a) *United States v. General Electric*, *supra*, is still good law. But this case goes beyond the *General Electric* case.

(b) It would be a clear violation where competitive, noninfringing patents combine and fix prices on all devices produced under any of the patents.

(c) But there is also a violation here where the devices are not commercially competitive since the patents are subservient. The motivation to seek competitive inventions is reduced by the price fixing. Price fixing in this type of cross-licensing is per se illegal.

(4) **Comments.**

(a) The rationale of *Line Material* is as follows:

1] The dominant value is competition; therefore, limit the patent monopoly as narrowly as possible.

2] Cross-licensing will not be deterred by the decision; where it has commercially useful results it will still occur.

3] The fair return from a patent, where it is dependent on others for a commercially successful product, is the royalty given by licensees (and in the cross-licensing situation the parties will set royalties based on the relative contribution of each patent). Cross-licensing and price fixing are too great a return to the patentees and too great a detriment to the public.

4] This policy will stimulate competitors to find competing products by continuing to invent until they have a way around the patents of others.

(b) Another rationale for *Line Material* is that the courts will allow the single patentee to exercise his "monopoly rights" because in reality a single patent normally does not have much of a monopoly. But when multiple parties are involved, then practically speaking there are generally anticompetitive effects.

5) **The *General Electric* doctrine in monopoly or oligopoly situations.** Query whether the *General Electric* doctrine will survive in the situation in which there are very few firms in the industry and the patentee licenses all or several of the firms and includes restrictive price agreements. For example, in *Newburgh Moire Co. v. Superior Moire Co.*, 237 F.2d 283 (3d Cir. 1956), there were five firms in the moire finishing business; Newburgh had a patent which it licensed to two other firms, with price fixing agreements. The court held the price fixing per se illegal. Query also in this situation whether substitute products will be included in defining the "relevant market."

b. **Division of markets.** Section 261 of the patent act provides that a patent may be licensed or the exclusive right thereunder may be assigned for any specified part of the United States. However, the same considerations that prevail in the price fixing area probably operate in the division of markets. Thus, where the evidence shows that possibly competing firms have combined in a licensing or cross-licensing arrangement with market divisions, this will be held illegal. Also illegal would be cross-licensing or patent pools with market division agreements. Presumably, however, the *General Electric* doctrine is applicable in the market division area.

c. **Vertical price fixing.**

1) **Introduction.** It may be difficult to characterize a patent licensing arrangement as vertical or horizontal and thus to square the holdings of the cases with principles from the horizontal or vertical antitrust cases. For one thing, the courts seldom characterize the patent cases in this manner. For another, elements of both are often present in the same situation. The cases are not always consistent in this area.

2) **Vertical price fixing after "sale" of the product.** In *United States v. Univis Lens Co.*, 316 U.S. 241 (1944), Univis (D) had a patent on a lens; it licensed wholesalers and finishing retailers to grind blanks and sell them to customers at prices fixed by D. It also licensed certain retailers to sell finished lenses only to consumers at fixed prices. Failure to comply resulted in cancellation of the licenses. No royalties were paid. The Court

held that this violated the antitrust laws. Once the patentee has "sold" the patented product (in its finished or unfinished state), it can no longer control the price at which it is sold. Query—how does this compare with the permissible horizontal restraint in *General Electric*, *supra*?

3) **Vertical territorial divisions after sale of the product.** In *Ethyl Gasoline Corp. v. United States*, 309 U.S. 436 (1940), Ethyl Gasoline manufactured and sold a patented fluid compound which, when added to gasoline, increased its efficiency in combustion engines. It was sold to oil refiners. The sale was connected with a license which prohibited the refiners from selling to anyone but Ethyl's licensees or to retail dealers and consumers. Jobbers were granted exclusive territories through the refiners. The Court held that this was illegal. By its sales to refiners, Ethyl lost its right to control territories of the jobbers.

C. USE RESTRICTED LICENSES

1. **Introduction.** When the patented invention has several separate uses or applications, the patentee can properly limit a licensee to one or more such uses and grant such rights exclusively or nonexclusively.

2. **Horizontal and Vertical Use Restrictions--General Talking Pictures v. Western Electric Co.,** 304 U.S. 175 (1938).

General Talking Pictures v. Western Electric Co.

a. **Facts.** The patentee had a patent on vacuum tube amplifiers, which were useful in several distinct fields. It gave a license to manufacture and use the amplifier to several companies in the commercial use area, and a license to several companies to use the product to make products for home uses. In both license agreements there was a restriction prohibiting the licensee from using the product to make other types of products than those allowed by the license. One of the companies licensed for home products made a commercial product. Action is against this company and its purchaser.

b. **Issue.** May a patentee restrict the use made of its licensed product?

c. **Held.** Yes.

1) An infringement action by the patentee is valid, both against the company that made and sold the amplifier to a user restricted by the license agreement and against the purchaser, which knowingly purchased the amplifier and used it in violation of the license.

d. **Comment.** Use restrictions may allow the patentee to engage in price discrimination. The elasticity of demand for the patented product or process may vary considerably among different uses. The patentee can then charge a higher royalty for the use where the elasticity of demand is lower. Thus, the Court might not reach the same conclusion in a modern case that it reached in *General Talking Pictures*.

Baldwin-Lima-Hamilton Corp. v. Tatnall Measuring Systems Co.

3. **Restrictions on Purchaser's Subsequent Use Illegal--Baldwin-Lima-Hamilton Corp. v. Tatnall Measuring Systems Co.,** 169 F. Supp. 1 (E.D. Pa. 1958), *aff'd*, 268 F.2d 395 (3d Cir. 1959).

   a. **Facts.** Baldwin (P) gave an exclusive license to Tatnall (D), who bought the patented gauge devices with a "notice" that they could not be used as part of another device. D then sold the gauges and licensed one manufacturer in each area to use the device as part of another product; D reserved some areas for itself.

   b. **Issue.** May a patentee limit the use of a patented product once the product itself is sold?

   c. **Held.** No. Where a "sale" has taken place, there can be no restrictions on use thereafter.

D. PATENT SETTLEMENTS

1. **Introduction.** In addition to cross-licensing between two or more firms, a "patent pool" can exist where the firms in an industry (which control most of the relevant technology) get together and cross-license each other to their technology. One of the dangers is that in effect a cartel (monopoly) will be established in the industry by the cooperation among these firms, excluding the entry of other firms or putting other firms in the industry that do not participate in the pool at a competitive disadvantage. These pools often result from disputes between persons holding various patent rights, where the parties get together and pool their patents rather than fight each other.

Standard Oil Co. v. United States (The Cracking Case)

2. **Patent Pooling and Cross-Licensing--Standard Oil Co. v. United States (The Cracking Case),** 283 U.S. 163 (1931).

   a. **Facts.** Four major oil companies had competing patents to cracking processes of refining oil to gasoline. Conflict developed concerning the scope, validity, and ownership of the patents; infringement suits began, and the Patent Office declared interferences. The companies formed a patent pool—each got the right to use the others' patents, each could license to others, and there was a sharing of license royalties. Many firms were licensed. Ds controlled 55% of the cracked gasoline refined and 26% of all gasoline. The government claimed that the pooling of royalties was illegal per se.

   b. **Issue.** May parties settle disputes over conflicting patent claims by cross-licensing and pooling of royalties?

   c. **Held.** Yes. There is no violation.

      1) There is no monopolization of the gasoline industry and no unreasonable restraint of competition. The pool was a legitimate settlement of disputes according to the value of patent claims.

   d. **Comment.** Most commentators think this case was wrongly decided.

1) Compare this case with *Line Material, supra*. It can be distinguished on the basis that here, there was no proved price fixing on the product, no price fixing on royalty licenses, no territorial divisions, and presumably competition between pool members continued.

2) No fixing of royalty rates was proven, but wasn't this a strong possibility? And if so, haven't the four companies insulated themselves from price competition among themselves over some price range and from competition with licensees over some range, and haven't they in general affected the supply of gasoline in the total market (and thus its price)? And aren't competing patents a "product line" and an agreement between competitors to fix royalty rates an unlawful restraint?

3) Alternatively, wouldn't it have been better to require that the four firms independently license each other? Also, wouldn't it have been better to let them fight out patent claims (some might have been proved invalid, they all would have worked on developing independent patent claims, etc.)?

3. **Improper Cross-Licensing--United States v. Singer Manufacturing Co.,** 374 U.S. 174 (1963).

United States v. Singer Manufacturing Co.

a. **Facts.** Singer was the only United States manufacturer of a zigzag sewing machine; it had 62% of the United States market, the Japanese had 22%, and European imports had 16%. Singer had conflicting patent claims with two European companies. They agreed to drop the disputes in return for royalty-free cross-licenses; one of the companies assigned its patent to Singer (taking a license back) in return for cash and a promise by Singer to enforce the patent. Singer then sued the Japanese companies importing into the United States.

b. **Issue.** May competitors settle patent disputes by a scheme intended to suppress competition?

c. **Held.** No. Violation of the Sherman Act.

1) The common purpose of the plan for licensing was to suppress the Japanese competition and to protect the two European companies.

4. **Monopolization.** Clearly, where a patent pool is used to gain a monopoly for member firms, the pool will be declared unlawful. In *Hartford-Empire Co. v. United States*, 323 U.S. 386 (1945), the parties locked up all patents pertaining to the manufacturing of glass containers and then granted licenses pursuant to a scheme designed to allocate markets among participants. The Supreme Court upheld a remedial order that outsiders be granted licenses at reasonable rates.

IV. MONOPOLY

A. BASIC CONCEPTS

1. **Introduction.** Section 2 of the Sherman Act prohibits monopolization itself. It provides: "Every person who shall monopolize, or attempt to monopolize, or combine or conspire with any other person or persons, to monopolize any part of the trade or commerce among the several states, or with foreign nations, shall be deemed guilty of a felony." The significance of this section becomes apparent when basic economic concepts are considered.

2. **Market Structure.**

   a. **Types of markets.** The structure of a market has an effect on the conduct and performance of the firms selling in the market. The three basic factors in defining market structure are as follows:

      1) Seller concentration;

      2) Product differentiation; and

      3) Condition of entry.

   b. **Seller concentration.** Markets may be defined by the concentration of sellers therein.

      1) **Atomistic industries.** Here, there are many sellers in competition. Each is so small that he takes the selling price in the market as given and beyond his control; therefore, he adjusts his output to the most profitable level at that price. Outputs cannot be controlled to increase price since no seller has an influence on price. It is impossible to work out collective agreements among sellers to restrict competition because there are too many sellers.

         As an industry, output is adjusted to demand until industry output reaches the point (and price is reduced to the point) where the marginal cost of supplying more output equals the selling price. Where production can be increased without increasing unit cost, or where there is ease of entry into the market, then the long-run equilibrium position for the industry will be where each firm is producing at minimum cost, market price is equal to this cost (which includes a normal profit), the industry output is what buyers demand at that price, the industry output is the largest that can be sold at a price covering cost, and there are no excess profits being made.

      2) **Monopolistic industries.** Here, there is a single seller supplying the entire output to the market. The monopolist can restrict output to the most profitable point (costs relative to price). The monopolist will tend to produce less and charge more than an atomistically competitive industry.

3) **Oligopolistic industries.** Here, there are a few large firms, each with enough of the market to influence price with output adjustment. These firms will anticipate and react to changes by other firms in the industry; hence, they are interdependent. Prediction of market behavior is difficult. Some possibilities:

(i) Express cooperation;

(ii) Imperfect cooperation;

(iii) A stalemate (each firm maintaining its existing position); or

(iv) Open price rivalry.

Market performance ranges from that of an atomistic industry to that of a monopoly.

c. **Product differentiation.** There are two types of markets: Those where the products are homogeneous, and those where there is product differentiation (*e.g.*, by design, quality, branding, etc.). Where differentiation exists, the following may occur

(i) Advertising and sales promotion;

(ii) Design and quality variations in order to obtain the most profitable adjustment of cost to demand and price; or

(iii) Price differences.

Thus, in this situation, an industry may be made up of a lot of firms, each having a little bit of monopoly power.

3. **Factors Favoring Consolidation.**

a. **Introduction.** There are a number of factors which favor consolidation of firms into oligopolies or even monopolies.

b. **Comparison with cartels.** The argument is made that where there are economic reasons for cooperation and limitation of competition, the consolidation method by a single firm is preferred to the use of a cartel. The principal business reason, of course, is that it is very difficult to manage a cartel effectively.

c. **Conditions necessary for consolidation to occur:**

1) The prospect that monopoly power, after acquired, will exist for a long time.

2) The ability of the potential monopolist to finance the acquisition of the other firms.

3) The prospect that the potential monopolist will be able to buy out the other firms (willingness to sell). Note that it is very difficult to obtain a monopoly by buying all competing firms (as the number is

reduced, the incentive for the remaining firms to sell out is reduced and the cost goes up).

4) Difficulty of entry of new competitors into the market. Monopoly does carry with it the ability to retard or prevent firms from entering the market (through higher advertising, lower prices, rebates, easier credit terms, etc.).

4. **Economies of Scale.**

a. **Introduction.** The argument is made that monopolies in many industries would benefit consumers since they would allow the existence of economies of scale not otherwise possible, and thus costs would be reduced, efficiency increased, and prices reduced.

b. **The meaning of "economy of scale."** There are a number of different meanings intended when "economy of scale" is talked about:

1) Lower average production costs. This may occur by using excess capacity (*e.g.*, around-the-clock use of machines, etc.).

2) Fewer but larger plants.

3) Larger firms acquiring capital and the factors of production at cheaper rates.

c. **Arguments relative to economies of scale.**

1) Introduction. In reality, most of the arguments either supporting or denying significant economies of scale have not been proved.

2) Lower production costs. It seems that most plants could operate more efficiently and produce at a lower average manufacturing cost. But little is known about selling and distributing costs, and so little is known about the possible effect on total average costs.

3) Inefficient selling costs.

a) Advertising expenses. Much advertising is used to create unreal (but consumer perceived) "product differentiation." This could be eliminated by a monopolist.

b) Producer- and advertiser-created consumer demand. The argument is also made that the "consumer is not king," that in fact the advertisers determine what the consumer wants. A monopolist could therefore persuade the consumer to buy what was most profitable to produce.

4) Factor costs. The argument is made that larger companies can obtain the factors of production at cheaper rates (*e.g.*, cheaper capital, labor costs, etc.). It is unknown why this is the case, although there is evidence that it is. It may be that there is less uncertainty associated with the larger firm, or less costs to market, handle, and deliver goods to a large company.

5) **Profit motive of the large firm.** There is an existing theory that the larger the firm gets, the more other motivations in addition to the profit motive become part of the firm's real objectives.

6) **Research size.** In recent years, there seems to be some evidence that real, continued technological progress is dependent on large aggregations of capital and research manpower.

7) **Small and large firms.** There is an argument that industries where both small and large firms exist together mean that efficiency exists in the smallest firm able to survive. There are too many variable factors for this theory to be proved (*e.g.*, whether these firms really sell the same product, the differences in management capabilities, etc.).

B. MONOPOLIZATION

1. Early Cases.

a. **"Rule of reason" in monopolization cases--Standard Oil Co. v. United States,** 221 U.S. 1 (1911).

Standard Oil Co. v. United States

1) **Facts.** The Rockefellers and others organized Standard Oil of Ohio (D) between 1870 and 1882, acquiring nearly all of the oil refineries near Cleveland (and many others) and the oil pipelines from the East. Finally, the group controlled nearly 90% of the trade in refined products, allowing them to set the price of crude oil. The company got preferential rates with the railroads, used price cutting against small (local) competitors, etc. Later, the parts of the organization were put into a trust, which was changed to a holding company after antitrust litigation in the State of Ohio. After the trust was formed, it continued to engage in predatory practices, and it was sued by the United States Government pursuant to sections 1 and 2 of the Sherman Act.

2) **Issue.** Have D's actions resulted in a restraint of trade or monopolization?

3) **Held.** Yes. D has violated both sections 1 and 2 of the Sherman Act.

a) The danger of a monopoly is from price fixing, limiting production, and allowing deterioration of the product.

b) Section 1 of the Act prohibits every contract, combination, or conspiracy in restraint of trade. Only undue or unreasonable restraints are prohibited.

c) Section 2 is an extension of section 1, prohibiting any monopolization or attempts to monopolize by any person of any part of the trade among the states. "Monopolization" is simply a form of restraint of trade. Section 2 makes sure that in no way could the basic prohibition of section 1 be evaded.

d) Section 2 is to be interpreted according to the "rule of reason."

e) "Monopolization" does not mean "monopoly." A monopoly is legal if it occurs by normal, proper business methods and practices.

f) Whether there has been improper "monopolization" depends on the intent and purposes of the defendant.

(1) Here, a prima facie presumption arises of improper intent and purpose (*i.e.*, to obtain and maintain market power by excluding others) by the fact of the defendant's total domination of the industry (existing market power).

(2) The presumption becomes conclusive that an improper intent exists due to the evidence of the improper ways in which market power was acquired and maintained.

g) The remedy is an injunction against any future improper acts and dissolution of the holding company.

4) Comment. There was evidence in the case that the defendant had actually driven competitors out of business by the business methods it used. Note also that this was a case where an actual monopoly existed (90% market power).

b. Similar case. In *United States v. American Tobacco Co.*, 221 U.S. 106 (1911), decided at about the same time as *Standard Oil*, the Court ruled against the American Tobacco Company, which became a monopolist of the cigarette industry through mergers then used its market power to dominate other sections of the tobacco industry, sometimes buying companies and shutting them down in order to preserve the monopoly position. The Court amplified on its statement in *Standard Oil* concerning the "rule of reason," indicating that the rule meant that freedom of contract (necessary to do business) was preserved; at the same time, giving the Sherman Act a reasonable construction did not mean that all of the acts and practices condemned by sections 1 and 2 of the Act could be permitted simply by finding that they were "reasonable."

c. The necessity of a "rule of reason" in monopolization cases. Note that it would appear impossible to say that a monopoly should be per se illegal. This is true because there are many situations which tend to create natural monopolies:

(i) The first firm to bring a product to market has a monopoly.

(ii) A small town may be able to support only one business of a certain type (such as a newspaper).

(iii) And as the Court hinted in *Standard Oil*, a firm might become a monopoly through normal industrial methods.

Thus, the courts have made the distinction between "monopoly" and "monopolize," the latter implying a drive to acquire, maintain, and exert monopoly power through methods other than normal industrial means. This analysis gets the courts into the question of the "intent or purpose" lying behind the achievement of market power.

d. **"Monopolization" vs. "attempting to monopolize."** Note the difference in these two situations, both prohibited by section 2.

1) "Monopolization" is using market power as a monopolist, to drive out competition, raise prices, etc.

2) "Attempting to monopolize" is a drive toward acquiring the market power to be able to monopolize.

e. **The intent requirement.**

1) *Addyston Pipe, supra*, indicates that it is illegal for a combination of firms to cooperate to fix prices. Later cases indicate that it is per se illegal for such combinations to attempt to fix prices. But it does not follow that it is illegal for a single firm, even in a monopoly position, to fix prices. The issue in this situation involves the intent or purpose of the firm in fixing its prices. That is, having a monopoly position does not mean that the firm's prices are per se unlawful. The issue is whether the monopoly position is being exploited so as to raise prices, exclude competitors, etc.; this constitutes illegal "monopolizing."

2) In the "attempting to monopolize" situation, it would appear that to win, the government would have to show (i) the intent to monopolize and (ii) a dangerous probability that monopolization will result if the firm's conduct is not prohibited.

3) In the criminal law, "intent" is usually implied from acts; *i.e.*, the person is held to intend the natural consequences of his acts. The same is true in antitrust law.

   a) Thus, intent may be shown from particular acts, a general course of conduct, etc.

   b) The court or the jury must draw inferences from the acts or course of conduct and draw conclusions as to the intent (*e.g.*, whether it was to "monopolize," etc.).

4) The problem with the "intent" standard is that it is difficult to ascribe bad motive or good motive to acts that can be characterized either way. For example, a firm with substantial market power may lower its prices in order (i) to drive out competitors or (ii) to be competitive, to the benefit of the consumer.

f. **Remedies in monopolizing cases.** Normally, a civil action is brought (either alone or in conjunction with a criminal action) asking the court to grant an equity decree to dissolve or break up the monopoly.

United States v. United States Steel Corp.

g. Effective power in the market--United States v. United States Steel Corp., 251 U.S. 417 (1920).

1) **Facts.** United States Steel (D) was formed by the acquisition of about 180 firms. At the time of suit, it controlled 41% of domestic steel production. It had engaged in a series of meetings over the years with other producers to discuss stabilizing "prices" (in effect, it had established a practice of "price leadership" for the industry). But the company had not engaged in predatory practices such as freight rebates, temporary price-cutting, etc. An action was brought under section 2 for "monopolizing" (no cause of action for attempting to monopolize" was brought, nor was a section 1 action for restraint of trade against the company and the other producers brought).

2) **Issue.** Do D's actions amount to monopolization in violation of section 2 of the Sherman Act?

3) **Held.** No. No violation of section 2.

   a) D did not have market power to fix prices; thus, it could not be guilty of "monopolizing."

   b) All of D's competitors testified that they have not been coerced into the prices they charge. And collusion with the other producers would not have been necessary if D had had market power.

   c) D is a huge company, but bigness alone is not illegal.

   d) The existence of unexerted market power alone is not enough; there must be other overt acts which are prohibited in order for "monopolization" to exist.

4) **Comment.** The government probably could have succeeded with a section 1 action, or an "attempt to monopolize" action. Note also that the case was probably wrongly decided even under section 2. The competing firms would not testify against United States Steel because together they really amounted to a cartel and they were cooperating on price under the direction of United States Steel.

h. Difference in treatment of cartels and monopolies. The Court seems to treat cartels and monopolies differently, although basically the ends of both may be or probably are the same. Cartels to fix prices, allocate territories, etc., are per se unlawful (*see infra*). Whether a monopoly is unlawful depends on "intent or purpose" (*i.e.,* the "rule of reason" is applied).

1) **Administrative differences.** Commentators have justified this difference on the basis of the inability of the courts administratively to conduct continuing surveillance of cartels.

2) **Acquisition of market power through normal means.** Another reason is the fact that conceptually, a monopoly can be created simply through normal business means exerted by a single firm, whereas a cartel can only exist by agreement among competing firms.

3) **Economic benefits.** Finally, a consolidation may result in economic efficiencies that do not occur in cartels. For example, in a consolidation, inefficient plants can be closed, the optimum manufacturing arrangement set up, etc.

i. **Tension in the intent or purpose test.** The problem with this test is that business conduct may be equally consistent with an inference of lawful competitive conduct or a purpose to drive out competition (*e.g.*, a large company cutting prices to meet lower prices by the few remaining firms).

1) The problem is that the courts feel economically and emotionally committed to the idea that a monopoly can legally develop and exist. Thus, the idea exists that a monopoly created by "normal business practices" is lawful.

2) But at the same time, politically and economically the courts fear the existence of monopolies. Thus, tension is never quite resolved.

2. Unlawful Acquisition of Monopoly Power.

a. **The intent problem revisited--United States v. Aluminum Co. of America,** 148 F.2d 416 (2d Cir. 1945).

United States v. Aluminum Co. of America

1) **Facts.** Aluminum Company of America (D), founded in 1888, controlled all production of ingot aluminum in the United States by patents until 1909, and for the next three years controlled all production by various restrictive agreements with foreign cartels and covenants not to supply electricity to competing firms. Thereafter it averaged over 90% market share (*see* discussion below). D also fabricated aluminum. Despite its market power, D only made a profit of 10%, which was far from an extortionate profit. The United States (P) brought an action under section 2 of the Sherman Act for "monopolizing." The trial court held that D did not violate the Act, and P appeals.

2) **Issue.** Where the defendant has the intent to achieve monopoly power and in fact achieves 90% of control of its relevant market, is this unlawful monopolization?

3) **Held.** Yes. Judgment reversed.

a) D's 90% market share constitutes a monopoly. Even assuming that it was not earning more than a "fair" profit, this is no excuse for monopolizing. It does not show that a fair profit could not be earned at lower prices.

b) Monopolies are illegal because, just like price-fixing arrangements, they deny to commerce the protection of competition. There are also noneconomic policies that argue against monopolies.

c) Although monopolies are generally forbidden, in some situations, a monopoly may be "thrust upon" a defendant; in such cases, it is not unlawful. One example of this is where there is a sole survivor by virtue of superior skill and industry.

d) Here, the monopoly was not thrust upon D; D was not a passive beneficiary. The facts show a persistent determination to create and maintain monopoly power:

(1) D always anticipated increased demand for the product and was ready to supply it, thus keeping competitors from entering the market.

(2) D was consistently determined to maintain control of the market. The only intent requirement is that relevant to any liability—did D intend to bring about the forbidden act? No monopolist monopolizes unconscious of what it is doing. By meaning to keep its hold on the market, D monopolized within the meaning of section 2.

b. **Comments.**

1) The case indicates that it is not necessary to show predatory acts to show intent to monopolize. Thus, the Court has moved some distance from *Standard Oil, supra*.

2) The case can be read as saying that despite a disclaimer, even normal aggressive business practices can show an intent to monopolize.

3) The case clearly states that actual exercise of monopoly power need not be shown to sustain a section 2 violation.

4) In effect, the burden is put on the defendant to show that it just could not help gaining monopoly power. And this burden seems heavy.

3. **Unlawful Use of Monopoly Power.**

a. **Introduction.** A series of cases are reviewed below in which the defendants have lawfully acquired monopoly power. The issue in each instance concerns how the defendants have thereafter used this market power.

United States v. Griffith

b. **Use of monopoly power without intent to monopolize--United States v. Griffith,** 334 U.S. 100 (1948).

1) **Facts.** Griffith (D) owned theaters in 85 towns; in 53 of these, it had the only theater. It negotiated with each film distributor for one contract covering all of its theaters; normally, the distributors would contract to D for all of their first-run movies to be released during the entire year. The United States (P) charged that this was an unlawful use of monopoly power (which exists in the one-theater towns) to restrain competition (in the competitive towns) by preventing competitors from obtaining first-run movies. P sued for an injunction pursuant to sections 1 and 2 of the Sherman Act. The district court found that D had no intent or purpose unreasonably to restrain trade or to monopolize, and P appeals.

2) **Issue.** Is it unlawful under the Sherman Act to use monopoly power even if the monopoly power is lawfully gained?

3) **Held.** Yes. Judgment reversed

a) Monopolies are generally the end products of section 1 violations, but even when they are not, monopoly power itself may violate section 2.

b) The use of monopoly power, even if lawfully acquired, to foreclose competition, gain a competitive advantage, or destroy a competitor is unlawful.

c) Here, D's monopoly power in the one-theater towns was used as a competitive weapon in the competitive towns. Even if D did not threaten the film distributors, and even if he had no specific intent to use his monopoly power to expand his empire, the end result is the necessary and direct result of D's actions.

4) **Remand.** On remand, the court issued an injunction requiring that D negotiate its contracts with distributors separately for monopoly towns and competitive towns.

5) **Comments.**

a) Does the case really accomplish anything? Distributors still know that the defendant has all of the theaters. Will the deals they make really be any different?

b) The issue seems to be the use of "monopoly leverage" in competitive situations. Is any use of monopoly power unlawful? How do you distinguish those uses that are proper from those that are not?

c) The defendant can still exact a monopoly rate in the one-theater towns and use the monopoly profits to bargain in the competitive towns. Is this any better for competitors than previously?

c. **Business practices normally permissible become illegal when conducted by a monopolist--United States v. United Shoe Machinery Corp.,** 110 F. Supp. 295 (D. Mass. 1953), *aff'd per curiam*, 347 U.S. 521 (1954).

United States v. United Shoe Machinery Corp.

1) **Facts.** United Shoe Machinery (D) supplied about 80% of the machines used to make shoes; it was the only company to make all of the necessary equipment, although there were competitors in specific areas and from foreign firms. It only leased its machines on 10-year leases; machine repair service was provided at no separate charge; if a customer turned the machine back early, there was a fee (which was smaller if the customer was taking another machine from D than if taking one from a competitor). D had a competitor in one type of process. In this area, D dropped its rate of return to a lower figure than in other areas. The government sued D under sections 1 and 2 of the Sherman Act.

2) **Issue.** May lawfully acquired monopoly power be used to maintain a monopoly?

3) **Held.** No. D violated the Sherman Act.

a) The market is defined as all machines (except dry thread sewing machines) used to make shoes.

b) D has monopoly power. It acquired this power lawfully (this conclusion was based on the court's analysis of previous cases against D).

c) But D has exercised its monopoly power unlawfully. The control is not maintained simply by ability, economies of scale, or adaptation to inevitable economic laws. D has erected barriers to entry and an anticompetitive environment by its business policies.

d) The system of leasing and the pricing policy (of lowering the margin of profit where competition exists) are unlawful.

e) None of these practices is immoral or anything that other honorable businessmen would not do. And, they are not, by themselves, a violation of the antitrust laws. But they are unlawful for a monopolist since they perpetuate market control rather than encouraging competition.

f) The following are the remedies imposed on D:

(i) D must sell machines (rather than just lease them) on favorable terms.

(ii) Where machines are leased, the term must be shortened.

(iii) Services must be priced separately.

(iv) But nothing can be done about the pricing policy. Pricing differences may be the result of the existence of patents, desirable for the consumer in that this creates a competitive environment, and the court cannot monitor every pricing change made by D.

These practices are all designed to loosen D's monopoly hold on the market.

4) **Comments.**

a) Thirteen years later, the Supreme Court reviewed the results of the remedy given in this case and stated that nothing had changed (United Shoe was still possessed of monopoly power). It therefore remanded the case to the district court for application of further remedies, with the instruction that the Sherman Act should "break up or render impotent the monopoly power found to violate the Act."

b) The problem is that monopolies are distrusted, but the court in *United Shoe* refused to hold that they are unlawful per se. The court left open the possibility that a monopoly could be achieved lawfully (by superior skill, inevitable economic conditions, etc.) and could be operated lawfully.

c) But at the same time, the court in *United Shoe* found that perfectly rational and honorable business practices constituted violations of the law when engaged in by a monopolist. Furthermore, the court in effect admitted that its decision was irrational by refusing in the remedy to proscribe the pricing policy of the defendant (one of the major bases for finding the violation), since the court stated that this was perfectly rational and even desirable business conduct. Hence, the question is, what conduct is improper by a monopolist? These decisions seem to say that a monopolist must bend over backwards to ensure that it encourages competition, even to the extent of engaging in irrational business behavior.

d) In short, the monopolist must ensure that it no longer remains a monopolist. This is, in effect, a holding that monopolies are unlawful. This is the end result of *United Shoe*, since the defendant did what was asked of it in the court's remedy (it changed the unlawful practices), but when this did not change its monopoly power, the review implied that the defendant should be broken up. In effect, this is saying that while there was no longer any unlawful conduct, a monopoly is bad and must be broken up.

4. **Vertical Integration and Relations with Competitors.** A firm is considered vertically integrated when it performs functions internally that it could have done by an outside firm. Common examples are manufacturers that also produce the raw materials that go into the goods, or that own the stores that sell the finished goods. Vertical integration may be an efficient way to organize a business. Many firms are vertically integrated to some extent, and this is not a significant antitrust issue. The problem arises when a monopolist in one market gains monopoly power in another market through vertical integration. Other concerns are the ability for a vertically integrated firm to institute price discrimination, the increased barriers to entry, and the general lessening of competition.

a. **Monopolists' control through vertical integration.** In *Otter Tail Power Co. v. United States*, 410 U.S. 366 (1973), Otter Tail controlled electrical transmission wires as well as wholesale power. When its franchise expired in specific communities, it prevented the communities from adopting municipal distribution systems by refusing to sell wholesale power to such systems and by refusing to permit the municipalities to purchase power from other producers through Otter Tail's transmission lines. This practice was considered a violation of section 2.

b. **Monopolists' control through new product development related to monopoly product.** In *Berkey Photo v. Eastman Kodak Co.*, 603 F.2d 263 (2d Cir. 1979), *cert. denied,* 444 U.S. 1093 (1980), Berkey won damages based on Kodak's failure to disclose the specifications for its new 110 size film before releasing its new 110 instamatic cameras. The jury found that because Kodak had a monopoly in the 110 camera market, it violated section 2 by failing to give competitors a chance to produce the new film. The court of appeals reversed, holding that it is an ordinary and acceptable business practice to keep new developments secret; Kodak had no duty to disclose the new film. The benefit to Kodak resulted not from monopolization but from integration.

Aspen Skiing Co. v. Aspen Highlands Skiing Corp.

c. **Monopolists' duty to cooperate with competitors--Aspen Skiing Co. v. Aspen Highlands Skiing Corp.,** 472 U.S. 585 (1985).

1) **Facts.** The Aspen Highlands Skiing Corporation (P) owned and operated a skiing facility on a mountain in Aspen, Colorado. The Aspen Skiing Company (D) owned and operated facilities on three other mountains in Aspen. For 15 years, P and D offered six-day, four-area ski tickets and divided the revenues on the basis of the usage of each resort. D then informed P that it would participate only if P accepted a fixed share of the revenues. P reluctantly agreed. The next year, D reduced the fixed share offer. D also made it virtually impossible for P to offer a multi-area package by refusing to sell P any tickets, refusing to accept vouchers from P's ticket pass, and discontinuing its three-day pass, leaving in effect only its six-day, three-area pass, thereby eliminating the opportunity for its customers to ski at P's resort. As a result, P's share of the skiing business at Aspen declined from 20% during the last year of the four-area tickets to 11% four years later. P sued for damages. The district judge instructed the jury that a monopolist is not barred from taking advantage of its efficiencies, and has no duty to cooperate with its business rivals, but it cannot unnecessarily exclude or handicap competitors, or use its monopoly power to further any domination of the relevant market. The jury found for P and awarded $2.5 million in actual damages. The court of appeals affirmed, holding that D had a duty to market jointly with P because the multi-area ticket was an "essential facility," and there was sufficient evidence to support a finding that D's intent in refusing to market the ticket was to create or maintain a monopoly. The Supreme Court granted certiorari.

2) **Issue.** Does a monopolist have a duty to market jointly with its competitors if the marketing had originated in a competitive market and had persisted for several years?

3) **Held.** Yes. Judgment affirmed.

a) D properly asserts that a monopoly has no general duty to engage in a joint marketing program with a competitor, but the verdict in this case was not based on that proposition. D's refusal to participate in the combined ticket plan is evidence of its purpose and could give rise to liability. A monopolist does not monopolize by mistake; exclusion that is not the result of superior efficiency is improper and is always deliberately intended.

b) In this case, D did not just reject a new idea proposed by P; D made a significant change in a pattern of distribution that had originated in a competitive market and had persisted for several years. In fact, the six-day, all-Aspen ticket was created when each mountain was separately owned and operated. Such tickets are available in other multi-mountain areas, which indicates that a free competitive market would lead to the use of such tickets. By eliminating the ticket, D as a monopolist made an important change in the character of the market.

c) The jury was properly instructed, and its conclusion that D's refusal to deal was not justified by valid business reasons should be upheld as long as it is supported by the evidence. This requires consideration of the effect of D's conduct on consumers as well as on P and D itself.

d) The evidence indicates that the six-day, four-area ticket was popular with skiers and was preferred to D's three-area ticket when both were available. Skiers also desired to ski P's mountain but did not solely because of the inconvenience when it was not included in the ticket. The evidence clearly shows that elimination of the ticket adversely affected P's business. D was unable to provide any efficiency justification for its practice. Thus, the evidence supports the verdict.

5. **Predatory Pricing.** Although one of the Sherman Act's basic objectives is low price levels resulting from competitive markets, the Act prohibits price cutting in certain circumstances. A firm might cut prices to unsustainably low levels (below "incremental" costs) in order to drive competitors out of business, and once it succeeds, raise prices higher than it could have if the competitors had remained in business. So-called predatory pricing is illegal. The challenge for the courts is to disallow predatory pricing while not discouraging ordinary price-cutting, which is desirable.

a. **No predatory pricing if higher than production cost--Barry Wright Corp. v. ITT Grinnell Corp.,** 724 F.2d 227 (1st Cir. 1983).

Barry Wright Corp. v. ITT Grinnell Corp.

1) **Facts.** Pacific was the only manufacturer of mechanical snubbers, used to build pipe systems for nuclear power plants. ITT Grinnell Corporation (D) was a major snubber user. Because of Pacific's strong market position, D sought an alternative supplier. D agreed to assist Barry Wright Corporation (P) in developing snubbers. D agreed to use P as its exclusive supplier from 1977 to 1979. Once Pacific learned of the arrangement, it offered D a specially low discount price based on quantity. D rejected the offer. Later, P was unable to meet its production schedule. D returned to Pacific and made a large order, extending through 1978. D then told P it breached its development contract. Later, D agreed to purchase additional snubbers from Pacific. Ultimately, D canceled its collaboration with P. P sued, claiming that Pacific's efforts to sell to D violated the Sherman Act. The district court found no violation, and P appeals.

2) **Issue.** Is it a violation of the Sherman Act for a monopolist to cut prices when the reduced price remains above the cost of production?

3) **Held.** No. Judgment affirmed.

a) Monopolization consists of (i) the possession of monopoly power in the relevant market and (ii) the acquisition or maintenance of that power by other than legitimate means. Here, Pacific had properly acquired monopoly power; the question is whether it improperly maintained that power. Pacific's methods would be improper if they were exclusionary or beyond the needs of ordinary business dealings.

b) P claims that Pacific acted in an exclusionary manner by giving special price discounts. However, the discount prices were still above Pacific's total cost of production. Some courts have held price cutting to be a violation of the Sherman Act when it is "predatory." This may arise when a firm can drive away all competitors through price cuts and then raise prices high enough to recoup the lost profits. The difficulty is determining when a price cut is predatory or when it is merely a response to market factors in accordance with the basic policy of the Sherman Act.

c) Most courts focus not on intent, but on the relationship between the discount price and the firm's costs. A firm that discounts prices below its marginal costs of production could not plan to maintain that price; it would be better off stopping production. Such a price cut may be considered predatory, as long as it is not justified by business reasons, such as promotions. Some courts examine the average total cost. But in this case, Pacific's price exceeds both the average cost and the incremental or marginal cost.

d) The Ninth Circuit follows an approach that varies depending on the price/cost comparison. A price below average variable cost is presumptively predatory; a price between average variable cost and average total cost requires proof by a preponderance of the evidence that the benefit of the price cut depends on its exclusionary tendency; and if the price exceeds average total cost, proof of exclusionary tendency by clear and convincing evidence is required. This test has some appeal, but it delves too deeply into economics and threatens to penalize procompetitive price cuts.

e) Because above-cost price cuts are typically sustainable, such prices are not forbidden by the Sherman Act.

f) P also claims that Pacific's requirements contracts were exclusionary, but they were not really requirements contracts; they required D to purchase specified amounts, not all of its requirements. The contracts reflected the industry practice of issuing advance orders, and there were valid business reasons for the contracts. All contracts are exclusionary, at least as to the parties and quantities involved.

g) The contracts contained noncancellation clauses that P claims were exclusionary because the incentive to fulfill its bargain was too great. If the clause was a penalty, then it would be unenforceable anyway. If it did reasonably reflect Pacific's likely actual damages, it was not unreasonable from an antitrust standpoint. Any anticompetitive effect is too speculative to transform the otherwise valid contracts into unlawful, exclusionary ones.

Brooke Group Ltd. v. Brown & Williamson Tobacco Corp.

b. **No predatory pricing if no probability of recoupment--Brooke Group Ltd. v. Brown & Williamson Tobacco Corp.,** 509 U.S. 209 (1993).

1) **Facts.** Brooke Group Ltd. (P) pioneered the economy segment of the cigarette market by introducing a line of generic cigarettes that was priced at 30% lower than branded cigarettes. By the time generics had captured 4% of the market, Brown & Williamson Tobacco Corporation (D) entered the

segment by underpricing P. P responded, and a price war ensued. D allegedly lowered its price below the cost of production. P sued, claiming that D's volume rebates to wholesalers amounted to price discrimination that had a reasonable possibility of injuring competition in violation of the Robinson-Patman Act. The jury found for P, but the district court granted D judgment as a matter of law on the ground that there had been no tacit coordination of prices in the economy segment (and thus no injury to competition). The court of appeals affirmed, and P appeals.

2) **Issue.** Is price discrimination illegal when there is no proof that the competitor had a reasonable prospect of recouping its investment?

3) **Held.** No. Judgment affirmed.

a) The Robinson-Patman Act prohibits price discrimination only to the extent that it threatens to injure competition. P claims that D has priced its products in an unfair manner in order to eliminate or retard competition and gain control over prices. To prevail, P would have to prove that:

(1) "The prices complained of are below an appropriate measure of its rival's costs"; and

(2) The competitor had a reasonable prospect of recouping its investment in below-cost prices.

b) Without recoupment by D, even if the low pricing causes P losses, D's lower costs produce lower aggregate prices in the market. D could recoup only if D's pricing is capable of producing the intended effects on its competition.

c) To determine whether recoupment was a reasonable prospect, the Court must inquire into the "extent and duration of the alleged predation, the relative financial strength of the predator and its intended victim, and their respective incentives and will." P would have to show that there is a likelihood that D's scheme would cause a rise in prices above a competitive level sufficient to compensate for the amounts expended on the predation.

d) The cigarette market is an oligopoly. An oligopoly's independent pricing may provide a means for achieving recoupment. However, predatory pricing schemes are implausible, especially when they require coordinated action among several firms. Where tacit cooperation is involved, as alleged here, there is a high likelihood that any attempt by one oligopolist to discipline a rival by cutting prices will cause an outbreak of competition. A predator suffers its present losses alone, but shares its later supracompetitive profits with all other oligopolists. But however unlikely the success of predatory pricing in an oligopoly, there is no per se rule of nonliability.

e) The scheme alleged by P does not provide an adequate basis for finding liability. Even if D did intend an anticompetitive course of events and sold its generics below cost, the evidence does not support a finding that D had a reasonable prospect of recovering its losses. No evidence suggests that D was likely to obtain the power to raise prices for its generics above a competitive level.

4) **Dissent** (Stevens, White, Blackmun, JJ.). The jury found for P after a 115-day trial. The evidence is sufficient to support its finding. D had a plan to harm P, and D lost millions of dollars during its price war. D's willingness to suffer these losses is powerful evidence that it believed it could eventually recoup its investment. When the price war ended, the price for generic cigarettes was raised even higher than the price for branded cigarettes was when the war started. Even if a predatory pricing program is unlikely to succeed in an oligopoly without actual conspiracy, the jury could have inferred that D reasonably believed it would have the cooperation of its fellow oligopolists. The jury could also properly infer that D's predatory plan entailed a reasonable possibility of injuring competition.

6. Patent Accumulation.

a. **Introduction.** There may be violations of the antitrust law in the accumulation by various means of patents in the hands of one company (or a group of companies), where such an accumulation controls a market that otherwise might be competitive. In this connection, otherwise lawful means of gaining patent rights (*e.g.,* assignment, purchase, etc.) might be unlawful due to the effect on competition. However, the mere accumulation of patents by a licensor is not illegal per se.

Transparent-Wrap Machine Corp. v. Stokes & Smith Co.

b. **Assignment of improvement patents--Transparent-Wrap Machine Corp. v. Stokes & Smith Co.,** 329 U.S. 637 (1947).

1) **Facts.** Transparent Wrap Machine Corporation (P) had a patent on a machine to make transparent packages, fill them with contents, and seal them. It licensed the patent to Stokes & Smith Company (D) and included a covenant that D would assign to P any improvement patents applicable to the machine or suitable for use in connection with it. D took out improvement patents but refused to assign them to P. P sought an injunction.

2) **Issue.** May a patentee require licensees to assign back improvement patents developed by the licensee?

3) **Held.** Yes. Injunction granted.

a) Patent law makes all patents assignable.

b) The law does not limit the consideration which may be paid for the assignment (hence, it could be the right to use another patent).

c) The effect on the public interest is the same in a license of one patent whether the licensee or the licensor controls all improvements.

d) The argument is made that enforcement of such a condition gives the licensee less incentive to make inventions; whatever force this argument has in other situations, it has none here since D, under the agreement, does not have to pay additional royalties on improvements and can continue to use the improvement patents as long as the agreement persists (it had five-year renewal options).

e) Conceivably, such licensing arrangements could be used to violate the antitrust laws; we only hold that the assignment of improvement patents in a license of a patent is not per se illegal.

4) **Comment.** Note that the language of the Court carefully limits the decision to its special facts. It is conceivable that expansion in any one of a number of directions could mean that the license with assignment of improvements would be unreasonable.

a) For example, under *Transparent Wrap*, at the end of the patent period of the basic patent, there would be no greater industry concentration if Transparent Wrap held the patent improvements than if Stokes did. But if Transparent Wrap had granted multiple licenses and controlled multiple improvement patents from the multiple licensees, there would be greater concentration if the patents were in Transparent Wrap's hands than in the hands of multiple licensees.

b) In other words, almost any fact situation which would create a less competitive environment might change the holding in *Transparent Wrap*.

c) These changes might be offset if the license agreement were to provide that licensees were to receive nonexclusive, royalty-free licenses to the improvements.

C. MONOPOLY AND THE PROBLEM OF DEFINING THE "MARKET"

1. **Introduction.** There are three major problems in the monopoly area:

a. **Relevant market.** The first is defining the relevant market.

b. **Market power.** The second is defining the point at which market power achieves monopoly status.

c. **Business conduct.** The third, assuming monopoly power exists, is defining what conduct is permitted by a monopoly.

2. **The Problem.** The problem with monopolies is the concern that they will raise prices above the levels that would exist in a competitive industry. Thus, in assessing whether monopoly power exists, the inquiry must be whether existing firms and potential competitors of the defendant have sufficient influence to limit defendant's ability to raise prices.

3. **Theoretical Considerations in Defining the Relevant Market.**

a. **Substitution of products.** The first consideration involves the ability and willingness of users of a product to use a substitute.

1) With any given product, there are many classes of users. Some could easily substitute other products, and some could not. Thus, elasticity of demand is really a weighted average of the demands of the various users.

2) The definition of the relevant market will thus depend on the degree of protection to be given to specialized users and to users generally.

b. **Geographic considerations.** The second issue concerns geography; *i.e.,* substitutability depends also on the location of the alternatives.

c. **Entry into the industry.** Finally, price adjustments will be limited by the factor of the ease of entry into the industry. This depends on many things—costs, amount of capital required, availability of needed expertise, etc.

4. **Tests for the Relevant Market.**

a. **Introduction.** Market definitions and estimates of market share can only approximate a firm's true market power, especially as applied by courts. To a large extent, a court's evaluation of a particular situation is colored by its view of the propriety of the challenged conduct.

b. **Department of Justice Guidelines.** The 1984 merger guidelines (discussed *infra*) also contain market definition guides which, though specifically applicable to mergers, also inform monopolization cases.

1) **Product market.** The objective is to find a group of products such that a hypothetical monopolist could profitably impose a small but significant and nontransitory price increase. If a price increase for the product of 5% for one year would cause so many buyers to shift to other products that the hypothetical monopolist would not find the increase profitable, the next-best substitute would be added to the market until a group of products is assembled for which the monopolist's price increase would be profitable.

2) **Available supply.** Estimates of supply responses to hypothetical price increases also include supplies provided by firms capable of producing and selling the product within one year.

3) **Geographic market.** Similar to the product market analysis, the objective is to find a geographic area in which the hypothetical monopolist could profitably raise prices without impact from goods produced elsewhere.

4) **Market share.** Market share analysis is based on available information, with a preference for dollar sales or shipments of product.

United States v. Aluminum Co. of America

c. **Application--United States v. Aluminum Co. of America,** 148 F.2d 416 (2d Cir. 1945).

1) **Facts.** The facts are set forth *supra*. This portion of the opinion considers Aluminum Company of America's (D's) market power. The possible markets for aluminum include virgin (new) aluminum,

secondary (scrap) aluminum, and imports. D did not sell all the virgin aluminum it produced because it fabricated some of it. Although D consistently produced more than 80% of the total domestic production of virgin aluminum, the trial court found that D's share of the market was only about 33%. The court included the secondary market, and excluded the portion of D's production that it fabricated itself. If all of D's virgin production was included, it would constitute 64% of the total market for virgin and secondary aluminum. However, if the secondary market were excluded, and all of D's virgin production were included, then D would have over 90% of the market.

2) **Issue.** In determining a production firm's market share, is it proper to consider the firm's control over the quantity of scrap material available in the market?

3) **Held.** Yes.

a) The differences between the alternative market share measures in this case are significant because 90% is enough to constitute a monopoly, 64% is unlikely to be enough, and 33% is clearly not enough.

b) It is proper to include all of D's virgin production, because D's sales of fabricated products reduces the demand for virgin production. In other words, if D did not fabricate products, other firms would, and would require the same inputs that D uses.

c) It is not appropriate to include the secondary market as part of the overall market. The reason is that because of its control over virgin production, D also controls the supply of scrap aluminum.

d) Consequently, D had a market share of over 90%. This would clearly be a monopoly were it not for the import supply. The threat of increased imports undoubtedly kept D's prices where they were. Still, within the limits of tariffs and transportation costs, D could raise its prices free of competitive restraint.

d. **The "reasonable interchangeability" test--United States v. E.I. du Pont De Nemours & Co.,** 351 U.S. 377 (1956).

United States v. E.I. du Pont De Nemours & Co.

1) **Facts.** The United States (P) brought an action under section 2 of the Sherman Act against du Pont (D) for "monopolizing" the market for cellophane, of which it controlled 75%. D's defense was that it only has 20% of the "flexible packaging market." The lower court held there was no market power since the market was flexible packaging. The lower court made the following factual findings: D entered cellophane production under patent licenses with a foreign company, giving D the United States territory; D later developed moisture-proof cellophane under a patent granting a license for limited production to only one United States competitor. D's sales of cellophane have risen dramatically over 20 years. The trend in prices has generally been downward, but there were exceptions to this.

2) **Issue.** What is the relevant product market for determining whether D has violated section 2 of the Sherman Act?

3) **Held.** The market is "flexible packaging materials" and D has no monopoly power of this market.

a) Monopoly is the ability to set prices and exclude competitors. D has a monopoly of cellophane since no one can manufacture it without access to D's patents.

b) Every manufacturer of a differentiated product has a monopoly of sorts, limited, however, by competitive products.

c) A product is competitive based on similarities in character and use and the extent to which buyers will be willing to substitute one for the other.

d) Products need not be fungible to be part of the relevant market.

e) The rule is that commodities that are reasonably interchangeable by consumers for the same purposes make up that part of the trade or commerce, monopolization of which may be illegal.

f) The market for flexible packaging materials is geographically nationwide.

g) The determining factor of substitutability is cross-elasticity of demand.

h) The beginning point of analysis is the use to which the product is put. Here, cellophane has a combination of characteristics which are not matched by others, but in each of these characteristics other flexible packaging materials are equal or superior, and all of these other materials are used by the same type of users as use cellophane. For example, cellophane supplies 7% of bakery good wrapping, 25% for candy, and 75% to 80% of cigarettes, etc. The interchangeability of uses makes the relevant market "flexible packaging materials."

i) The fact that cellophane's price is two to three times that of its chief and most similar competitors in the flexible packaging market does not establish monopoly power. Some users are sensitive to price and some are not.

j) It is the variable characteristics of the materials and the marketing of them that determines choice.

k) D had an average of 15.9% after-tax return on capital; this does not demonstrate a monopoly without a comparison of the rates of return of other flexible packaging companies.

l) The market is composed of products having a reasonable interchangeability for the purposes for which they are produced—price, use, and qualities considered. The application of the test remains uncertain.

4) **Dissent** (Warren, C.J., Black, Douglas, JJ.). Cellophane combines certain elements more definitely than any other packaging material. For example, its lower-priced substitutes do not have the qualities of cellophane. Furthermore, sales increased dramatically over the years despite the fact that cellophane was priced substantially higher than its so-called competitors. D also cut prices but lower priced substitutes did not, and yet they retained their market position. D itself considered cellophane a separate market and worked to maintain a monop-

oly in it. D made tremendous profits, yet only one competitor entered the cellophane market. In one year, D raised prices in order to keep its rate of profit at a desired level; thus, D had substantial control over price. The majority holds that because cellophane has competition for many end uses, those users who can use only cellophane are not entitled to protection (*e.g.*, cigarette industry was monopolized by cellophane).

5) **Summary analysis.**

a) **Majority opinion.** The majority takes one view, that reasonably interchangeable products should not be arbitrarily eliminated in defining the relevant market. This is an economic approach to antitrust, and introduces a very complex factual inquiry into deciding antitrust cases.

(1) Every differentiated product is unique and thus has a monopoly over price in some price range. And every product has competition after some price level is reached.

(2) The issue becomes one of over what price range a company has monopoly power.

(a) If the company raises its prices and loses customers, does this prove it has substitute competition? Not by itself, since it may have lower costs than the substitute, higher profits, and enjoy a range of price monopoly up to the point where it loses customers by an increase. Costs versus competitors' costs is some indication of this situation, and unusual profits may be an indicator of such a situation.

(b) If price is decreased and D gains customers, does this indicate that it is not monopolist? No. It may have all kinds of customers with which it can maintain its prices, since there may be no substitutes for these customers.

(c) There is also the issue as to whether there may be no substitutes for some users and whether the interests of these users should be protected (*e.g.*, the cigarette manufacturers in this case). In this situation, a further question arises. For those users where there is not a close substitute, is it possible that the product can be differentiated in some way so that to other users it has characteristics which make it unusable for the user who has no substitutes? If so, then there is a monopoly. If not, then the user who has no substitutes is still protected because he can buy at the same competitive prices as other users (*i.e.*, the competition that the product receives from substitutes in other uses keeps the price of the product from being monopolistic). Presumably, this was the situation in the cellophane case.

(d) So the issue for the majority is, what amount of actual market power does the defendant have (*i.e.*, over what price range does it exercise control)? Note that defining this, determining it, and deciding how much is too much is incredibly difficult. Thus, the majority (if this is its approach) has chosen a very sophisticated, very difficult, and very time-consuming standard for the courts to administer. Note, for example, that there was no discussion in the case of comparable costs, profit margins, etc., among the supposed competitors.

b) **Dissenting opinion.** The dissent may be saying that it will look at a simpler test: are the products exactly alike? There is justification for such a test, theoretically in the Sherman Act, and practically from the administrative problems of the courts. Of course, if this test is adopted, there is always the case where the defendant appears to have a monopoly in his product but is losing sales to other products and really has no market power and hence is not a monopolist. In addition, the dissent argued that the majority was wrong on its facts. Compare the dissent with the *Aluminum Co.* opinion, *supra*, where secondary, scrap ingot was eliminated in the definition of the market.

Note that even if this test of "exactly alike products" were used, the courts would still have to examine carefully such factors as price behavior, profits, conditions of entry, etc., at least in situations where the defendant has considerably less than 100% of the market.

D. ATTEMPT TO MONOPOLIZE

1. **Introduction.** A company having market power might use that power in an attempt to monopolize. Such a situation differs from one in which a monopolist exercises its monopoly power. Behavior that would ordinarily be considered good business practice amounts to monopolizing when used with controlling market power. Thus, the extent of a company's market power may be determinative in characterizing its conduct as an attempt to monopolize.

Lorain Journal Co. v. United States

2. **Refusals to Deal--Lorain Journal Co. v. United States,** 342 U.S. 143 (1951).

a. **Facts.** Lorain Journal (D) operated a newspaper in Lorain, a town of 50,000. The paper reached about 90% of the population. A radio station was set up in a town eight miles away. D refused to allow advertising in the paper if the customer was also advertising on the radio station, and it monitored the radio programs to enforce its policy. The United States sued under section 2 of the Sherman Act.

b. **Issue.** Is the refusal of a monopolist newspaper to accept ads from advertisers who also advertise on a competing radio station an attempt to monopolize?

c. **Held.** Yes.

1) The right to refuse to deal is not absolute. Here, D's acts amounted to an attempt to monopolize.

d. **Comment.** Normally, a firm may refuse to deal with anyone (*see* the discussion of refusals to deal, *infra*). But in the context of monopoly power in some relevant market, such refusals may be unlawful.

3. **Requirement of Dangerous Probability of Monopolizing--Spectrum Sports v. McQuillan,** 506 U.S. 447 (1993).

Spectrum Sports v. McQuillan

a. **Facts.** McQuillan (P) was a distributor of athletic and equestrian products made with sorbothane, an elastic polymer. The manufacturer notified P that P had to sell its athletic distributorship to maintain its equestrian distribution rights. P refused and was terminated. Shortly thereafter, Spectrum Sports (D), which was partly owned by the son of the manufacturer's president, became the national distributor of sorbothane athletic products. P's business failed, and P sued for damages for alleged violations of section 2 of the Sherman Act. The jury found that D had violated section 2 by "monopolizing, attempting to monopolize, and/or conspiring to monopolize." The court of appeals upheld the verdict on the ground that the evidence established a case of attempted monopolization because the jury could infer two elements of that offense—a specific intent to achieve monopoly power and a dangerous probability of monopolization of a relevant market—from evidence of D's unfair conduct, without proof of relevant market or D's market power. The Supreme Court granted certiorari.

b. **Issue.** May parties be held liable for attempted monopolization under section 2 without proof of a dangerous probability that they would monopolize a relevant market and had specific intent to monopolize?

c. **Held.** No. Judgment reversed.

1) The courts have generally required a plaintiff in an attempted monopolization case to prove three elements: (i) that the defendant has engaged in predatory or anticompetitive conduct with (ii) a specific intent to monopolize and (iii) a dangerous probability of achieving monopoly power.

2) Unfair or predatory conduct may prove the necessary intent, but intent alone is insufficient to prove the dangerous probability of success. This element requires inquiry into the relevant product and geographic market and the defendant's economic power in that market.

3) The Sherman Act is intended to protect the public from a failure of the market. Therefore, the courts have avoided interpretations of section 2 that might chill competition. The concern about applying section 2 in a manner that would further anticompetitive ends is not met where the courts inquire only whether the defendant has engaged in unfair or predatory tactics.

4) The jury in this case could have based its verdict on the attempt-to-monopolize theory alone. Since that theory did not apply on these facts, the verdict cannot stand.

V. VERTICAL RESTRAINTS

A. RESTRICTED DISTRIBUTION

1. The Economics of Resale Price Maintenance.

a. **Definition.** Resale price maintenance is a practice whereby those who supply goods to distributors set prices to be charged on resale.

b. **Conditions necessary for resale price maintenance.** Where dealers want it, they must represent a fairly high percentage of the available outlets. Also, most manufacturers making closely competitive brands must agree to it or the attempt to establish that it will fail.

c. **Arguments for resale price maintenance.**

1) **Political argument.** Without it, the small merchant may be put out of business by large chains able to cut prices on "loss leader" national brand goods.

2) **Dealers.** Resale price maintenance allows dealers to be more competitive by advertising, effective merchandising, etc.

3) **Manufacturers.** Resale price maintenance ensures protection of goodwill, product differentiation, protection from elimination of retail outlets by loss leaders, and assurance of dealer services necessary to market the product.

d. **Arguments against resale price maintenance.** Resale price maintenance amounts to price fixing at the retail level and thus dampens competition between those at this level of the distribution chain. Possibly, this results also in less pressure on manufacturers with regard to price.

2. The Antitrust Laws and Resale Price Maintenance.

a. **Vertical price fixing and state action.**

Dr. Miles Medical Co. v. John Park & Sons Co.

1) **Early case law--Dr. Miles Medical Co. v. John Park & Sons Co.,** 220 U.S. 373 (1911).

a) **Facts.** Dr. Miles Medical Company (P) manufactured proprietary medicines under a secret but unpatented formula and sought in its express contracts with wholesalers to prescribe prices for both wholesale and retail sales and to forbid sales to "cut rate" chemists. P here sues a wholesaler for getting supplies of the medicines at reduced prices by inducing others to break their contracts.

b) **Issue.** May a manufacturer set a minimum resale price for wholesalers and retailers?

c) **Held.** No. No injunction will issue; the price maintenance contracts are invalid restrictive agreements.

(1) When a manufacturer parts with control over his goods and sells them to others, he is not entitled to lay down conditions by express contract which restrict competition in future sales at other levels in the distribution system (as in price fixing).

(2) It makes no difference whether the product is patented or made pursuant to a secret formula.

d) **Comment.** It appears that such express contractual vertical price fixing restraints are per se illegal.

2) **Other vertical price fixing cases.** The United States Supreme Court has indicated in many contexts that vertical price fixing violates the Sherman Act.

a) It makes no difference that the manufactured product is made pursuant to a patented process or machine. [United States v. Standard Manufacturing Co., 226 U.S. 20 (1912)]

b) It makes no difference that the article is patented or subject to copyright. [United States v. Univis Lens Co., *supra*; Bobbs-Merrill Co. v. Straus, 210 U.S. 339 (1908)]

c) It makes no difference that the article is being sold in competition with articles of the same general class. [United States v. Bausch & Lomb Optical Co., 321 U.S. 707 (1944)]

3) **Agency systems.** Note that the way around the problem for companies that wished to maintain retail prices was to either integrate and do retailing as well as manufacturing, or to establish an "agency" system so that retailers were in effect "employees" of the manufacturer.

4) **Maximum prices--Albrecht v. The Herald Co.,** 390 U.S. 145 (1968). Albrecht v. The Herald Co.

a) **Facts.** Albrecht (P) was the exclusive distributor for The Herald Company (D) in a particular area. P charged customers more for D's newspapers than D's suggested price, and D ceased selling to P. P sued and lost. The court of appeals affirmed, reasoning that a price ceiling was necessary to protect the public from price gouging by dealers who had monopoly power in their own territories. P appeals.

b) **Issue.** May a producer set maximum prices for its dealers who have exclusive sales territories?

c) **Held.** No. Judgment reversed.

(1) The *Kiefer-Stewart* case, *supra*, held that agreements to fix maximum prices cripple the freedom of traders and thereby restrain their ability to sell in accordance with their own judgment.

(2) Maximum prices may be set too low to allow small dealers to participate. Or they may have the attributes of fixed minimum prices if everyone charges the set price. Therefore, D's practice is illegal.

d) **Concurrence** (Douglas, J.). This is a "rule of reason" case. The price fixing might be permissible depending on the legality of the territorial allocation, but since the latter question was not tried, the price fixing cannot be upheld.

e) **Dissent** (Stewart, Harlan, JJ.). This case involves monopoly products, unlike the *Kiefer-Stewart* case. D's practice prevents P from raising his price above a competitive price. This is consistent with the purpose of the antitrust laws. The justification for a per se rule prohibiting fixing of minimum prices has not been shown to exist in the case of maximum prices. D's practice prevents P from reaping monopoly profits. The Court has decided that exclusive territories and consequent market power can never be a justification for dictation of maximum prices because exclusive territories are sometimes illegal. But they are neither always unlawful nor have they been shown to be unlawful here.

b. **The Miller-Tydings amendment.**

1) **Introduction.** Associations of small retailers led the way in trying to achieve legislation recognizing retail price maintenance. States began by giving manufacturers the right to enforce contracts prescribing resale prices on branded goods. The problem was that these laws were enforceable only when there was a direct contract between the manufacturer and the retailer, and it was an intolerable burden for a manufacturer to sign contracts with all distribution outlets. States then passed laws which indicated that once a resale price had been prescribed by contract with any distributor, it was unlawful for any other distributor to knowingly undercut that price (non-signer clause contract). In *Old Dearborn Distributing Co. v. Seagram Distillers Corp.*, 299 U.S. 183 (1936), the Court held that a state fair trade law based on these principles was constitutional. This took care of the problem with state law, but whenever interstate commerce was involved, federal antitrust law was a problem.

2) **The federal law—Miller-Tydings Act.**

a) **Substance of the Act.** The Miller-Tydings Act provided that nothing in the Sherman Act or the Federal Trade Act should "render illegal contracts or agreements prescribing minimum prices for the resale of a commodity . . . which is in free and open competition with commodities of the same general class produced or distributed by others, when contracts or agreements of that description are lawful as applied to intrastate transactions under any statute . . . now or hereafter in effect in any State . . . in which such resale is to be made, or to which the commodity is to be transported for such resale."

b) **Comment.** It appeared that resale price maintenance could be enforced by manufacturers even on retailers who did not sign and did not wish to sign specific contracts undertaking to maintain prescribed prices, and this right of enforcement could be exercised in all the states which had fair trade acts even in respect of branded goods which entered those states from outside. This was true from 1937 to 1951.

c. **The McGuire Act (1952).** In the McGuire Act, Congress stated that nothing in federal law should make unlawful a "nonsigner" provision in state law. Furthermore, the Act allowed agreements with respect to stipulated prices as well as minimum prices, and permitted the first purchaser of the goods (*i.e.,* wholesalers) to enter into resale price agreements with subsequent purchasers.

d. **Repealed.** Both the Miller-Tydings Act and the McGuire Act were repealed in 1975.

3. **Territorial and Customer Restraints.**

a. **Introduction.** A manufacturer may wish to set resale prices, the problems of which have been discussed above. Or, it may wish to appoint dealers to sell its products and wish to appropriate to each dealer a specific territory or allocate specific customers. That is, the manufacturer may wish to prevent "intrabrand" competition in order to promote "interbrand" competition with competing products.

Typically in these situations the dealers will agree not to sell the product to other than designated customers or outside the allocated territory.

Actions in this area under the antitrust laws are brought under the Sherman Act or section 5 of the FTC Act. Section 3 of the Clayton Act does not apply.

b. **Horizontal restraints.** Horizontal territorial or customer restraints among competitors are per se illegal. Therefore, if it can be shown that a division of territories between dealers has been agreed upon and imposed on the manufacturer as a result of concerted action by the dealers, this will be an unlawful horizontal restraint.

c. **Vertically imposed restraints.**

1) **Right of manufacturer to choose to whom it will sell.** It is clear that a manufacturer, where there are competing brands or close substitutes, may select the dealers through whom it will sell and market its products. Thus, if A, a manufacturer, selects only one distributor in each major city, there is no violation. Note that thus far nothing has been said about exclusive territories. In practice, the selection of retailers by the manufacturer may work out this way (*i.e.,* to be exclusive territories).

a) This is analogous to the case of *United States v. Colgate & Co., infra* (*i.e.,* simple statement of price and refusal to deal).

b) On analogy to *Colgate*, it should also be appropriate to unilaterally grant exclusive territories or exclusive customers. Like *Colgate*, however, anything that goes beyond the manufacturer's unilateral simple statement of territory or customers and a refusal to deal (and involves the dealers in an "agreement or combination") would be a violation.

Packard Motor Car Co. v. Webster Motor Car Co.

2) **Sole outlet--Packard Motor Car Co. v. Webster Motor Car Co.,** 243 F.2d 418 (D.C. Cir. 1957), *cert. denied*, 355 U.S. 822 (1957).

a) **Facts.** The largest dealer of Packard's (D's) three dealers in Baltimore told D that it would go out of business unless it got an exclusive dealership in the city. D agreed and notified Webster (P), another dealer, that its one-year contract would not be renewed (D then offered P one more year). P declined the one-year extension and sued under the Sherman Act.

b) **Issue.** May a manufacturer create a sole outlet if it does not control the relevant market?

c) **Held.** Yes. No violation.

(1) The relevant market is automobiles; others are reasonably interchangeable with D's; there is no monopoly and no tendency to create one, even though this eliminates intrabrand competition.

d) **Dissent.** There is no unilateral action by D, but rather a conspiracy to eliminate P.

3) ***White Motor Co.* and subsequent cases.**

a) In *United States v. White Motor Co.*, 372 U.S. 253 (1963), the Court indicated that it did not know whether such territorial allocations should be illegal per se; therefore, the Court reversed a district court verdict giving summary judgment in favor of the government and ordered the district court to hold a full trial, taking account of the commercial effects of such allocations.

(1) The trial never took place since White Motor Company signed a consent decree.

(2) The Court indicated that territorial allocations might be justified where a company was first starting, or where necessary for "financial reasons."

b) In *Sandura Co. v. FTC*, 339 F.2d 847 (6th Cir. 1964), and *Snap-On Tools Corp. v. FTC*, 321 F.2d 825 (7th Cir. 1963), vertical allocations of dealer territory were upheld under a rule of reason.

4) **Note.** These cases deal only with the situation where the manufacturer is attempting to allocate territories or customers for its products; the manufacturer is not attempting to prevent dealers from dealing in the products of competitor manufacturers.

Continental T.V. v. GTE Sylvania

d. **Effect of passage of title--Continental T.V. v. GTE Sylvania,** 433 U.S. 36 (1977).

1) **Facts.** Continental (D) was a retailer of consumer electronic products and had a franchise for the sale of televisions produced by GTE Sylvania (P). P marketed its television sets by awarding limited franchise arrangements

which restricted the retail outlets through which the franchisees could sell the television sets. P awarded a franchise to a store within one mile of D's store and D protested, simultaneously requesting approval to sell television sets through another retail location. P refused the request and D canceled a large order with P and placed it with a competing company. P substantially reduced D's credit line and brought an action to recover the price of television sets already delivered to D. D counterclaimed for treble damages for Sherman Act violations. The trial court awarded damages to D, and the court of appeals reversed.

2) **Issue.** May a manufacturer seek to restrict and confine areas or persons with whom an article may be traded after the manufacturer has parted dominion over it?

3) **Held.** Yes. Judgment affirmed.

a) *United States v. Arnold, Schwinn & Co.*, 338 U.S. 365 (1967), is reversed insofar as it held that a manufacturer could exercise control as long as he retained title (a per se rule).

b) The test is now the general test for Sherman Act violations (*i.e.*, the rule of reason).

c) The rule of reason as applied to these facts would allow reasonable restraint of intrabrand competition to increase the competitive advantage in a strongly competitive interbrand market.

d) Distinguishing competitive effects on the legal implications of the passage of title is not supported by the economic policies enunciated by the Sherman Act.

4) **Concurrence** (White, J.). *Schwinn* should not have been overruled since P was an insignificant factor in the market and adopted its less restricted marketing plan to survive in the market, while Schwinn was the dominant producer and adopted more restrictive methods to increase its market share. *Schwinn* also should be maintained as standing for the invalidity of restraints on alienation after title had passed, thus giving vitality to the importance of the passage of title distinction.

4. Agency and Similar Relationships.

a. **Introduction.** Use of agency and consignments is one way around the prohibition in *Dr. Miles* (*supra*) against setting vertical resale prices.

1) **Agencies—The *General Electric* case.** In *United States v. General Electric Co.*, *supra*, the company organized a system of distributing electric lamps under which the wholesale and retail dealers never purchased or owned the lamps but held and sold them as "agents" for the company. It was claimed that the company's instructions to the retail dealers to sell only at specified prices could not run afoul of the Sherman Act, for these retail prices were not "resale prices" but were the company's prices (*i.e.*, the retailer as the company's "agent" was

making the first sale of the goods). The company won on this issue. The Court found that the delivery of the goods to the retailers was simply a consignment to an agent for custody and sale.

2) **Consignment arrangements.** Numerous companies tried to follow the *General Electric* example. They shipped goods on consignment, retaining title in themselves until the goods were sold. However, the Court has been suspicious of these arrangements and in a number of cases has found that the consignment arrangement was simply a dodge and really amounted to a "device to fix and maintain prices."

Simpson v. Union Oil Co.

b. **Consignment approach limited--Simpson v. Union Oil Co.,** 377 U.S. 13 (1964).

1) **Facts.** Union Oil (D) had leases with its distributors (gas stations), leasing the stations for one year and consigning its products for sale at fixed prices. The consignment provided that title was in D but that the distributor bore the risk of destruction or loss except when due to certain acts of God. Simpson (P), a distributor, sold at prices below those set by D; D refused to renew the lease and canceled the consignment contract. P sues under the Clayton Act and Sherman Act.

2) **Issue.** May a company fix prices of products of which it is not the patentee by using a consignment arrangement?

3) **Held.** No. Unlawful price fixing found.

a) *General Electric*, *supra*, applied only to patented articles.

b) A supplier may not coerce a retailer in order to maintain prices. Here, the consignment arrangement was used as a "cloak" to avoid the antitrust laws.

c) A vast distribution system is involved; in this situation, where the potential anticompetitive effects are great, a consignment system cannot be used to avoid retail price fixing. Otherwise, the antitrust laws could be avoided by a "clever manipulation of words."

4) **Dissent** (Stewart, J.). The General Electric case with respect to consignments has been overruled, even though that case specifically indicated in its language that it had broader application than to patented products.

c. **Comments.** This case may be read several ways:

1) The fact that the consignment was incomplete (in that the retailer still had the risk of loss) may be a deciding factor (*i.e.,* this was not a "consignment" at all). Thus, it was a blatant attempt to violate the rule of the *Dr. Miles* case, *supra* (*i.e.,* that you cannot fix resale prices).

2) Consignments are unlawful when retail price maintenance is involved, except in the situation of patented articles, such as in the *General Electric* case. This would mean that, except for a patent situation, consignments connected with setting of resale prices go beyond *Colgate, infra*, and violate *Dr. Miles*.

3) Consignments are unlawful when large, economically important distribution systems are involved. This raises a "market power" argument, which was earlier eliminated in the horizontal price-fixing cases. [*See* Socony-Vacuum, *supra*] The rationale would have to be that there are different factors to consider in the vertical situation that are not present in a horizontal situation. If this is true, it means that an additional factor to common law agency principles has been added in considering application of the antitrust laws.

4) The distinction between lawful and unlawful consignment arrangements is (i) whether price restrictions are imposed on consignees who would otherwise be in competition with each other, and (ii) whether the consignor has such economic leverage over his consignees that his refusal to deal with them except on the price-maintained basis is in effect "coercive." This was the fact situation as the Court described it in *Simpson*.

   a) Query why "coercion" is relevant. Does it make any difference that a dealer willingly or unwillingly involves himself in an anticompetitive situation?

   b) This again would imply that agency-consignment relationships are permissible, but that additional factors (*e.g.*, "coercion") are considered (in addition to the usual common law factors) in determining whether a consignment really exists. If coercion is found, and thus no true consignment, then the rule in *Colgate* provides no protection, and *Dr. Miles* controls since the illegal consignment goes beyond the mere setting of resale prices and a refusal to deal.

5) It might be argued that on the facts the dealers in *Simpson* were more like "independent" merchants and hence a true agency did not exist. In other factual contexts, "agents" might be involved; for example, an artist might commission an agent to sell his paintings, setting prices at which they are to be sold. This might be lawful.

6) Note that it is probable that something remains of the consignment exception.

d. **Last alternative—Vertical integration.** For the manufacturer interested in maintaining resale prices, the last alternative after (i) fair trade laws, (ii) *Colgate* (*infra*), or (iii) consignment is to integrate vertically by either buying or setting up retail outlets. But query—what value is the United States Supreme Court trying to maintain by preserving the option of manufacturers to set their retail prices? And are there significant differences in the vertical situation from the horizontal one? And do true consignments preserve the significant differences to the degree that it should be a recognized exception to the general rule against vertical price fixing? Note that one value being upheld is the prevention of vertical integration and thus the further concentration of industry. Another value is the preservation of the manufacturer's ability to design and implement a product and marketing strategy to compete with competing products.

5. **Refusal to Deal and Resale Price Maintenance.**

a. **Introduction.** The antitrust laws do not go so far as to prevent a manufacturer from refusing to deal with a distributor whose marketing practices the manufacturer dislikes. This section discusses the issue of whether a manufacturer may refuse to deal when the distributor refuses to maintain prices which have been set by the manufacturer.

United States v. Colgate & Co.

b. **Absence of a contract--United States v. Colgate & Co.,** 250 U.S. 300 (1919).

1) **Facts.** Colgate (D) had a comprehensive resale price maintenance program and all of its products sold at uniform prices across the country. The indictment brought by the United States (P) listed the ways in which such prices had been maintained, including distribution of price lists and an announced policy that D would refuse to sell to anyone who sold at different prices. The district court quashed the indictment, and P appeals.

2) **Issue.** May a manufacturer refuse to deal with dealers who fail to follow its suggested price scheme?

3) **Held.** Yes. Judgment affirmed.

a) There was an absence of any contractual arrangements between D and the distributors and each was free to set its own prices, at the risk of incurring D's displeasure. D did not control the market, and there was no purpose to create or maintain a monopoly.

4) **Comment.** This decision was taken as holding that a manufacturer could announce a resale price and enforce it by refusing to sell to those that did not maintain the set prices, as long as there were no explicit contracts between the parties (in effect leaving the distributor free to choose not to maintain the set prices).

United States v. Parke, Davis & Co.

c. **Definition of "agreement" or "combination"--United States v. Parke, Davis & Co.,** 362 U.S. 29 (1960).

1) **Facts.** Parke, Davis & Company (D) was a manufacturer of drugs; it issued price lists with the announcement that it would refuse to deal with wholesalers or retailers who did not maintain D's prices. There were no fair trade laws in Washington, D.C. or Virginia; five retail drug chains in these areas refused to maintain the prices. D visited the wholesalers and told them they would be cut off if they sold to price-cutting retailers; they agreed not to. The retailers were also visited and told that they would be cut off (and that all other retailers were being similarly informed). The retailers continued price-cutting; D again visited them and worked out an arrangement where they could continue their pricing policy if they would stop advertising cut prices; all agreed. Action under Sherman Act for a combination in restraint of trade.

2) **Issue.** May a manufacturer go beyond mere price announcements and refusals to deal in enforcing price limitations?

3) **Held.** No. Violation of the Sherman Act.

a) *Colgate*, *supra*, alleged only that there was a simple announcement of a price policy and an intention not to deal with price-cutters. There were no agreements, express or implied.

b) Here, D "entwined" the wholesalers and retailers in a program to promote compliance with its price policy; this went beyond "mere announcement" and refusal to deal.

4) **Dissent.** D's unilateral action is no less unilateral simply because it is done simultaneously at the wholesale and retail levels.

5) **Comment.** Thus, again, the courts are faced with a characterization problem. When does a manufacturer's conduct go beyond a "mere announcement and refusal to deal?" It appears from *Parke* that almost anything beyond the simple announcement will constitute "an agreement or combination" in restraint of trade. Thus, *Colgate* has been very narrowly circumscribed. Where wholesalers are asked to play a role in disciplining retailers, or where the manufacturer "negotiates" compliance by wholesalers or retailers, there would appear to be a violation. In short, ***anything*** in addition to an announcement of prices and a refusal to deal is suspect.

d. **Setting maximum prices--Albrecht v. Herald Co.,** 390 U.S. 145 (1968). Albrecht v. Herald Co.

1) **Facts.** Herald Company (D) publishes a newspaper, distributed by independent carriers who buy at wholesale and sell at retail. D suggested a maximum price and indicated it would discontinue its practice of granting exclusive territories (or cancel the route altogether) where there was noncompliance. Albrecht (P), a distributor, raised its prices. D then sent a letter to P's customers indicating that it would deliver the paper at its lower price; a paper solicitation firm was hired to solicit away P's customers, and the customers that were solicited were given to another carrier (all of this was done with the understanding that the customers would be returned if P would cut its price). P sued under the Sherman Act and appealed the lower court denial of a motion for judgment notwithstanding the verdict.

2) **Issue.** May a publisher terminate an independent carrier for refusal to honor the publisher's maximum subscription price?

3) **Held.** No. Judgment reversed.

a) There was an unlawful combination between D, the solicitation firm, and the carrier (that took over the portion of P's customers). D exceeded the *Colgate* limits.

4) **Dissent** (Harlan, J.). There was no violation because there was no conspiracy, nor was D a monopolist. Merely hiring a new distributor is not a conspiracy.

5) **Comment.** After *Albrecht*, it appears that once a combination or agreement is shown to exist to set resale prices, a per se violation exists.

Monsanto Co. v. Spray-Rite Service Corp.

e. **Complaints by dealers to manufacturer--Monsanto Co. v. Spray-Rite Service Corp.,** 465 U.S. 752 (1984).

1) **Facts.** Spray-Rite Service Corporation (P), a discount wholesaler, was the 10th largest distributor of chemical agricultural herbicides produced by Monsanto Company (D). D refused to renew P's distributorship. P sued, claiming that D and its other distributors conspired to fix the resale prices of D's products and terminated P's distributorship in furtherance of the conspiracy. D claimed that it terminated P because P failed to hire trained salesmen and promote sales adequately. The court denied D's motion for a directed verdict. The jury found for P, and awarded $3.5 million in damages. The court of appeals affirmed, holding that P could survive the directed verdict motion by showing that D terminated P following complaints by other distributors relating to P's price-cutting practices. The Supreme Court granted certiorari.

2) **Issue.** Is evidence of complaints by distributors to a manufacturer about the price-cutting tactics of a particular distributor, followed by the termination of the price-cutting distributor, sufficient proof to support a finding of an antitrust violation?

3) **Held.** No. Judgment affirmed on other grounds.

a) In distributor-termination cases, there are two important distinctions: (i) the distinction between concerted action and independent action, and (ii) the distinction between concerted action to set prices and concerted action on nonprice restrictions. Independent action is permissible; concerted action is not. Concerted action to set prices is per se illegal, but concerted action on nonprice restrictions is judged under the rule of reason.

b) These basic principles are not always easily applied to a given set of facts, because a manufacturer and its distributors frequently exchange specific market information for legitimate reasons. A manufacturer may have legitimate concerns about retail prices so its distributors can afford to provide necessary customer service. Complaints from distributors, by themselves, cannot justify an inference of illegal concerted action. There must also be evidence to exclude the possibility that the manufacturer and nonterminated distributors were acting independently.

c) In this case, there was evidence that after P was terminated, D approached other price-cutting distributors and stated that their supplies of a new corn herbicide would be reduced if they did not maintain the suggested retail price. One resisted, but complied after D complained to that distributor's parent company. Shortly before P was terminated, another distributor wrote a newsletter to his customers explaining D's attempts to "get the marketplace in order." This evidence supports the inference of concerted action, and the fact that D had relayed to P the complaints about P's price-cutting but never the post-termination justifications supports the conclusion that D terminated P as part of its concerted action, not independently.

4) **Comment.** The approach taken by the court of appeals ignored the danger of eroding the *GTE Sylvania* and *Colgate* doctrines, *supra*.

f. **No proof of agreement on pricing--Business Electronics Corp. v. Sharp Electronics Corp.,** 485 U.S. 717 (1988).

Business Electronics Corp. v. Sharp Electronics Corp.

1) **Facts.** Business Electronics Corporation (P) and Hartwell were retailers authorized by Sharp Electronics Corporation (D) to sell D's calculators in the Houston area. D published suggested minimum retail prices, but both P and Hartwell sold below those prices. Hartwell complained about P's prices, and threatened to stop carrying D's products unless D terminated P. As a result, D terminated P's dealership. P sued, claiming that Hartwell and D had conspired to terminate P. The jury found that D and Hartwell had an agreement to terminate P's dealership because of P's price cutting. The court of appeals reversed on the ground that such an agreement is illegal per se only where the dealer expressly or impliedly agrees with the manufacturer to set its prices at some level. The Supreme Court granted certiorari.

2) **Issue.** Is a vertical restraint of trade per se illegal if it does not include some agreement on price or price levels?

3) **Held.** No. Judgment affirmed.

a) Courts apply a per se rule instead of the normal rule of reason principles only for conduct that is manifestly anticompetitive. Vertical agreements on resale prices are illegal per se. However, other vertical restraints must be evaluated by the existence of demonstrable economic effect.

b) In *Continental T.V. v. GTE Sylvania*, *supra*, the Court held that vertical nonprice restraints are not per se illegal and have the potential to stimulate interbrand competition. For example, in this case, D may have agreed to the vertical restriction to allow Hartwell to provide better services to its customers.

c) The Sherman Act's term "restraint of trade" refers to a particular economic consequence, not a particular list of agreements. The type of agreement involved in this case was not illegal prior to adoption of the Sherman Act, and there has been no case law since then that makes these agreements per se illegal.

4) **Dissent** (Stevens, White, JJ.). The agreement between Hartwell and D should be considered per se illegal because it was motivated by Hartwell's desire to eliminate a price competitor instead of by any wish to maintain an orderly and efficient distribution system.

B. TYING ARRANGEMENTS

1. **The Clayton Act.** Section 3 of the Clayton Act provides as follows:

> It shall be unlawful for any person engaged in commerce, in the course of such commerce, to lease or make a sale or contract for sale of goods, wares, merchandise, machinery, supplies or other commodities, whether patented or unpatented for use, consumption or resale . . . or fix a price charged therefor, or discount from, or rebate upon, such price, on the condition, agreement or understanding that the lessee or purchaser thereof shall not use or deal in the goods, wares, merchandise, machinery, supplies, or other commodity of a competitor or competitors of the lessor or seller where the effect of such lease, sale or contract for sale or such condition, agreement or understanding may be to substantially lessen competition or tend to create a monopoly in any line of commerce.

2. **Definition.** "Tying" may take several forms.

   a. Express conditions against handling a rival firm's product.

   b. A requirement that the buyer buy only from a certain supplier ("exclusive dealing").

   c. The tying of one commodity to another; for example, a manufacturer of a machine may say to its customer that as long as the machine is used by the customer, she must use it with some other product of the manufacturer.

3. **Requirements.** There are three basic requisites for an illegal tie:

   a. There must be separate tying and tied products;

   b. The seller must have sufficient economic power to restrain competition appreciably in the tied product; and

   c. The tying arrangement must affect more than an "insubstantial" amount of commerce.

4. **Initial Development in the Patent Cases.**

   a. **Misuse of patents to restrain competition.**

      1) **Introduction.** A patentee may use the patented product as the tying product in a tie-in (*i.e.,* if the buyer wants the patented product, it must also buy the tied product). As a matter of patent law, the courts have held that the inclusion of such a tying provision in patent licenses may constitute a misuse of the patent. Where misuse is found, the patentee will be denied relief against infringement of the provisions of the license or of the patent itself.

2) **Application--Motion Picture Patents Co. v. Universal Film Manufacturing Co.,** 243 U.S. 502 (1917). Motion Picture Patents Co. v. Universal Film Manufacturing Co.

a) **Facts.** Motion Picture Patents Company (P) brings a patent infringement action; it has the patent on the motion picture projector and has imprinted on the machine the statement that it may not be used except with films covered by another of P's patents, which had expired.

b) **Issue.** May a patentee restrict the use of its patented product by specifying that only another product made by the patentee can be used with it?

c) **Held.** No.

(1) The patent covers only the machine itself, not materials that may be used with it. The use of materials other than P's will not impair P's patent on the machine.

d) **Dissent.** A patent allows the patentee to determine how the patented product may be used; there is thus no reason why the patentee cannot limit the materials that are used with the machine.

b. **Action against infringer of the patented tying product.** In *Morton Salt Co. v. Suppiger Co.*, 314 U.S. 488 (1942), the plaintiff had a patent on a machine used to deposit salt tablets in commercial canning operations; it leased the machines with a requirement that the lessee use only the plaintiff's salt tablets. The defendant sold a machine that infringed the plaintiff's patent. The Court denied the plaintiff an injunction, on grounds that the plaintiff had exceeded the scope of its patent grant, using the patented machine to engage in anticompetitive conduct. Therefore, the Court held that equity would not provide the plaintiff with relief against the defendant for patent infringement, at least until it was clear that the plaintiff had discontinued its unlawful conduct (the "unclean hands" doctrine).

c. **Action against supplier of the tied product.** In *Carbice Corp. v. American Patents Development Corp.*, 283 U.S. 27 (1931), the Court denied relief to a patentee in an action against a party supplying the tied product (dry ice to be used in the plaintiff's patented machines).

5. **Clayton Act Analysis.**

a. **Early cases--United Shoe Machinery Corp. v. United States,** 258 U.S. 451 (1922). United Shoe Machinery Corp. v. United States

1) **Facts.** United Shoe Machinery Corporation (D) controlled 95% of the shoe machinery business in the United States; its machines were covered by patents. It leased its machinery, and as part of the lease it had every type of tying contract imaginable (*e.g.*, to lease any machinery, lessee must lease all from D; use of competitor's machinery was basis for cancellation of leases; all supplies used with machines had to come from D, etc.). The government brought a section 3 action.

2) **Issue.** May a dominant supplier require customers to use its products exclusively or not at all?

3) **Held.** No. Violation of section 3 of the Clayton Act.

a) D here controls nearly the entire industry and the tying arrangements clearly tend to create a monopoly. Although the conditions do not contain specific agreements not to use the machinery of a competitor of D, the practical effect is to prevent such use.

International Salt Co. v. United States

b. **Quality standards--International Salt Co. v. United States,** 332 U.S. 392 (1947).

1) **Facts.** International Salt (D) was the leading producer of commercial salt in the United States. D owned patents on two machines used in connection with salt in industrial processes. D leased these machines, providing that the lessee had to buy salt from D. It had maintenance contracts on the machines. On one machine, it allowed lessees to find cheaper salt, but the lessee had to give D the chance to meet the lower price. An action was brought under section 1 of the Sherman Act and section 3 of the Clayton Act.

2) **Issue.** May a patentee impose as a condition for use of its patented machines a requirement that the licensee purchase all supplies from the patentee?

3) **Held.** No. This is a per se violation.

a) A patent does not allow a tying arrangement with an unpatented product.

b) In one year, $500,000 of salt was sold with the machines. This is not an "insignificant volume of business." Salt is the relevant market.

c) Tendency toward a monopoly is a creeping one, but is nevertheless clear.

d) The lessor may impose reasonable standards of quality, in good faith, as to products used in connection with its machines. But there was no evidence here that competitors were not producing salt of comparable quality to D's salt.

6. **Sherman Act Analysis.**

Times-Picayune Publishing Co. v. United States

a. **Sherman Act vs. Clayton Act--Times-Picayune Publishing Co. v. United States,** 345 U.S. 594 (1953).

1) **Facts.** D published the only morning newspaper in New Orleans, and one of the two evening newspapers. It only accepted advertising when ads were put in both of its papers. An action was brought under sections 1 and 2 of the Sherman Act.

2) **Issue.** Does the Sherman Act prevent tying if the company acts alone and does not enjoy a monopolistic position?

3) **Held.** No. No violations found.

a) The Clayton Act applies either if the seller enjoys a monopolistic position in the market for the tying product, or if a substantial volume of commerce in the tied product is restrained. In either case there is the required lessening of competition.

b) Both conditions must be met to satisfy the Sherman Act, however. The government proceeded under the Sherman Act. But D controlled only about 40% of the advertising space in the relevant market. (Note that the Court also found that advertising in both papers was really only one product since most commonly owned papers sold advertising this way.)

c) Under the rule of reason the "unit" plan is not an unreasonable restraint of trade since there is no substantial adverse effect on competition.

4) **Comment.** Note that the government did not proceed under the Clayton Act, probably because the Clayton Act, section 3, is inapplicable to tying contracts for the sale of services (it applies only to goods, wares, etc.). Thus, there was an important issue as to whether section 3 applied to advertising.

b. **Definition of market power under the Sherman Act--Northern Pacific Railway v. United States,** 356 U.S. 1 (1958). Northern Pacific Railway v. United States

1) **Facts.** Northern Pacific Railway (D) had 40 million acres of land which it sold under contracts which required buyer to ship by D's railroad all products manufactured on the land, provided that D's rates were equal to those of competing carriers. United States (P) brought a Sherman Act action.

2) **Issue.** If an entity controls a product considered unique, may it have sufficient market power to make tying arrangements illegal?

3) **Held.** Yes. Violation of the Sherman Act.

a) Tying contracts are per se illegal where D has sufficient economic power with respect to the tying product to appreciably restrain free competition for the tied product and a not insubstantial amount of interstate commerce is affected. (Note that this standard is less than the "monopoly position" required in *Times-Picayune, supra.*) Here D had the requisite power.

b) The very existence of a tying arrangement is compelling evidence of the required market power, at least where there is no other business explanation. (Note that the Court seems to be referring here to the possible defense suggested in *International Salt, supra.*)

4) **Dissent.** There is insufficient evidence of D's dominance in landholdings as compared with other landowners, or of the uniqueness of D's land.

United States v. Loew's, Inc.

7. **Package Transactions--United States v. Loew's, Inc.,** 371 U.S. 38 (1962).

a. **Facts.** Loew's, Inc. (D), a producer of movies, put packages of old copyrighted films together for sale to television stations. It required the station to buy some unwanted films to get the best ones. United States (P) brings an action under section 1 of the Sherman Act.

b. **Issue.** May a seller offer only package transactions" which combine desirable and undesirable products at one combined price?

c. **Held.** No. Violation of the Sherman Act.

1) The seller must have sufficient economic power with respect to the tying product to appreciably restrain competition in the market for the tied product. Such economic power is inferred from the tying product's desirability or uniqueness. For example, the requisite economic power is presumed when the tying product is a patented or copyrighted product.

2) By offering only package deals, D is actually tying sales of unwanted films to sales of wanted films. D will be required to produce an individual price list for each film available separately.

IBM v. United States

8. **Specify Standards, Not Brands--IBM v. United States,** 298 U.S. 131 (1936).

a. **Facts.** IBM (D) manufactures data processing machines which use tabulating cards manufactured by D. The cards must meet certain specifications to work properly. D leases its machines on the basis that only D's cards will be used with them, but it leased to the government on the basis that with a 15% increase in lease costs the government could use its own cards.

b. **Issue.** May a patentee whose equipment requires supplies meeting exact specifications condition use of the equipment upon use of the patentee's supplies?

c. **Held.** No. Violation of section 3 of the Clayton Act.

1) The lease to the government shows that others could manufacture cards that would work satisfactorily (*i.e.,* meet IBM's specifications).

2) Tying tends toward a monopoly; D has 81% of the market, the only competitor has 19%.

3) The volume in cards is over $3 million annually.

4) The fact that the machines are patented makes no difference. Also, the patent on the cards does not cover them as they are purchased by users (unperforated).

9. **New Industry Rule--United States v. Jerrold Electronics Corp.,** 187 F. Supp. 545 (E.D. Pa. 1960), *aff'd per curiam*, 365 U.S. 567 (1961).

United States v. Jerrold Electronics Corp.

a. **Facts.** Jerrold Electronics Corporation (D) manufactured, sold, and installed a variety of television antenna systems, including community television antenna systems. D sold only complete systems, including installation and service. D generally prohibited the use of anyone else's equipment to add capacity. The United States (P) challenged D's business arrangements as unlawful tying contracts.

b. **Issue.** May a company making and selling new equipment that is unproven and highly sensitive require that it be the exclusive provider of service for the equipment?

c. **Held.** Yes.

1) D clearly had a majority of the business in community television antenna systems. D also had economic power because its equipment was the only equipment available that met all the problems that arose at the antenna sites. This power gave D significant leverage to persuade customers to agree to D's service contracts and was sufficient to invoke the doctrine of "per se unreasonableness."

2) Although P has established both of the prerequisites for finding D's practices unreasonable per se, the per se rule is not conclusively binding in a case with facts different from those in the cases giving rise to the per se rule.

3) Because the technology involved here was new, both D's reputation and the growth of the entire industry was at stake if the systems did not operate correctly. If D had allowed others to provide services, customers would have purchased D's equipment and done their own service, a system which would have likely failed. Accordingly, D's practice of selling its equipment only in conjunction with a service contract was reasonable.

4) As D's systems became better established in various parts of the country, D discontinued its policy. However, D did not discontinue its policy quickly enough. With regard to full system sales, a community television antenna system is not a single product. Other companies offered such systems without requiring a purchase of a full system. D's policy of selling full systems was reasonable at first, as was the mandatory service contract, but it became unreasonable once the need for compulsory service contracts disappeared.

10. **Leverage--United States Steel Corp. v. Fortner Enterprises,** 429 U.S. 610 (1977).

United States Steel Corp. v. Fortner Enterprises

a. **Facts.** Fortner (P) was a corporation formed by an experienced real estate developer for the purpose of developing a tract of homes. United States Steel Corporation's (D's) home division desired to market its prefabricated homes and formed a subsidiary corporation solely for the purpose of extending credit to customers for the prefabricated homes. P sought financing from D and credit was extended to cover all of the development costs as well as the price of purchasing prefab homes. The contract specified that the loan was for the purpose of purchasing homes from D. P became dissatisfied with the agreement and sued for treble damages under the tying arrangement doctrine of the Sherman Act. The district court granted summary judgment for D, but the United States Supreme Court reversed and remanded the case for a trial on the issue of D's economic power. The trial court found that the credit arrangement was unusual in that it involved a high degree of risk to D and that 100% financing of real estate development was seldom available. The court also found that the price of D's homes was at the most 15% above competitors and that D held an insignificant share of the market for prefabricated homes. Based on these facts, the court rendered judgment for P, and the court of appeals affirmed. D appeals.

b. **Issue.** Is the measure of "appreciable economic power" used to determine if an illegal tying arrangement exists to the competitive advantage of the party seeking the tying arrangement?

c. **Held.** Yes. Judgment reversed.

1) The competitive advantage must be an economic, physical, legal, or similar advantage which prevents competitors from offering a competing product. Here, D was willing to offer financing in a higher risk contract but no evidence was adduced to show that it had an advantage in terms of cost or other factors as compared with other financers.

2) The fact that a financing arrangement is unique does not support an inference of appreciable economic power absent a showing of competitive advantage in ability to provide the financing.

d. **Concurrence** (Burger, C.J., Rehnquist, J.). This holding is limited to credit offerings by one company with tying arrangements with the product of another company and is not intended to cast its influence on single product financing by the same company.

Jefferson Parish Hospital District No. 2 v. Hyde

11. Two Approaches to Tying Arrangements--Jefferson Parish Hospital District No. 2 v. Hyde, 466 U.S. 2 (1984).

a. **Facts.** Hyde (P), a board certified anesthesiologist, sought admission to the medical staff of a hospital within Jefferson Parish Hospital District No. 2 (D). D rejected the application because of an exclusive contract for anesthesiological services between the hospital and Roux & Associates, a four-person firm of anesthesiologists. The court of appeals held that the contract was illegal per se, and the Supreme Court granted certiorari.

b. **Issue.** Must a firm have market power in the tying product market before a tying arrangement may be considered illegal per se?

c. **Held.** Yes. Judgment reversed.

1) Tying arrangements are per se unreasonable because they present an unacceptable risk of stifling competition. Not every refusal to sell two products separately restrains competition, however. When each

product could be purchased separately in a competitive market, a combined package would not restrain competition.

2) The essential element of an invalid tying arrangement is the use of market power in the tying product to force buyers to take the tied product. The impairment of competition in the market for the tied product is a violation of the Sherman Act.

3) Application of the per se rule depends first on the requirement that the volume of commerce foreclosed must be substantial, then on the likelihood of anticompetitive forcing taking place. Where a patent is used to force buyers to purchase separate tied products, the per se rule applies. The focus is on the markets for the two products involved because there must be two separate product markets to have a tying arrangement.

4) In this case, the focus is on D's sale of services to its patients, including anesthesiological services. D claims that it provides a functionally integrated package of services, but the evidence demonstrates that consumers differentiate between anesthesiological services and the other services provided by D. Thus, there are two markets. However, the hospital to which P applied handles only 30% of the patients in its area, which is insufficient market power to permit forcing. For that reason, the per se rule does not apply.

5) D's practice could still violate the Sherman Act if it unreasonably restrained competition, but the evidence in this case does not establish how the practice affected consumer demand for separate arrangements with anesthesiologists such as P.

d. **Concurrence** (O'Connor, J., Burger, C.J., Powell, Rehnquist, JJ.).

1) The per se rule should not be used in tying cases because it requires analysis of the economic effects of the tying arrangement before it can be applied. In effect, the courts must conduct a rule of reason inquiry before determining whether the per se rule applies. This has the result of ignoring economic benefits that a particular arrangement may have.

2) Instead, the courts should apply the rule of reason and determine whether (i) the seller has power in the tying product market; (ii) there is a substantial threat that the tying seller will acquire market power in the tied-product market; and (iii) there is a coherent economic basis for treating the tying and tied products as distinct, such that consumers would wish to purchase the tied product separately without also purchasing the tying product. Once these requirements are met, the arrangement would be held illegal only if its anticompetitive impact outweighs its contribution to efficiency.

3) In this case, the third element was not satisfied because there is no sound economic reason to treat surgery and anesthesia as separate services. Patients purchase anesthesia only as part of hospital services. At the same time, the arrangement confers significant benefits on

patients by insuring availability, and by making the hospital responsible to select and monitor anesthesiologists.

4) Even though the contract with Roux is exclusive dealing, it does not unreasonably enhance the hospital's market position relative to other hospitals, or unreasonably permit Roux to acquire power relative to other anesthesiologists. Thus, it is permitted under the rule of reason.

Eastman Kodak Co. v. Image Technical Services

12. Tying Within One Brand's Market--Eastman Kodak Co. v. Image Technical Services, 504 U.S. 451 (1992).

a. **Facts.** Eastman Kodak Company (D) manufactured and sold photocopiers and micrographic equipment, as well as service and replacement parts for its equipment. Image Technical Services and other independent service organizations (Ps) serviced D's equipment. Ps purchased parts from D. D started a new policy of selling replacement parts only to buyers of D's equipment who used D's service. D also limited Ps' access to other sources of D's parts by having other manufacturers of D's parts agree not to sell parts to anyone other than D. As a result, Ps' customers were forced to switch to D for service and Ps lost their business. Ps sued, claiming that D had unlawfully tied the sale of services for its machines to the sale of parts in violation of section 1 of the Sherman Act and had unlawfully monopolized and attempted to monopolize the sale of service and parts for such machines in violation of section 2. The district court granted summary judgment for D, but the court of appeals reversed.

b. **Issue.** If a manufacturer lacks power in the equipment market, must a court assume it also lacks power in the market for service and parts for its equipment?

c. **Held.** No. Judgment affirmed.

1) A tying arrangement is an agreement by a party to sell one product on the condition that the buyer also purchase a different product (the tied product), or at least agrees not to purchase that product from another supplier. A tying arrangement violates section 1 only if the seller has "appreciable economic power" in the tying product market.

2) Ps produced sufficient evidence of a tying arrangement to defeat D's motion for summary judgment. The facts could support findings that service and parts are two distinct products because each has been sold separately and that D has tied the sale of the two products by selling parts to third parties only if they agree not to buy service from Ps.

3) "Appreciable economic power in the tying market" is defined as the power "to force a purchaser to do something that he would not do in a competitive market." This power may be inferred from a seller's possession of a predominant share of the market. In this case, Ps must be allowed to show that D has sufficient power in the parts market to force unwanted purchases of the tied services from D.

4) D claims that it lacks market power in the primary equipment market, and therefore could not have market power in the derivative after-

markets for parts and service. This theory is based on the assumption that if it raised its parts or service prices above competitive levels, potential customers would stop buying its equipment. However, the alleged facts show that D's equipment sales did not drop after it raised its service prices. Ps attributed this result to the significant information and switching costs that created a less responsive connection between aftermarket prices and equipment sales. In other words, once customers purchased D's equipment, they were locked in. The high parts and service costs were not factors customers considered when making the initial purchases.

5) Ps have also presented genuine issues for trial regarding D's alleged violation of section 2. D controls nearly 100% of the parts market and up to 95% of the service market, with no readily available substitutes. This shows possession of monopoly power. Courts have indicated that one brand of a product can constitute a separate market in some instances.

6) Ps have also presented evidence that D took exclusionary action to maintain its monopoly over parts and used its control over parts to strengthen its monopoly over the service market. None of D's asserted business justifications are adequate to justify a summary judgment for D.

d. **Dissent** (Scalia, O'Connor, Thomas, JJ.). Every manufacturer of durable goods with distinctive parts has the market power held by D in this case. The majority has lowered the threshold for the per se rule against tying and for monopolization too low if it can reach a defendant with no power in the interbrand market. D could have taken other actions to make the tying product original equipment with no tying implications.

13. **Summary.** This area is much like that of attempting to define the "relevant market"—the cases present a comfortable gloss of language that hides complex problems requiring an analysis that does not appear to have been attempted by the courts.

a. **Characterization problem.** In the first place, there exists the problem of characterizing a fact situation as to whether it involves tying. For a tying situation to exist, there must be two products (tying and tied product). For example, are an automobile and its tires one product or two? Some of the factors to consider:

1) Are the parts "functionally" one product?

2) Are they sold separately and used in various markets separately?

3) Does the amalgamated sale of the "components" result in cost savings other than saving in distribution expenses?

4) Do the products sell to entirely different consumers? (This occurs in the reciprocity cases.)

5) Do important groups of consumers prefer to have them treated as different products (*i.e.,* would they prefer to buy the components from separate suppliers)?

6) What trade practices exist (*i.e.,* in practice are the components priced separately, etc.)?

b. **Leverage effect.** The rationale of preventing tying is to prevent a party with market power in one product from using this "leverage" to foreclose competition in other markets. The factors that are examined in this regard are:

1) **Market power.** The cases indicate that the seller must have economic power in the tying product. They further indicate that this need not be a specific market share, or monopoly power. The problem is that this factor has not been carefully examined in the cases in regard to its relationship to anticompetitive effects. For example, it is not clear from the *Loew's* case, *supra*, that competitors would be injured by the package film deals of the defendant. Thus, what the case seems to result in is giving the buyer a wider range of choice. In short, most of the cases slight the issue of what anticompetitive effects are being prohibited. But it appears that any substantial tie-in is unlawful, however market power is defined.

2) **A "not insubstantial amount of business."** The additional prong of the test is a showing that a "not insubstantial amount of business" has been foreclosed from competitive forces. This factor and market power work together. In effect, a court may hold that where a not insubstantial amount of business has been affected, market power exists; or where market power can be shown to exist, it may be presumed that a not insubstantial amount of business is affected. In any event, it seems clear that "not insubstantial" need not be a large amount (*e.g.,* $200,000 in *United States Steel Corp. v. Fortner Enterprises*, *supra*).

3) **Justification and the per se rule.** Some of the courts talk about a per se rule. However, it appears that the courts really are applying a rule of reason, since they allow defendants to show business justifications (such as in *Jerrold*, *supra*) for tying and characterization and market power hurdles must be overcome.

C. EXCLUSIVE DEALING

1. Introduction.

a. **Vertical integration.** It is impossible to say exactly what the effect of vertical integration may be in any given case (*i.e.,* integration into one company of the supplier of raw materials, the manufacturer, and the retailer). In some instances, integration is more efficient; a lower unit cost of the end product may result. In other instances, there may be no greater efficiency involved. And in some instances, there may be diseconomies.

There are, of course, anticompetitive implications possible in the integration situation. For example, an integrated firm is normally its own customer, and integration may therefore cut off possible customers for nonintegrated firms. Also, where there are cost savings involved, the tendency of an industry is to integrate, and fewer and fewer firms result (*i.e.,* the industry structure becomes more concentrated). Finally, integrated companies may control all facilities available at one level of the integrated structure, which may act as a deterrent for firms to enter or compete at other levels.

b. **Exclusive dealing arrangements.**

1) **Introduction.** Section 3 of the Clayton Act is set forth in detail, *supra*. This section is discussed there in connection with tying contracts, which are conceptually analogous to exclusive dealing arrangements in that an attempt is made to tie a supplier to a customer on an exclusive basis. Both types of agreements are proscribed by the language of section 3.

2) **Definition.** An exclusive dealing arrangement is one where by contract the buyer agrees that it will buy only from a certain supplier. Note that to be unlawful, such a contract must be something more than simply a contract to buy goods; every contract excludes other suppliers. This "something more" must be a substantial adverse effect on the competitive opportunities for other firms to supply the ultimate consumers.

2. **A Quantitative Test--Standard Oil Co. of California v. United States,** 337 U.S. 293 (1949).

Standard Oil Co. of California v. United States

a. **Facts.** Standard Oil (D) was the largest refiner and supplier of gas in the western states. D sold gas through its own stations and independent dealers, selling 7% of the market's volume through the dealers and 7% in its own stations. There were six other major competitors and 70 small ones. D used exclusive-supply contracts with the dealers (as did all competing gas companies with their dealers). The independent dealers constituted 16% of the stations in the area. Sixty million dollars of gas was sold in 1947 through these dealers. The contracts were from year-to-year. The United States (P) brought a section 3 action under the Clayton Act.

b. **Issue.** May an anticompetitive effect be presumed if an exclusive dealing arrangement involves a substantial dollar amount?

c. **Held.** Yes. Violation section 3 of the Clayton Act.

1) Where tying contracts are involved (such as in *International Salt, supra*), all that need be shown is that a "not insubstantial amount of business" is involved. But requirement contracts serve purposes which are not necessarily anticompetitive. Often both buyer and seller wish to use such a contract. By such a contract the buyer can be assured of a source of supply, protect against price rises, avoid the risk of storage, etc. Sellers can reduce selling expense, plan production, etc.

2) Thus, requirement contracts might justify a rule of reason analysis. Here D has not increased market share in the past several years, but it might have lost market share without such contracts. In short, courts are not set up to conduct such detailed economic analysis.

3) Therefore, section 3 of the Clayton Act is violated when competition has been foreclosed as to a "substantial amount" of business. Here, no one will disagree that a substantial amount of business was involved.

FTC v. Motion Picture Advertising Service Co.

3. **Unfair Trade Practice--FTC v. Motion Picture Advertising Service Co.,** 344 U.S. 392 (1953).

a. **Facts.** Motion Picture Advertising Service (D) produced and distributed advertising films which were displayed in theatres on an exclusive contract basis. D had exclusive contracts with 40% of the theatres in its operating area. D and three competitors together had exclusive contracts with 75% of all theatres which showed such advertising. The FTC found that D's contracts unreasonably restrained competition and tended to monopolize. It prohibited D from entering any such contract lasting more than a year. The court of appeals reversed.

b. **Issue.** May the FTC restrict the use of exclusive dealing even when there is no proof of conspiracy?

c. **Held.** Yes. Judgment reversed. A practice restricting competition that is indulged in by competitors who, combined, dominate the market is an unfair method of competition, even though there is no conspiracy.

d. **Dissent** (Frankfurter, J.). For the first time, the Court holds that separate exclusive contracts may be aggregated to support a charge of Sherman Act violation. This case is unlike *Standard Oil, supra*, which involved a producer's power over retailers.

Tampa Electric Co. v. Nashville Coal Co.

4. **A Qualitative Test--Tampa Electric Co. v. Nashville Coal Co.,** 365 U. S. 320 (1961).

a. **Facts.** Tampa Electric Company (P) is an electrical utility in Tampa, Florida, supplying electricity to an area of the state. It built a new plant and contracted with Nashville Coal Company (D) for all its requirements for a 20-year period, to be not less than 225,000 tons per year. Just prior to delivery, D refused to perform. It was estimated that the total requirements of P would reach 2.25 million tons annually; the contract was worth about $128 million over its life. P sued D to enforce performance. The lower courts held that the relevant market was peninsular Florida, where P's requirements constituted a significant percentage of the total need. Accordingly, the lower courts held that the contract violated section 3 of the Clayton Act. P appeals.

b. **Issue.** Is the relevant market that in which the suppliers compete rather than the location in which the buyer is based?

c. **Held.** Yes. Judgment reversed.

1) The contract does not substantially lessen competition and should be enforced.

a) First, there must be a determination of the line of commerce; *i.e.,* coal.

b) The second question is the "relevant market." Here, it is the geographical area of the seven states where producers of coal compete for customers. In this market, P's requirements amount to less than 1% of the total output.

c) Third, there must be a determination of a substantial lessening of competition. Several factors should be considered:

(i) Probable effect of the contract on the relevant area of effective competition.

(ii) Percentage of the total volume of commerce involved.

(iii) Probable effects on competition of the share of commerce involved being preempted.

The amount of commerce quantitatively is of little consequence.

2) The case is distinguished from *Standard Oil, supra*, in that there the whole industry was using requirement contracts and numerous retail outlets were involved (over 6,000 stations).

d. **Comment.** This case rejects the approach of *Standard Oil* (*i.e.,* a purely quantitative amount of business), but it does not give anything much more concrete.

1) Note the critical importance of the definition of the "relevant market."

2) Note also that in *Tampa Electric*, the utility was the end user of the coal, so the requirements contract was not preventing other sellers from using a distribution system to get to consumers. This is the point the Court was making when it distinguished *Standard Oil*. In *Standard Oil*, the Court was trying to protect the consumer by seeing that alternative products could get to market through the established distribution system. In *Tampa,* the utility was the ultimate consumer.

5. **Business Reasons.** Note also that the business reasons for the contract may be determinative. In *Tampa*, an electric utility was involved, which needed to count on a source of supply, and the public interest was involved. In other words, where it appears that there is a substantial motivation on the part of the buyer to have a requirements contract for compelling business reasons, the contract may be upheld. For example, exclusive dealing contracts might be allowed in the situation where a new company is getting started and needs to have the assurance that its distributors will sell only its products.

6. **Buyer's Motivation.** Another factor may be whether (i) the buyer wants the exclusive contract or (ii) the exclusive contract is imposed by the seller, and the

buyer (while it would like to handle additional competitor's brands) accepts the exclusive arrangement in order to get the seller's product.

7. **Alternative Distribution Systems.** Finally, note that if an alternative distribution system can be easily created (such as with many door-to-door salespersons systems), exclusive arrangements may not create a barrier to competing firms who have the option of creating their own distribution systems.

FTC v. Brown Shoe Co.

8. **Federal Trade Commission Actions--FTC v. Brown Shoe Co.,** 384 U.S. 316 (1966).

   a. **Facts.** FTC (P) brought an action against Brown Shoe Company (D), the second largest manufacturer of shoes, enjoining D from continuing its "franchise" contracts with 650 shoe stores to sell Brown shoes and "no other competing lines." The franchise could be canceled on short notice. D also provided some special services to shoe stores accepting the franchise (low cost group insurance, special marketing assistance, etc.). D argued that there had to be a showing that there was a substantial lessening of competition.

   b. **Issue.** May the FTC declare a practice unfair even if it does not specifically violate the antitrust laws?

   c. **Held.** Yes. Judgment affirmed.

      1) The FTC can bring an action for unfair competition against practices which conflict with the central polices of the Sherman Act or Clayton Act even though specific proof of the elements required by these acts is not shown.

   d. **Comment.** It seems unfortunate to have different standards for the various acts applied to the same facts. Also, it seems unclear what this case stands for, since the opinion is not clearly written.

9. **Rule of Reason.** It seems that the Court has really espoused a rule of reason test in this area. The tests put forth in the cases are conflicting, or at least not uniform.

   a. But it does seem clear that the defendant can argue business justifications, and if there is not a substantial lessening of competition in a relevant market, the contract will be upheld (note that with a substantial business justification, the market may be defined so as not to find a lessening of competition).

   b. Alternatively, the defendant can show that there has not been a substantial lessening of competition. This may be shown by demonstrating that only a small proportion of the relevant market is involved, or only a small amount of business (or both), or that in effect there is little or no lessening of competition (such as where the defendant shows that other, alternative distribution systems could easily be created or are available).

10. **Agency Arrangements.** Note that a company may attempt to avoid the ban on exclusive dealing arrangements by formulating its arrangement with its distributor or buyer as an "agency."

VI. MERGERS AND ACQUISITIONS

A. COMPETITIVE EFFECTS

One of the most difficult problems in antitrust law is whether market structure ***alone*** can be illegal; *i.e.,* does it violate the antitrust laws for a firm to grow so large (through mergers, acquisitions, or otherwise) that it has the ***power*** to restrain competition, etc., even though such power has not been exercised, and no intent or attempt to monopolize is shown? Or must there be some ***abuse*** of power—*e.g.*, some attempt to fix prices, restrain trade, or other predatory practice—before a violation can be found? There is a valid interest in keeping the market structure diverse and competitive, for as a market becomes oligopolistic, it becomes easier for firms to restrain competition.

1. **Application.** In *Reynolds Metals Co. v. FTC*, 309 F.2d 223 (D.C. Cir. 1962), the court found that there was an anticompetitive effect. Reynolds produced 40% of the aluminum foil; converters (200 firms) used 192 million pounds annually for certain purposes. Arrow was one of eight converters who supplied decorated foil to the florist market; it had 33% of the decorated foil florist market. Reynolds bought Arrow, then lowered Arrow's prices, allowing it to take over a larger share of the market. The court found an anticompetitive effect in the exclusion of other manufacturers of raw foil from selling to Arrow. Also, Reynolds's acquisition gave Arrow significant financial resources over its competitors in the florist foil market.

B. INTRODUCTION TO MERGER LAW

1. **The Sherman Act.**

   a. **Per se rule.** In its earliest decision on this issue, the United States Supreme Court seemed to indicate that any mergers (horizontal or vertical) which had the ***effect*** of restraining competition were illegal per se under section 1 of the Sherman Act. In *Northern Securities Co. v. United States*, 193 U.S. 197 (1904), the Court did not require a showing of predatory practices; it was enough that the merger destroyed the competition that had previously existed between the firms in question.

   b. **Size alone not illegal.** Another line of United States Supreme Court cases indicated that size alone was ***not*** per se unlawful and that mergers or acquisitions would not be dissolved, absent a showing of an attempt to monopolize or commit other predatory practices. For example, in *United States v. United States Steel Corp.*, *supra*, the Court held that an unexercised power to fix prices did not violate the Sherman Act. The Court declared that "the law does not make mere size an offense . . . it requires ***overt acts*** (some predatory practice)."

   c. **The objective of a competitive market--United States v. Columbia Steel Co.,** 334 U.S. 495 (1948).

   United States v. Columbia Steel Co.

      1) **Facts.** United States Steel sought to acquire Consolidated, a West Coast manufacturer of fabricated steel products (tanks, welded pipe, etc.); Columbia Steel, a wholly owned subsidiary

of United States Steel, was to make the acquisition. United States Steel was the largest producer of rolled steel products in the United States (33% of the market); Columbia was the largest producer of rolled steel products on the West Coast. Rolled steel was used by Consolidated in fabricating its products. United States Steel had two fabricating companies that operated in the East. The government challenged the acquisition on the basis that it would lessen competition, in that it would exclude all sellers except United States Steel from supplying Consolidated's requirements of rolled steel.

2) **Issue.** May a merger be prohibited based solely on the size of the acquiring company?

3) **Held.** No. The merger is not unreasonable.

   a) Vertical integration is not illegal per se.

   b) Exclusive dealing (as between parent and subsidiary) is unlawful only when it is an unreasonable restraint on trade. The restraint becomes unreasonable only when it unreasonably restricts the opportunities of competitors to market their products.

   c) Economic and technological factors may make vertical integration essential in some industries.

   d) Thus, it is the intent and purpose of the parties that is critical. Where the intent is a legitimate business purpose, integration may not be unlawful; where the intent is to eliminate competition or to create a monopoly, it is unlawful.

   e) Where integration can be explained by normal commercial motives, factors such as the amount of commerce affected, the strength of the remaining competition, and other facts are relevant to determine whether the intent is to restrain competition or exclude competitors.

4) **Dissent.** D's purpose in acquiring Consolidated is to insure itself a market. Buying the customer for whose business D was competing is a clear elimination of competition.

5) **Comment.** It is clear that any vertical integration restrains some competition. But the Court is saying that there may be economic and business justifications for the restraint. Thus, the issue is whether the restraint is unreasonable. To determine this, the Court will look to the strength of the firm's actual competitors to see if the market remains competitive.

   a) In this area, cases are judged on the basis of the actual competitive situation, not some theoretical model of competition.

   b) This means that even though the industrial structure may make it impossible for new firms to enter, vertical integration may be upheld if the existing condition between competing firms is judged to be sufficiently competitive.

   c) This is the notion of "effective competition."

2. **The Clayton Act.**

a. **Introduction.** There was adverse reaction to the *Columbia Steel* case (*supra*). Section 7 of the Clayton Act was amended and now is the section normally applied to attempt to prevent vertical integration; it is, of course, also relevant to monopolization cases.

1) **Wording of section 7 of Clayton Act.** Section 7 provides:

> No corporation engaged in commerce shall acquire, directly or indirectly, the whole or any part of the stock or other share capital, and no corporation subject to the jurisdiction of the Federal Trade Commission shall acquire the whole or any part of the assets of another corporation engaged also in commerce, where in any line of commerce in any section of the country, the effect of such acquisition may be to substantially lessen competition, or to tend to create a monopoly. . . . This section shall not apply to corporations purchasing such stock solely for investment and not using the same by voting or otherwise to bring about, or in attempting to bring about, the substantial lessening of competition. Nor shall anything contained in this section prevent a corporation engaged in commerce from causing the formation of subsidiary corporations for the actual carrying on of their immediate lawful business, or the natural and legitimate branches or extensions thereof, or from owning and holding all or a part of the stock of such subsidiary corporations, when the effect of such formation is not to substantially lessen competition.

2) **Rule of reason.** This section of the Clayton Act essentially states a rule of reason approach.

3) **May substantially lessen competition.** Obviously, under the wording of this section, it is not necessary to prove that the restraint involved actually has restrained competition. It is enough that it "may" tend to substantially lessen competition.

4) **Types of mergers and acquisitions.** Section 7 applies to mergers of horizontal competitors, vertical mergers or acquisitions, and conglomerate mergers and acquisitions (those between firms in unrelated markets).

5) **Application of section 7.** In determining the legality of vertical mergers under section 7, courts proceed as follows:

a) First, the relevant geographic and product markets must be determined.

b) Next, the probable effect of the merger is considered by measuring the share of the market which will be foreclosed.

c) If more than a de minimis share is foreclosed or potential competition is eliminated, the court must then consider any economic and historical factors peculiar to the case, including any trend toward concentration in the industry, barriers to new entry created by the merger, and the nature and purpose of the merger.

C. VERTICAL INTEGRATION BY MERGER OR ACQUISITION

1. **Introduction.** The motivation for vertical integration is two-fold:

   a. **To reduce costs.** Integration may reduce market transaction costs, such as time and money spent in shopping, buying, negotiation, etc. It may be easier and possibly cheaper to coordinate the effort to make component parts come together properly, and the firm may be able to respond more rapidly to competitive changes.

   b. **Control.** The second motivation is to control what happens to the company (control over markets, over supplies, etc.).

   c. **Adverse competitive effects.** There may also be adverse competitive effects from integration. For example, where an integrated firm wants to compete at the retail level, it may use the profits coming from other levels of the integrated company to reduce the prices at the retail level and drive out competition; when competition is reduced, it may then raise prices.

2. **Effect on the Industry.** Many case histories have shown that once one or several firms in an industry begin to integrate, the others do also, for fear of being foreclosed from critical supplies or markets. Thus, to preserve a competitive environment, limits must be set on the integration process in order to avoid undue market concentration.

United States v. Yellow Cab Co.

   a. **Monopolization action--United States v. Yellow Cab Co.,** 332 U.S. 218 (1947).

      1) **Facts.** Checker (D), a cab manufacturing company, acquired cab operating companies in several major cities (owning, for example, 86% of the cab licenses in Chicago, 100% in Pittsburgh, etc.). The government charged that there was a contract between the manufacturing company and the operating companies in restraint of trade, since the cab operating companies agreed to buy cabs only from the manufacturing company. The district court had dismissed the complaint.

      2) **Issue.** May vertical integration violate the Sherman Act?

      3) **Held.** Yes. Case remanded for a full trial.

         a) Restraints of trade under section 1 of the Sherman Act are unlawful no matter how much commerce is involved. And section 2 makes it unlawful to monopolize "any appreciable amount of commerce."

         b) There is a substantial amount of commerce involved where the operating companies have agreed to buy cabs only from the manufacturing companies (a replacement market for about 5,000 cabs). Other cab manufacturers are foreclosed from competing for this market.

c) It makes no difference that the market is foreclosed because the companies are affiliated (*i.e.,* vertically integrated).

d) The issue is whether the intent of the defendant is to integrate in order to restrain commerce or create a monopoly. There should be a trial on this issue.

4) **Remand.** On remand, the court found that the relationship between the manufacturer and the operating companies was not a deliberate plan to restrain trade or monopolize. Also, the operating companies were not compelled to buy cabs from the manufacturer but could exercise their business judgment.

5) **Comment.** This was the first case to argue that vertical integration amounted to monopolization.

b. **Rule of reason.** In *United States v. Paramount Pictures*, 334 U.S. 131 (1948), the Court held that the legality of vertical integration under the Sherman Act depends on the purpose for the integration and the power it creates. The Court condemned the joint ownership of movie theatres by production companies because each producer gave the other a preference in the exhibition of movies.

c. **Threat to integrate.** In *United States v. New York Great Atlantic & Pacific Tea Co.*, 67 F. Supp. 626 (E.D. Ill. 1946), *aff'd*, 173 F.2d 79 (7th Cir. 1949), A & P had obtained special discounts from suppliers by threatening to change suppliers or to produce goods itself. A & P did actually integrate vertically in some instances. While recognizing that vertical integration alone was not illegal, the court held that A & P had violated the Sherman Act by unreasonably restraining competition. Its improper actions "tainted" its vertical integration.

3. **Partial Stock Interest--United States v. E.I. du Pont De Nemours & Co.,** 353 U.S. 586 (1957). United States v. E.I. du Pont De Nemours & Co.

a. **Facts.** In 1917, du Pont (D) bought 23% of the common stock of General Motors ("G.M.") and began supplying G.M. with finishes and fabrics. The government brought an action under section 7 of the Clayton Act. It was shown that G.M. had 50% of the car market; in one year it bought $18 million worth of car finishes from D (67% of its needs) and $3 million worth of fabrics (52% of its needs).

b. **Issue.** May section 7 bar the acquisition by a supplier of the stock of a customer?

c. **Held.** Yes. There is a violation.

1) The relevant market is automobile finishes and fabrics.

2) This market is substantial. G.M. is 50% of the market.

3) Competition is foreclosed in a substantial share of the substantial market (this is shown by the large percentage of the market supplied by D and by the large dollar amount of this percentage of the market).

4) It makes no difference that D only owns a part of G.M.'s stock; section 7 covers this situation.

5) There can be no logical inference that D bought the stock merely as an "investment."

Brown Shoe Co. v. United States

4. **The Test for "Substantially Lessening" Competition--Brown Shoe Co. v. United States,** 370 U.S. 294 (1962).

a. **Facts.** Brown Shoe Company (D) bought Kinney Shoes for stock; both were manufacturers and retailers of shoes (men's, women's, children's). The district court finding that the merger of the manufacturing operations did not violate the antitrust laws was not appealed. D was the fourth largest manufacturer (4%), and Kinney was the 12th largest (.5%). D was the third largest retailer (6%), and Kinney was eighth with 2%. The district court found the following:

(i) Men's, women's, and children's shoes generally were produced in separate factories.

(ii) A definite trend existed in the industry for manufacturers to acquire retailers.

(iii) The number of manufacturers was declining.

(iv) Manufacturers increasingly tended to supply a greater percentage of shoes to owned retail outlets.

(v) Brown Shoe was involved in each of these trends itself.

(vi) At the time of the merger, Kinney did not buy any of its retail shoes from D; at the time the action was brought, D supplied 8%.

The district court found that the merger violated section 7 of the Clayton Act. D appeals.

b. **Issue.** May trends toward oligopoly be stopped in the early stages before any firms actually reach oligopolistic size?

c. **Held.** Yes. Judgment affirmed.

1) As to the ***vertical aspects*** of the merger (Brown's acquisition of Kinney's retail outlets):

a) The relevant product market is defined by reasonable interchangeability or cross-elasticity of demand between the product and substitutes. Submarkets may be defined based on practical indicia such as industry or public recognition, a product's peculiar characteristics and uses, unique production facilities, distinct customers, distinct prices, and specialized vendors. Section 7 prohibits lessening of competition in any of these submarkets.

b) The relevant product markets are men's, women's, and children's shoes. D argues for price/quality and age/sex distinctions, but none of these would help its case.

c) The relevant geographical market is the entire nation. Manufacturers can distribute on a nationwide basis.

d) The effect of the merger must be tested as to whether in any relevant market in any section of the country there may be a substantial lessening of competition. Considerations:

(1) The size of the market share foreclosed. Unless the share is a monopoly, this by itself is not determinative. Here, the share is neither a monopoly nor de minimum. Other factors must be looked at.

(2) The purpose of the arrangement. Courts require different effects on competition, depending on purpose (*e.g.*, tying contract vs. requirements contract). Here, the legislative history indicates that Congress wanted to preserve the "failing company" exception and to allow small companies to merge in order to enable them to compete better. But here, it is obvious that large companies are involved and the purpose was to foreclose competition by putting more Brown shoes in Kinney outlets.

(3) The trend toward concentration in the industry. Section 7 has one purpose of preserving industrial structures with numerous competitors.

2) As to the ***horizontal aspects*** of the merger (*i.e.*, merger of the retail stores of Kinney and Brown), *see infra* next section.

d. **Comment.** Note that the majority opinion obscures some important questions on market shares. First, most of Brown's retail locations were franchises, not owned by Brown. Second, in computing Kinney's retail sales, all of Kinney's retail purchases were lumped together; however, it might have been more proper to consider what percentage of the independent manufacturer's sales Kinney's purchases represented, since this would be a more accurate reflection of the market share foreclosed by the merger.

5. **Department of Justice Merger Guidelines—1984.**

a. **Introduction.** The Justice Department has a major role in enforcing antitrust merger policy because in many cases, competitors lack incentive to bring an action. This may be due to a common interest in higher prices resulting from oligopolistic trends, or may result from the lack of financial incentives to seek an injunction (no damages to treble). In any case, in

1968, the Justice Department issued merger guidelines for the benefit of potential merging parties. More lenient guidelines were issued in 1982; these were relaxed further in 1984. The guidelines give prominent attention to market definition as discussed *infra*. The FTC generally follows the guidelines, but some states apply stricter tests.

b. **Herfindahl-Hirschman Index ("HHI").** Formerly, the Department applied a concentration ratio based on the market shares of the top four firms. This was replaced with the HHI, an index consisting of the sum of the squares of the individual market shares of all firms in the market. The HHI reflects the market share concentration of all firms, giving proportionately greater weight to the market shares of the larger firms. A merger always increases the HHI. For example, two firms having 10% market shares would enter the HHI at 200 ($10^2 + 10^2$). After a merger, the merged firm would add 400 to the HHI (20^2).

c. **Application of the guidelines to vertical mergers.** A vertical merger is subject to challenge if it increases barriers to entry. This requires the satisfaction of three conditions:

1) ***Degree of integration***: The two markets must be so extensively integrated that entrants to the primary market would have to simultaneously enter the secondary market. This condition is not met if post-merger sales by unintegrated firms in the secondary market can service two minimum-efficiency-scale primary market plants.

2) ***Difficulty of entry***: The requirement of entry into the secondary market must make primary market entry significantly more difficult and thus less likely.

3) ***Market structure***: The structure of the primary market must be otherwise so conducive to noncompetitive performance that the increased difficulty of entry is less likely to affect its performance. This is generally met if the HHI exceeds 1800.

d. **Other considerations.** The Department is more likely to challenge a vertical merger if it would facilitate collusion among vertically integrated firms, or if it is used to avoid rate regulation. The Department recognizes the potential efficiencies from vertical integration and gives relatively greater weight to this factor than it does to horizontal mergers.

D. HORIZONTAL MERGERS

1. **Introduction.** Here, mergers between competitors at the same level of manufacture or distribution are considered.

2. **Measures of Concentration.** There are basically two measures of concentration.

a. **Overall concentration.** For example, the top 500 corporations in size control X% of the total assets. These measures can be used as indicators of certain broad aspects of the social-economic structure of society, or serve as measures of concentration of economic power.

b. **Concentration ratios for individual industries.** For example, the top four firms control 75% of sales. These measures are important for measuring the competitive structure of individual industries and markets.

3. **Concentrated Industries.**

a. **Presumption of anticompetitive structure.** The objective is to prevent industries from becoming oligopolistic in nature, where such a structure leads to price and output cooperation and higher prices than would exist in a purely competitive market. The presumption is that the fewer the firms in an industry, the less the competition in the industry and the higher the profitability of the firms. Empirical evidence seems to lend support to this conclusion.

b. **Competing considerations.**

1) Bigness is not by itself badness. Normally, there are certain economies of scale involved in reaching a certain efficient size.

2) Scarcity of firms does not necessarily lead to an anticompetitive environment.

3) It is impossible just to count firms in an industry and determine the nature of the competitive environment.

a) Defining the market is difficult. Firms producing close substitutes might have to be included to get an accurate picture.

b) Sometimes there are many firms but the market is anticompetitive (*e.g.*, A = 90%; 100 other firms have total of 10%).

4. **Defining the Relevant Market.**

a. ***Brown* considerations.** In *Brown Shoe Co. v. United States, supra*, the Court disposed of the horizontal aspects of the merger (merger of the retail stores of Kinney and Brown) as follows:

1) Section 7 is to prevent the lessening of competition between the acquiring and the acquired companies.

2) The product market is the same as vertically.

3) The geographical market is where the stores competed prior to the merger, which are those towns exceeding 10,000 population and their surrounding territory in which both Brown and Kinney had a retail store. (Note that D argued for central business districts of large cities, or standard metropolitan areas that included smaller communities.)

4) There are many situations where Brown and Kinney now have a large share of the relevant markets. Market share is a very important

factor; even 5% may be too much, since one of the objectives is to preserve competitive markets of many smaller competitors.

5) Another factor is the trend toward concentration in the industry.

6) Here, the integrated company might be able to market its own brands at lower prices than the competition, which might benefit the consumer but injure competitors; even though the Act protects competition and not competitors, still another purpose of the Act is to insure that markets, even though less efficient, are characterized by many competitive units.

United States v. Philadelphia National Bank

b. **Quantitative test--United States v. Philadelphia National Bank,** 374 U.S. 321 (1963).

1) **Facts.** Philadelphia National Bank (D) had a merger agreement with Girard Bank. Both had their home offices in Philadelphia and branches in three surrounding counties (this was the area to which state law permitted branching). D was the second largest bank in the area; Girard was third. D had 22% of the assets; Girard 15%. Thus, the top two banks together had 45% of the four-county market; the top three had 60%; the top four 70%. If the merger were permitted, D-Girard would be the largest bank with 36%; the top two would then have 59%; and the four largest would have 78%. There had been a noticeable trend of bank mergers in Philadelphia (the number of banks dropping from 108 to 42 in 15 years). The government brings a section 7 action.

2) **Issue.** May illegality be presumed if the merger results in an undue percentage of the relevant market and an increased concentration in that market?

3) **Held.** Yes. Merger violates section 7.

a) Product market is commercial banking services.

b) Geographical market is the four-county area. Geographical markets are determined by supplier-customer relations, and banking is primarily based on convenience of location. The market definition here is not perfect since some larger borrowers do banking nationwide and smaller customers bank in their neighborhood; but this is the best market definition possible.

c) The purpose of section 7 is to prevent concentration in its incipiency. Thus, a merger producing a firm controlling an undue percentage of the market and resulting in a significant increase in concentration of the market is inherently likely to lessen competition and will be enjoined unless there is a clear showing that the merger is not likely to have anticompetitive effects.

(1) Here, the merger would result in a firm controlling more than 30% of the market. This is a large enough share to raise the inference of illegality.

(2) We do not indicate what the smallest percentage would be to raise such an inference.

(3) There is no evidence to rebut the inference of anticompetitiveness.

d) Entry into the banking field is far from easy.

e) It is no justification that the merger would allow the combined banks to compete with New York banks on larger loans, or that a larger bank would help with the industrial development of the Philadelphia area. A court cannot weigh all of the ultimate consequences of a decision. Section 7 states the purpose of preventing the lessening of competition in a line of commerce in any section of the country.

4) **Comment.** Note that *Brown Shoe, supra*, apparently involved more factors than market share and industry concentration. Thus, *Brown Shoe* indicated that the Court would follow a policy of attempting to qualitatively assess the effect on competition of the merger. This case indicates that when the market share of the merged firms gets large enough, a presumption of illegality will be made. Note also in all of these cases that the definition of the relevant market is critical to the outcome. This case may follow the notion that a geographical market is any submarket where there is a substantial number of consumers who would prefer to do business in their "local" area.

c. **Trends toward concentration.**

1) **Introduction.** As shown above, a "substantial lessening of competition" may be shown by a merger between firms having a substantial market share. Another factor to be considered is the trend in the industry—whether it is toward concentration.

2) **Example--United States v. Von's Grocery Co.,** 384 U.S. 270 (1966). United States v. Von's Grocery Co.

a) **Facts.** The market was defined as the retail grocery business in the Los Angeles area. Von's Grocery Company (D) had 4.7% of the market; the acquired company had 4.2% (they were the third and sixth largest chains). The four largest had 24% of the market; the eight largest had 41%; and the 12 largest had 49%. Ten years previously, the corresponding percentages had been 26%, 34%, and 39%. The number of single-store grocers had dropped in the same period from 5,300 to 3,800; the number of two-store or more chains had increased from 96 to 150; and nine of the top 20 firms had acquired in the aggregate 126 stores. Both D and the acquired company were very aggressive and had grown substantially in the past five years.

b) **Issue.** Are mergers of leading companies in industries characterized by oligopolistic trends illegal?

c) **Held.** Yes. Violation of section 7.

(1) Section 7 looks to the possible future effect on competition.

(2) A trend toward concentration is to be arrested in its incipiency.

(3) The purpose of the Act is to maintain many small competitors.

(4) Here, there is a merger between two large firms in a market which is becoming increasingly concentrated.

d) **Concurrence** (White, J.). In a market that is moving toward concentration, any merger between the largest firms (or between one of the largest and a lesser company) is unlawful where the top eight firms have 40% or more of the market.

e) **Dissent** (Stewart, Harlan, JJ.). The majority relied simply on counting the decline in the number of stores. This is too simple a rationale; we must look behind these numbers to determine the actual state of and trend of competition in the market. The decline in the number of single-store owners is a result of the rise of the combined supermarket. The acquisitions that took place by the 20 largest firms were mostly of failing firms. There have been numerous new one-store start-ups. Seven of the top 20 firms were not even in existence 10 years ago. And there are no barriers to entry into the market.

f) **Comment.** Query whether a showing of economic efficiency through the merger would be a defense. Query also what the majority is really holding. The dissent is probably correct that it is dangerous to rely simply on one factor (a declining number of firms). A group of factors should probably be looked at together: (i) the number of firms; (ii) the trend among the top eight or 10 firms; (iii) the reasons for trends; and (iv) the share represented by the combined firms.

3) **Geographical market.** In *United States v. Pabst Brewing Co.*, 384 U.S. 546 (1966), Pabst, the 10th largest brewer, acquired Blatz, the 18th largest brewer. They had a combined 24% of the Wisconsin market; 11% in the three-state area of Wisconsin, Illinois, and Michigan; and 4.5% of the nation's sales. The Court held that the relevant geographical market is "any section of the country" where the government can show a substantial lessening of competition. In this case, there was a lessening of competition because the number of breweries went down from 714 to 229 in five years and the number of companies from 206 to 162, and the percentage share of the market controlled by the leading brewers was going up. Since there was a trend toward concentration, these percentages were high enough to indicate a violation.

5. **Interpretation of Statistical Information.**

a. **Introduction.** The dissent in *Von's Grocery, supra*, argued that the Court should not look blindly at statistical information but should attempt to determine underlying causes so that a more realistic estimate could be made of the state of the competitive market.

b. **Example--United States v. General Dynamics Corp.,** 415 U.S. 486 (1974).

United States v. General Dynamics Corp.

1) **Facts.** Freeman Coal's parent company bought control of United Electric Coal in 1959. Freeman produced coal from deep shaft mines, United from strip mining. In 1966, General Dynamics Corporation (D) gained control of Freeman and therefore of United also. The government argued that the product market was coal and the geographical market either a region, of several midwestern states or the state of Illinois. In these regions, the industry showed high concentration and a trend toward concentration:

	Region		**Illinois**	
	1957	**1967**	**1957**	**1967**
Top two firms	29.6	48.6	37.8	52.9
Top four firms	43.0	62.9	54.5	75.2
Top ten firms	65.5	91.4	84.0	98.0

Also, the number of coal-producing firms in Illinois dropped from 144 to 39. And the firm's share of the coal market was increased:

	Region			**Illinois**		
	Rank	**Year**	**%**	**Rank**	**Year**	**%**
Freeman	2	1959	7.6	2	1959	15.1
United	6	1959	4.8	5	1959	8.1
Combined	2	1959	12.4	1	1959	23.2
Freeman	5	1967	6.5	2	1967	12.9
United	9	1967	4.4	6	1967	8.9
Combined	2	1967	10.9	2	1967	21.8

2) **Issue.** May nonstatistical factors be considered in determining whether a merger will result in a substantial lessening of competition?

3) **Held.** Yes. There is no violation of section 7.

a) Inferences may be drawn from statistical data. But here, there were other pertinent factors which require a conclusion that there has been no substantial lessening of competition.

b) These factors concern the developments in the coal industry.

(1) Coal is losing its market share to other sources of energy, so the product market may not be coal.

(2) Electric utilities are the main purchasers of coal—they buy their coal on long-term contracts. So the issue is not how much coal the acquired company sells (since this has been committed long ago), but what reserves the company has that are not committed and thus subject to sale. United held less than 1% of the coal reserves in the regional area and only four million tons were uncommitted at the time of trial. Also, it appears that there is

no substantial possibility that United can acquire more strip-mined coal and United does not have the expertise to mine deep shaft coal.

c) Normally, evidence of what happens to competition after a merger is not probative (it would allow postmerger conduct to influence decisions), but here it has value since it reflects the actual structure of the industry, which is not subject to manipulation.

d) It makes no difference how the relevant market is defined. There could be no substantial lessening by United in any market.

4) **Dissent** (Douglas, Brennan, White, Marshall, JJ.). Coal is the relevant product market (it has distinct customers who are not price sensitive). The geographic market is the State of Illinois or the region, because the government suggests that Freeman and United sold at least one-half of their output to the same customers. The argument that United had no substantial reserves to sell is the "failing company" defense; however, this must be assessed at the time of merger, not at the time of trial, and United did not qualify at that time. No time of merger findings as to competitive effect were made. Also, it appears that many companies bought new coal reserves in the 1960s and United had an additional 27 million tons of deep shaft reserves. Five years previous to the merger it had been mining deep reserves. The record of the district court is devoid of the findings necessary to make a decision in this case; the case should be remanded.

6. Department of Justice Merger Guidelines—Horizontal Mergers.

a. **Application of HHI to horizontal mergers.** The Department of Justice considers factors other than the HHI. For example, when entry is easy, a merger would not likely be challenged. However, the Department begins analysis of a merger by assessing its impact on the HHI. The applicable standards depend on the nature of the market involved:

1) ***Low concentration (post merger HHI less than 1000)***: No challenge except in extraordinary circumstances.

2) ***Moderate concentration (post-merger HHI between 1000 and 1800)***: No challenge unless merger increases HHI by more than 100 points.

3) ***High concentration (post-merger HHI greater than 1800)***: No challenge unless merger increases HHI by more than 50 points.

4) ***Large firm (market share of at least 35%)***: Challenge likely if firm merges with another firm having 1% or greater market share.

b. **Other factors.** Besides ease of entry, the Department will consider other factors including technology, the potential for collusion, efficiencies, and the failing company defense.

c. **Impact.** The new guidelines, being more favorable to mergers, probably would have kept the Department from suing in *Brown Shoe* and *Von's Grocery*, *supra*.

E. CONGLOMERATE MERGERS AND JOINT VENTURES

1. **Introduction.** Here, consideration is given to situations where a firm or firms move into areas where they are not currently competing. For example, a firm may extend its "product market" by acquiring another company with entirely different products, or a firm may extend its "geographical market" by acquiring a firm with similar products but doing business in a different geographic area.

2. **Preventing Competition—Joint Ventures.**

   a. **Barriers to entry.** When competition is discussed, it normally revolves around the theme of competition among firms already established in the market. But it is important also to consider the barriers to entry into the markets.

      1) "Barrier to entry" may be defined as the advantages of the sellers in an industry over potential new entrants. Advantages are reflected in the extent to which these sellers can raise their prices over a competitive level without attracting new firms to the market.

      2) Existing firms in an industry clearly take potential entry and new entrants into account in establishing their business practices.

      3) For easy entry, there are three necessary conditions. These conditions give insight into what might prevent entry or make it difficult.

         a) Existing sellers must have no cost advantages over the entrant. This requires that entrants be able to buy materials at similar prices, that the new entry does not affect factor prices, and that existing firms have no superior production methods.

         b) There should be no product differentiation advantages.

         c) The new entrants will add so little to industry output that it will not affect industry prices.

   b. **Joint ventures--United States v. Penn-Olin Chemical Co.,** 378 U.S. 158 (1964).

      United States v. Penn-Olin Chemical Co.

      1) **Facts.** Penn-Salt, with $100 million in assets, manufactured and sold chemicals. It had 9% of the sodium chlorate industry and a plant in the Northwest. Olin, with $860 million in assets, had many divisions, one of which was a chemical division. It did not manufacture sodium chlorate but sold it in the southeast for Penn-Salt. It had a process, which it licensed to paper manu-

facturers, that made use of the chemical in the bleaching process. Because of this process, the demand for the chemical was growing fast. Two companies (located in the southeast) controlled 90% of the sodium chlorate market (one had $200 million in assets, one $100 million). Both Penn-Salt and Olin had done studies about building a plant in the southeast, and they formed a joint venture and built the plant. The next year, another company entered the market in the southeast with a new plant. The district court found that both Penn-Salt and Olin had the resources and the expertise to enter the market by themselves, and that each thought the venture could be profitable. But the court held that the issue was whether both companies would have entered the market if the joint venture had not been formed; only if both would have entered would competition have been foreclosed. The district court dismissed the complaint, and the United States appeals.

2) **Issue.** May section 7 prevent a joint venture which eliminates a potential competitor in the market?

3) **Held.** Yes. Case remanded for new findings.

   a) The district court should make findings about whether even one firm would have entered the market, with the other remaining as a potential competitor.

   b) If the district court finds that this was probable, then it must be determined whether there could be a substantial lessening of competition because the two formed a joint venture and thus foreclosed the probable competitive state that would have existed. Factors to consider include (i) the number and power of competitors in the market; (ii) the market power of the joint venturers; (iii) the relationship of the lines of commerce of the joint venturers; (iv) the reasons and necessities of the joint venture; and (v) the adaptability of the lines of commerce of the joint venturers to anticompetitive activity.

4) **Dissent** (Douglas, Black, JJ.). The joint subsidiary constituted a horizontal agreement to divide markets, and therefore is illegal per se under the Sherman Act.

5) **Remand.** Neither Penn-Salt nor Olin would have entered the market by itself. No violation.

6) **Comment.** The situation in *Penn-Olin* needs to be broken apart conceptually:

   a) Even if neither company would have entered the market alone, there can still be a violation if they enter together (for example, perhaps the market power formed would have an anticompetitive effect on the market).

   b) There are situations where both companies might have entered by themselves so that there may be no violation if they enter together (*i.e.*, perhaps a combination is needed to develop a competitive company, given the market concentration that exists).

c) If only one would have gone in, the issue becomes whether the existence of the other still would have added significantly to the competitiveness of the market (as a possible entrant).

d) Note that in solving each of these situations, the analogy to the horizontal merger area is helpful. What is the condition of the market? Its concentration? Its concentration trends? Would the other firm be a possible "substantial competitor" if it did come in?

e) Note that where neither firm would have come in, there is substantial motivation to create a presumption of legality to the joint venture since this creates competition in the market.

(1) Assume that this was a correct factual finding by the district court on remand. Given the oligopolistic market that existed, the joint venture would add to the competitiveness of that market.

(2) The issue of proof about the intentions of the individual joint venture partners is interesting. The issue is whether they would individually enter the market. This is shown by circumstantial evidence. The evidence in this case was that both firms had the resources, capital, management, and expertise, and had done feasibility studies about entry. Thus, there was good evidence that they would have entered the market. Possibly, the holding stems from the fact that given the current condition of the market (oligopolistic), the joint venture would have a substantial and immediate beneficial effect.

3. Conglomerate Mergers.

a. Introduction.

1) **Product extension.** In some instances where a company makes a product extension merger, efficiencies may be involved in the acquisition, even though the two firms sell different products. For example, the products may be close enough (although not substitutes) that the distribution system used by one company can be used for both products (*i.e.,* the customers are the same). An example is soap and bleach. In other instances, there is absolutely no way that marketing efficiencies can result; the products involved may be entirely different (*e.g.,* movies and insurance).

2) **Efficiencies.** There are possible economic efficiencies involved in conglomerate mergers, even where there is no relationship in the marketing processes. For example, there are management personnel efficiencies; size may be such that the cost of capital comes down, etc.

3) **Concentration.** There is evidence that the business assets of the United States are increasingly being controlled by fewer and fewer companies. For example, between 1950 and 1962, the 200 largest

manufacturing companies increased from 46% to 54% their share of total manufacturing assets. This is of concern since one objective of the antitrust law is to maintain a society with multiple sources of economic power.

FTC v. Procter & Gamble Co.

b. **Product extension merger--FTC v. Procter & Gamble Co.,** 386 U.S. 568 (1967).

1) **Facts.** Procter and Gamble Company (D) bought Clorox, the leading manufacturer of liquid bleach with 48.8% of the market and sales of $40 million. The next largest competitor had 16% of the market; the top four firms had 65%; the top six had 80%; and the remaining 20% of the market was held by 200 firms. Clorox had $12 million in assets; only eight firms had more than $1 million. All bleach is chemically the same; advertising is the key to sales. It is marketed through grocery stores. D had over $500 million in sales and 55% of detergent sales, also sold by advertising, to the same customers as bleach, and through the same outlets. The advertising budget of D was $80 million per year. D had been considering entering the bleach market; it found that buying Clorox was better, and it expected to be able to expand Clorox's market share (which it did, to 52%, in the four years after the merger).

2) **Issue.** If a conglomerate merger eliminates a potential market entrant, may it be prevented?

3) **Held.** Yes. Violation of section 5 of the FTA.

a) The merger diminishes competition in the bleach market since it eliminated D as a potential competitor (but there was no finding that D would have entered the market by itself). It also destroys whatever restraining effect D's presence at the edge of the market might have had on those already in it.

b) The merger also makes entry into the market less likely (a huge firm like D makes firms less likely to try to compete).

c) Firms in the market already will be unlikely to try price competition against D.

d) Clorox might be given more favorable shelf space due to its connection with D.

e) D might subsidize underpricing with profits from other areas, including advertising discounts.

f) The market is already oligopolistic and this merger will intensify this.

4) **Concurrence** (Harlan, J.).

a) The state of economic knowledge about conglomerate mergers is not at the point where rules of thumb can be used to decide cases. There are both beneficial aspects (*e.g.,* they allow a company to sell out and allow the buying company to diversify to protect against fluctuations, etc.) and harmful aspects. A full analysis is required.

b) Four guidelines should be relied on:

(1) An analysis of premerger market structure should be made.

(2) A presumption may be made that the market operates according to generally accepted economic principles, but the defendant must be given the chance to show that in fact it does not (*i.e.,* the defendant might argue that there is no price leadership even though the structure is made up of only a few firms).

(3) A showing of reasonable probability that there will be a change in market structure allowing the exercise of substantially greater market power establishes a prima facie case.

(4) The defendant may show that there are countervailing economies from the merger that should be weighed against the adverse effects.

c. **Geographical extension and potential competition--United States v. Falstaff Brewing Corp.,** 410 U.S. 526 (1973).

United States v. Falstaff Brewing Corp.

1) **Facts.** Falstaff Brewing Corporation (D) bought Narragansett Brewing Company ("N"). N had 20% of the New England beer market (the eight largest firms had 81% of this market), an increasingly concentrated market. D had 6% of the national market (the fourth largest) but did no business in New England. It had studied the possibility of entering the New England market, but decided on the merger instead. The district court found that since D would not have entered the market without a merger, there was no violation.

2) **Issue.** May a merger be prevented solely because the acquirer's presence outside the market has a competitive effect, even if the acquirer would not have entered but for the merger?

3) **Held.** Yes. Case remanded.

a) It is error to decide that because D would not have otherwise entered the market, it was not a "potential competitor," and that a merger therefore does not lessen competition. The trial court should consider D as a potential competitor and consider whether there has been the requisite lessening of competition due to its elimination.

4) **Comment.** In geographical extension cases, where the potential acquiring company has the necessary resources and potential to enter a market it is not in, there will be a strong tendency to find that it cannot merge with a firm already in the market, unless this firm is a small firm and gives the acquiring company only a "toehold" in the market. This will particularly be true where the market structure is oligopolistic in nature. Furthermore, even though regional markets exist, courts may give some weight to the larger market structure (such as the national market) and its trends in determining whether to permit a firm to merge with another firm in a regional market.

United States v. Marine Bancorporation

d. Market extension merger where potential competition unlikely--United States v. Marine Bancorporation, 418 U.S. 602 (1974).

1) **Facts.** Marine Bancorporation, Inc. (D), a national bank with its principal office in Seattle, having $1.8 billion in assets (the second largest in the state) and 107 branches, bought WTB, a bank located in Spokane (where D had no branches), having assets of $112 million and 19% of the Spokane market. The five largest banks in the state had 75% of the market. In the Spokane market, the top two banks held 74% of the market (WTB had an additional 19%). State law prevented banks from branching except into new markets, but after a merger no branching was permitted. The government challenges the merger under section 7.

2) **Issue.** Is a merger of entities with significant market shares legal if the acquiring firm could not enter the market without merging, and a merger with a small entity could not have a significant future deconcentration effect?

3) **Held.** Yes. No violation.

   a) Commercial banking is the product market; Spokane is the geographical market. (The government argued that the entire state should be considered the market since the trend was for a few large banks to expand by merger into every market in the state, creating an oligopolistic market in banking services in each state.)

   b) A market extension merger may be unlawful if the target market is substantially concentrated; if the acquiring firm has the characteristics, capabilities, and economic incentive to render it a perceived potential de novo entrant; and if the acquiring firm's premerger presence on the fringe of the target market in fact tempered oligopolistic behavior on the part of the existing participants in that market.

   c) The Spokane market was concentrated, but there were no feasible means of D making a de novo entry into the market that would have had an appreciable procompetitive effect on the market, (*e.g.*, there would have been no such effect if D had purchased instead one of the very small banks in the Spokane market). Since there was no such feasible method of entry short of a merger, D could not have been perceived by those already in the market as a possible competitor-entrant.

4) **Comment.** Note that the Court did not buy the government's argument about the trend in statewide banking markets. Since one motivation of the antitrust laws is to maintain a large number of competitors, and the government is inevitably right that the trend is toward a few large banks controlling all markets in a state, it seems that the Court's rationale about market definition is short-sighted.

Ford Motor Co. v. United States

e. Buying a supplier to enter a new market--Ford Motor Co. v. United States, 405 U.S. 562 (1972).

1) **Facts.** Champion had 50%, Autolite 15%, and G.M. 30% of the spark-plug market. Plugs were sold cheaply to Ford (D) and Chrysler as original

equipment, but the replacement market (after-market) was profitable. Normally, the after-market replaced the same type of plug put in the original equipment. D was going to start its own manufacture of plugs, but bought Autolite instead. D represented 10% use of the plug market. The trial court ordered D to divest its Autolite original equipment assets, and D appeals.

2) **Issue.** Is the loss of a potential entrant into an oligopolistic industry a sufficient reason to prevent a merger?

3) **Held.** Yes. Merger is unlawful.

a) D was a potential entrant into the industry. The merger foreclosed 10% of the plug market to other sellers. The tie with original equipment totally controlled the after-market; to allow the acquisition would mean that the plug market would become exactly like the concentrated car market. The barrier to entry to any new firms would be impossible.

f. Reciprocity.

1) **Introduction.** "Reciprocity" is the situation where A buys from many companies (suppliers), and A buys B which sells to many of these suppliers. Now, A may use its leverage with the suppliers to see that they buy from B.

2) **Application--FTC v. Consolidated Foods Corp.,** 380 U.S. 592 (1965). FTC v. Consolidated Foods Corp.

a) **Facts.** Consolidated Foods Corporation (D) owned food processing plants and a network of wholesale and retail food stores. It acquired Gentry, Inc., a manufacturer of dehydrated onion and garlic. The FTC brought a section 7 action on the basis that there existed a possibility of reciprocal buying (*i.e.,* D would buy from food processors for its wholesale and retail operations if the processors would buy from Gentry). The dehydrated onion and garlic industry was an oligopoly (Gentry and one other firm had 90% of the market).

b) **Issue.** Is a merger illegal if it involves potential reciprocity?

c) **Held.** Yes. Violation of section 7.

(1) The merger prevents competition from existing in the oligopolistic dehydrated onion and garlic market, since D's buying power can be used to protect Gentry's business.

d) **Concurrence** (Stewart, J.). Mere opportunity for reciprocity is not enough to invalidate a merger. However, the record indicates that in fact reciprocity has occurred.

3) **Acquired company not dominant in markets--United States v. ITT Corp.,** 324 F. Supp. 19 (D. Conn. 1970). United States v. ITT Corp.

a) **Facts.** ITT, the ninth largest industrial company in the United States, bought Grinnell, the 268th largest with sales of $341 million. ITT was a conglomerate that had purchased hundreds of companies in the past 10 years; Grinnell was in several lines of commerce.

b) **Issue.** May a merger be barred because it may have anticompetitive consequences in numerous undesignated individual lines of commerce?

c) **Held.** No. Complaint dismissed.

(1) Each of several product lines of Grinnell are the "lines of commerce."

(2) The geographical market is a national market and two regional areas.

(3) Although Grinnell is the largest company in several product markets (*e.g.*, power piping, automatic sprinkler devices and systems, etc.), it does not have a dominant position in any of these markets (the most it has is 23% of any one of these markets). (The court looked at concentration, trends, and entry conditions.)

(4) The primary issue is whether a "dominant competitor in a relatively oligopolistic market is acquired by a much larger company so that the acquired company acquires marketing and promotional and other advantages that will further entrench its position of market dominance by raising barriers to entry in the relevant markets." We look to see if any of these advantages exist:

(a) The sprinkler systems are sold separately and there will be no advantage in being combined with a mechanical contracting company.

(b) We reach the same conclusion with respect to being combined with ITT's fire insurance company.

(c) Grinnell has sufficient financial resources on its own so that combination with ITT will not give it any more advantage than it already has.

(d) Grinnell also has already expanded abroad so that affiliation with ITT is no added advantage.

(e) There is no vertical foreclosure since ITT's purchases of Grinnell's product line are de minimis.

(f) ITT has huge buying power, but the potential for reciprocity is small: (i) ITT has a company "policy" against it; (ii) no evidence has been shown that ITT kept a list of suppliers; (iii) ITT is run on a profit center approach, which means that individual managers look for the best deals they can get; (iv) most of Grinnell's business comes in competitive bidding; and (v) there is no substantial evidence of Grinnell's ever having relied on reciprocity.

d) **Comment.** The court would not accept the idea of concentration in industry as a basis for finding the acquisition unlawful. It indicated that there had to be shown a lessening of competition in specific industries in specific areas of the country.

4. **Interlocking Directorates.** Section 8 of the Clayton Act prohibits a person from being a director of two or more corporations when any one of them has capital and surplus in excess of $1 million if such corporations are competitors, so that elimination by agreement of competition between them would be a violation of the antitrust laws.

5. **Deconcentration.** Most of the antitrust cases have been about preventing further concentration in an industry. In addition, over the years several proposals have been made by members of Congress for legislation aimed at deconcentrating oligopolistic industries. Also, many have urged that the executive branch take the initiative in bringing actions to break up certain industries. To this point, nothing has come of the legislative efforts, and there is some question as to whether the current antitrust laws would support such an attempt.

VII. PRICE DISCRIMINATION

A. INTRODUCTION

1. **Motivation of Sellers.** The most profitable way to sell a product is to sell for the price that reflects its value to each customer. In many cases, this type of pricing is impossible since the purchaser getting the lowest price would sell to others. With services (medical, etc.), however, it is somewhat easier to charge discriminatory prices.

2. **Price Discrimination in the Antitrust Laws.** Note that many business practices that are unlawful under the antitrust laws have as their eventual objective the charging of discriminatory prices.

3. **Political Equality vs. Economic Equality.**

   a. **Political equality.** Political equality is the idea that persons in the same situation should be treated similarly, or that discrimination should be based only on the dissimilarities of their situations. This idea is applied in the antitrust laws.

   b. **Economic discrimination.** In economics, under classical theory, price should follow cost or there is a misallocation of resources. This means that if there is a price difference without a cost difference, there is discrimination; or if there is a cost difference without a price difference, there is discrimination. This concept is not fully applied in the antitrust laws; *i.e.,* where a commodity is sold at a uniform price to all purchasers there is no political discrimination (and maybe no antitrust violation), but there could be an economic discrimination if, for example, the same price were charged to all when in fact the costs to some were higher.

   c. **Inclusion of the economic idea in the antitrust laws.** In the price discrimination area, the antitrust laws recognize that a lower cost will justify a lower price. Note also that price differences that naturally arise from everyday bargaining in a competitive market are not condemned by the antitrust laws.

B. THE ROBINSON-PATMAN ACT

1. **Basic Provisions of the Act.**

   a. **Section 2(a).** That it shall be unlawful for any person engaged in commerce, in the course of such commerce, either directly or indirectly, to discriminate in price between different purchasers of commodities of like grade and quality, where either or any of the purchasers involved in such discrimination are in commerce, where such commodities are sold for use, consumption, or resale . . . and where the effect of such discrimination may be substantially to lessen competition or tend to create a monopoly in any line of commerce, or to injure, destroy, or prevent competition with any person who either grants or knowingly receives the benefit of such discrimination, or with customers of either of them:

Provided, that nothing herein contained shall prevent differentials which make only due allowance for differences in the cost of manufacture, sale, or delivery resulting from the differing methods or quantities in which such commodities are to such purchasers sold or delivered:

Provided, however, that the FTC may, after due investigation and hearing to all interested parties, fix and establish quantity limits, and revise the same as it finds necessary, as to particular commodities, where it finds that available purchasers in greater quantities are so few as to render differentials on account thereof unjustly discriminatory or promotive of monopoly in any line of commerce; and the foregoing shall then not be construed to permit differentials based on differences in quantities greater than those so fixed and established. . . .

b. **Section 2(b).** Upon proof being made, at any hearing on a complaint under this section, that there has been discrimination in price or services or facilities furnished, the burden of rebutting the prima facie case thus made by showing justification shall be upon the person charged with a violation of this section, and unless justification shall be affirmatively shown, the Commission is authorized to issue an order terminating the discrimination.

Provided, however, that nothing herein contained shall prevent a seller rebutting the prima facie case thus made by showing that his lower price or the furnishings of services or facilities to any purchaser or purchasers was made in good faith to meet an equally low price of a competitor, or the services or facilities furnished by a competitor. . . .

c. **Section 2(f).** That it shall be unlawful for any person engaged in commerce, in the course of such commerce, knowingly to induce or receive a discrimination in price which is prohibited by this section.

2. **Summary of Elements.** Under section 2(a), it is unlawful for any person:

(i) Engaged in commerce;

(ii) To discriminate in price between different purchasers;

(iii) Of commodities of like grade and quality;

(iv) Where the effect may be substantially to lessen competition in any line of commerce, or tend to create a monopoly; or

(v) To injure, destroy, or prevent competition with any person who either grants or knowingly receives the benefits of such discrimination, or with the customers of either of them.

Both the seller who offers and the buyer who knowingly receives discriminatory prices are guilty of a violation.

3. **Other Sections of the Act.** Sections 2(c), (d), and (e) will be outlined *infra*. Section 3 is a separate law.

4. **Major Issues.**

a. **Goods of like grade and quality.** What are they?

b. **Price discrimination.** What is it?

c. **Substantial lessening of competition.** Note that a lessening of primary competition (*i.e.,* the supplier and its competitors), secondary competition (*i.e.,* the buyer and its competitors), or third-line competition (*i.e.,* the customers of the buyer) is sufficient.

d. **Defenses.**

1) Difference due to costs.

2) Difference due to good faith effort to meet competition.

3) Discrimination induced by the buyer.

5. **Primary-Line Effects.**

a. **Introduction.** "Primary-line" effects are anticompetitive effects between suppliers at the same level of the distribution system (*e.g.,* anticompetitive effects on one manufacturer by price discrimination practiced by another competing manufacturer).

Moss v. FTC

b. **Diversion of business test--Moss v. FTC,** 148 F.2d 378 (2d Cir. 1945), *cert. denied*, 326 U.S. 734 (1945).

1) **Facts.** Samuel Moss (D) sold rubber stamps of the same size and quality in the same markets at different prices to different customers. The FTC ordered D to cease its price discrimination, and D appeals.

2) **Issue.** Once the FTC proves that D has used price discrimination, must D prove that there was no anticompetitive effect?

3) **Held.** Yes. Violation of section 2(a).

a) Selling at discriminatory prices shifts the burden of proof to the defendant to show that such discriminatory prices did not divert business from competitors.

4) **Comment.** This case has not been widely followed.

Anheuser-Busch, Inc. v. FTC

c. **Predatory intent--Anheuser-Busch, Inc. v. FTC,** 289 F.2d 835 (7th Cir. 1961).

1) **Facts.** Anheuser-Busch, Inc. (D) was the leading brewer in the United States with 7% of the market; most local markets, however, were dominated by local companies. The St. Louis market had four other competitors; in 1953, D was last with 12.5% of this market. A new labor contract was signed at the end of 1953; D raised its prices except in St. Louis. D's St. Louis competitors did not raise their prices. D began to lose sales all over the nation; it tried to cut its prices but wholesalers would not pass on the savings. In St. Louis, D cut its prices since it had no wholesalers and the retailers passed

the savings on. Over a two-year period, D cut prices again and market share went to 36%; then it raised its price above that of its competitors and introduced a lower-priced beer under a different label. Its market share fell to 17%. It also raised advertising expenditures and changed its sales distribution system. The FTC ordered D to cease and desist, and D appeals.

2) **Issue.** To prove a primary-line injury violation of section 2(a), must the FTC prove a substantial and sustained drop in price in a local area by a large competitor, with the intent or known effect of destroying, injuring, or "disciplining" a smaller-scale rival?

3) **Held.** Yes. No violation of section 2(a).

a) D's market share rose, but this alone is not enough. Nor was the rise over the long term very substantial. D's major competitors still controlled over 75% of the market.

b) D's price changes were made necessary by competitive conditions.

c) Change in market shares can be accounted for by other factors taking place with D's competitors. Also, one competitor, Falstaff, increased its share from 29% to 43% of the market.

d) There is no predatory misconduct shown on D's part, aimed at destroying a competitor. There is no proven use of profits in another area to subsidize price competition in St. Louis.

4) **Comment.** This case can be seen as one where the court goes back to the original intent of the Robinson-Patman Act and rationalizes the decision on the basis of whether there have been acts which appear to have been motivated by a "predatory intent." In addition, the amount of business diverted to D was small, and the market remained very competitive.

d. **Lessening of competition--Utah Pie Co. v. Continental Baking Co.,** 386 U.S. 685 (1967). Utah Pie Co. v. Continental Baking Co.

1) **Facts.** Utah Pie Company (P) is in the frozen dessert pie business, with a plant in Utah. The three defendants (Continental, Carnation, and Pet (Ds)) are large companies in the same business with their closest plants in California. The Utah market grew 500% in four years; P maintained about 45% of the market and its volume, sales, earnings, and profits grew. P sold to several grocery chains under brand labels and sold under its own brand. The major competitive weapon in the market was price, and during the four-year period, the price in the market dropped about 33%. Pet sold its pies in Utah to Safeway at prices lower than it sold in markets closer to its California plant and lower than its other sales in Utah. Safeway had 6% of the Utah market. For seven of the 44 months, it sold its own label pies at prices in Utah cheaper than in other areas closer to its plant.

2) **Issue.** Are predatory price cuts below cost in a local area violations of section 2(a)?

3) **Held.** Yes.

a) An injury may be found even though the sales volume of P is growing and P continues to operate at a profit. It is not necessary that it be shown that the price discriminators are consistently undercutting P's prices (although there was some evidence of predatory intent by Ds against P). Here, the destructive impact of price discrimination was on the price structure of the market.

b) There is evidence from which the jury could have found that for periods of several months Pet was charging less in Salt Lake than in the California and other closer markets. With respect to sales to Safeway, the burden of proof of proving cost justification is on Pet. Pet only showed evidence of such justification for one year, and this evidence was not particularized for the Salt Lake market. The jury could also have found this evidence insufficient to prove cost justification. The jury could also have found that Pet's actions amounted to a reasonable possibility of lessening of competition. It makes no difference whether P itself would have gotten the Safeway business, or whether P itself was the company that suffered from the anticompetitive actions (although there was evidence that showed that Pet's actions were aimed at P, such as information in Pet's files that it considered P an unfavorable factor, and it had sent an industrial spy into P's plant).

c) Continental had 1.8% of the market in 1960; in 1961, it cut its prices below what it was selling in other areas and got 8.3% of the market. It sold pies to some of the same chains where P had been selling pies. Its prices were below direct cost plus overhead allocation. The jury could have found this to be anticompetitive. It makes no difference that P's sales volume grew; it had to cut its prices to a point it would not otherwise have done.

d) Carnation sold at less than its costs and at lower prices than in other markets closer to its plants. The jury could find a violation here.

4) Comment. Note that on the facts, a substantial lessening of competition was found where Utah Pie had the lowest prices and the largest share of the market, and its sales and profits were increasing. There is something to the argument of the dissent.

e. **Market analysis.** It is clear that the analysis on the issue of a "substantial lessening of competition" must be aimed at determining the long-run effect of price discrimination practices. Many factors should be considered.

1) Factors showing an anticompetitive effect.

a) Strong market power by seller in wider markets.

b) Predatory practices toward smaller competitors.

c) Long-term price cutting below competitor's price levels.

d) Prices below costs (this supports an inference of predatory intent).

e) Possible demise of significant rivals or large numbers of competitors.

2) **Factors tending to disprove conclusion of anticompetitive effect.**

a) Decline in the defendant's market share, or an insignificant market share.

b) Growth of the defendant's competitors in market share, sales, etc.

c) Pattern of price variations with competitors.

d) Ease of entry into the market.

e) Strength of competition in the market: price and otherwise.

f) Reasons for price discrimination, such as need to bolster market position, etc.

f. **Conflict in policy.** There is an inherent conflict in the Robinson-Patman Act and the policy of the antitrust laws. Antitrust policy favors vigorous price competition; yet vigorous enforcement of the Robinson-Patman Act may impair such competition. A policy which prevents an interstate firm from cutting prices to enter a local market against local competitors (unless the interstate firm cuts prices in all its markets) is insulating these local markets.

g. **Section 3.** Section 3 makes it a criminal offense punishable by fines or imprisonment to be a party to a discriminatory transaction, engage in local price cutting, or sell goods at unreasonably low prices for the purpose of destroying competition or eliminating a competitor.

6. **Secondary-Line Effects.**

a. **Introduction.** Here, the charge is that price discrimination by a seller to a buyer affects competition at the buyer level, *i.e.*, injures competition with "any person who knowingly receives price discrimination." Secondary-line injury accounts for the majority of Robinson-Patman cases.

b. **Proving substantial injury to competition--FTC v. Morton Salt Co.,** 334 U.S. 37 (1948). FTC v. Morton Salt Co.

1) **Facts.** Morton Salt Company (D) sold salt and gave a 6% discount for those who bought in carloads. This might have been justified on cost savings (99% of its salt sold was by this method). But it also offered additional discounts to those who bought large quantities over the course of a year. No justification based on cost savings was offered for these discounts. Only five companies qualified. It was shown that smaller purchasers were selling at retail at higher prices than the quantity discount purchasers.

2) **Issue.** May competitive injury be inferred from the practice of selling at different prices to different buyers?

3) **Held.** Yes. Violation of section 2(a).

a) All that need be shown is a "reasonable possibility" of a substantial lessening of competition.

b) Where goods are sold "substantially cheaper" to one buyer over another, there is evidence that this is a substantial lessening of competition. (Note that "substantially cheaper" is satisfied if the price difference would cause a buyer to switch to the cheaper product.)

c) It makes no difference that the sale of salt is a very small part of the total business of a grocer.

4) **Comment.** Note the analogy to the tying cases. If there is a substantial difference in price to buyers, there is really no further inquiry into the amount of commerce involved. Any amount of commerce (above a de minimis amount) is substantial enough to be a "substantial lessening of competition."

Texaco v. Hasbrouck

c. **Functional discounts--Texaco v. Hasbrouck,** 496 U.S. 543 (1990).

1) **Facts.** Texaco (D) sold gasoline at its retail tank wagon prices to Hasbrouck and other independent retailers (Ps), but granted substantial discounts to distributors Gull Oil and Dompier Oil, who picked up gas at D's plant and delivered it directly to their retail outlets. Gull resold the gas under its own name, without disclosing to anyone that D supplied it. Dompier paid a price slightly higher than Gull paid, but resold its gas under D's brand names. Dompier also owned a bulk storage facility, which it seldom used, and received a delivery fee from D in addition to its price discount. Dompier entered the retail business directly, and its stations regularly sold gas at prices lower than Ps'. Dompier's sales increased from 20% of the market to almost 50%. D's management knew that Dompier's growth was attributable to the large discount, but told Ps that they could not understand why Dompier was pricing gas so cheaply. Ps sued D under the Robinson-Patman Act. The jury found for Ps, and the district court denied D's motion for judgment n.o.v. The court of appeals affirmed, and the Supreme Court granted certiorari.

2) **Issue.** May a manufacturer offer functional discounts if they are not reasonably related to the cost of the functions performed?

3) **Held.** No. Judgment affirmed.

a) D claims that it did not "discriminate in price," but the Court has previously held that a price discrimination within the meaning of section 2(a) is simply a price difference. Functional discounts are not necessarily exempt from the Robinson-Patman Act, because the Act is concerned with competitive consequences at different levels of distribution.

b) In *FTC v. Morton Salt Co.*, *supra*, we held that an injury to competition can be inferred from evidence that some buyers had to pay their suppliers substantially more for their goods than competitors had to pay. D argues that this presumption should not apply to the differences between prices charged to wholesalers and prices charged to retailers. In fact, a legitimate functional discount that constitutes a reasonable reimbursement for the purchasers' actual marketing functions does not violate the Act. Such a discount raises no inference of injury to competition under *Morton Salt*.

c) In this case, there is no evidence to connect Gull's and Dompier's discounts to any savings enjoyed by D. Both received wholesaler discounts even though most of their sales were directly to consumers. The *Morton Salt* presumption of adverse effect applies here because Gull and Dompier competed directly with Ps in the retail market. D was fully aware of the impact of Dompier's discount on the retail market.

d) Ps evidence about damages may have included some injury attributable to the conduct of independent retailers, but antitrust plaintiffs are excused from an unduly rigorous standard of proving injury in antitrust cases.

4) **Concurrence** (White, J.). The majority incorrectly states that a price differential is not illegal if it merely accords due recognition and reimbursement for actual marketing functions. This would exempt a manufacturer who sells to a distributor at a price low enough that the distributor could sell to its customers at a lower price than other retailers can buy directly from the manufacturer.

5) **Concurrence** (Scalia, Kennedy, JJ.). The majority appears to have created an exemption for functional discounts that are "reasonable," even if such discounts are prohibited by the Act. Congress should be the one to exempt functional discounts, not the courts.

d. **Factors to consider.** The following factors would be relevant in proving anticompetitive effects (their opposites would tend to indicate that there was little anticompetitive effect):

1) Substantial difference in price;

2) Standardized product;

3) Product sold to competing buyers selling to the same market; and

4) Keen competition among the buyers (because their sales and profit margins are low).

e. **Increasing complexity.** Historically there have been several distinct levels in the distribution system, from supplier to customer. Each level had performed certain specific tasks and taken certain risks, which other levels did not perform. However, in more recent years, these distinctions in the distribution systems have blurred and the antitrust questions are much more difficult.

1) For example, in *In re Mueller Co.*, 60 F.T.C. 120 (1962), the defendant sold products for water and gas distribution systems to jobbers of two classes; it gave limit jobbers an additional 10% discount on some items. The limit jobbers inventoried these items and the regular jobbers did not. The court found that this was a violation. By subsidizing certain jobbers, the defendant had given them a business advantage (by having the high

volume items on hand for immediate delivery to customers). Also, the evidence supports the conclusion that the opportunity to be a limit jobber is not open to all jobbers but only to those selected by the defendant.

2) "Commodities of like grade and quality" is a requirement under section 2(a). Generally, physical differences in two products which affect their acceptability to buyers will preclude the products from being of "like grade or quality." However, mere differences in the brand name or label under which the product is sold are not sufficient to justify price discrimination. [*See, e.g.,* FTC v. Borden, 383 U.S. 637 (1966)—Borden sold its own label evaporated milk nationally, then sold the same milk, at a cheaper price, to supermarket chains to be sold under their private labels]

3) Wholesalers and retailers may not always be treated differently. A vendor who sells at a lower price to a wholesaler than to a retailer is guilty of price discrimination if the wholesaler passes the lower price on to controlled retail subsidiaries. Thus, price discrimination charges cannot be avoided simply by incorporating a captive subsidiary. [*See, e.g.,* Perkins v. Standard Oil Co., 395 U.S. 642 (1969)] Standard sold to the plaintiff at a higher price than it charged Signal Oil, a wholesaler; Signal passed its lower price on to oil dealers in competition with the plaintiff.

C. AFFIRMATIVE DEFENSES TO ROBINSON-PATMAN ACT ACTIONS

1. Cost Justification.

a. **Introduction.** The burden of proof is on the party claiming cost justification for the difference in prices charged.

1) In some instances, this justification might be easy to prove, as where a quantity discount is offered and direct costs of packaging and freight can be shown.

2) However, in many other instances proof is very difficult, *e.g.,* with respect to discounts given for large total purchases over time. Delivery practices may vary with the individual customer, and alleged differences in manufacturing costs, advertising costs, and others will be difficult and complex accounting questions, even when such accounting data is available.

3) The courts seem to have developed a rule of reason approach on this issue.

United States v. Borden Co.

b. **Application--United States v. Borden Co.,** 370 U.S. 460 (1962).

1) **Facts.** Borden and Bowman (Ds) sold their milk products on a volume discount basis to independent grocers and at a flat discount to the large chains (which discount was larger than any

volume discount given to the independents). A section 2 action was brought. Ds rely on the cost justification defense.

2) **Issue.** May a seller classify his customers into reasonable categories based on the average costs of selling to the customers in each group, then charge all customers in each group an appropriate price?

3) **Held.** Yes. Case remanded for further findings. Cost justification studies are not adequate to provide a defense.

a) Borden put the large chains into one category; the independents were placed in four other categories by volume of purchases. Then cost data was considered, including direct personnel costs, truck expenses, losses on bad debts, and returned milk. Various formulas were used to make the allocations. Bowman used a study of driver time in various operations and costed these operations. It was not shown, however, that all independents used these extra operations and that the chains did not.

b) It is not necessary to establish cost differences with respect to each customer. It is permissible to put customers into classes. But these classes must be divided by the relevant criteria that determine cost differences.

c) Here, the classes were not shown to have sufficient relevant homogeneity. With respect to Borden, some of the independents had higher volume than some of the chains, and all independents were assigned added cost factors which were not shown to have been possessed by all (such as cash collections). Bowman had similar defects in its classifications.

2. **Good Faith Meeting of Competition.**

a. **Introduction.** The defendant may also defend a section 2 action by proving that the lower price offered to some purchasers was simply a good faith attempt to meet the competition offered by another seller.

b. **Cases and comments.**

1) **Good faith attempt to meet competition is a complete defense--Standard Oil Co. v. FTC,** 340 U.S. 231 (1951). Standard Oil Co. v. FTC

a) **Facts.** Standard Oil Company (D) sold gas to large jobbers and retail stations; the jobbers got tank-car loads (8,000 to 12,000 gallons). Jobbers got the gas at 1½¢ per gallon less; hence, the jobbers could sell gas to their retail stations at prices less than the other retail stations who got the gas from D. The FTC brought a section 2 action.

b) **Issue.** Is a good faith effort to meet competition a complete defense, even when others are injured by the price reduction?

c) **Held.** Yes. Case remanded.

(1) Section 2(b) provides a complete defense when it can be shown that the discrimination in price by the seller is a good faith effort to meet competition.

(2) A seller can meet a lower price offered to his buyer in order to retain the buyer as a customer, even though the seller's price to its other customers remains the same.

(3) Where the seller sustains the burden of proof of showing the 2(b) defense, the defense is not destroyed because it appears that the beneficiaries of the seller's price reductions may derive a competitive advantage from the price reduction, or it may reduce its own prices so that its customers derive a competitive advantage. (Note that the Court is saying that the defense is not lost because the seller's buyer has a competitive advantage against other buyers—secondary-line competition—or might sell at a lower price to its customers and thus affect a third-line competition.)

d) Comment. The difficulty with this defense is that the courts cannot allow a defendant to evade the Act simply by saying that it was just following the discriminatory practices of its competitors. This is too frequent and too easy a defense. But on the other hand, to require much more places the responsibility on the defendant to see that the prices of its competitors that it is meeting are lawful and not discriminatory (*i.e.,* to stand by and be hurt by the competitors unless the competitors are proceeding in a lawful, nondiscriminatory manner). The defense is a difficult one to rationalize and for the courts to apply in a manner that makes much sense.

United States v. United States Gypsum Co.

2) Price verification--United States v. United States Gypsum Co., 438 U.S. 422 (1978).

a) Facts. United States Gypsum Company (D) exchanged presale price quotations with a competitor, a violation of the Sherman Act under *United States v. Container Corp. of America, supra*. D claimed that this activity was justified by the need to verify rival prices to make sure it would satisfy the requirements of a "good faith" defense under section 2(b).

b) Issue. May competitors exchange price information to assure that they are meeting each others' prices?

c) Held. No. Violation of Sherman Act.

(1) The 2(b) defense may be satisfied by a good faith belief. Absolute certainty is not necessary.

(2) When a buyer's reliability is suspect and the seller wants verification, it is understandable that the seller would want to obtain price information directly from competing sellers. However, exchange of such price information would seriously impinge on other important antitrust policies. Since the good faith defense does not require precision, an exception to the Sherman Act is not necessary.

3) **Reliance on buyer information--Great Atlantic & Pacific Tea Co. v. FTC,** 440 U.S. 69 (1979).

Great Atlantic & Pacific Tea Co. v. FTC

a) **Facts.** Borden submitted a bid to Great Atlantic & Pacific Tea Company (D) which D did not like. D took competing bids and told Borden that its first bid was "out of line." Borden could get no specific information from D, so it submitted a substantially lower bid.

b) **Issue.** May a seller rely solely on buyer information in making a good faith effort to meet the competition?

c) **Held.** Yes. No violation.

(1) Borden could not verify the prices offered by its competition, so it was justified in relying on the meager information provided by D.

4) **Legality of competitors' prices--FTC v. A.E. Staley Manufacturing Co.,** 324 U.S. 746 (1945).

FTC v. A.E. Staley Manufacturing Co.

a) **Facts.** A.E. Staley Manufacturing Company (D) had a plant in Decatur, Illinois; most competitors had their plants in Chicago. When D started business, it followed the single point price basing system of the industry, based on Chicago as the shipping point. The FTC brought a section 2 action. D defends that it was simply following competition in good faith.

b) **Issue.** May a good faith attempt to meet competition involve a pricing system which is unlawful?

c) **Held.** No. Violation of section 2.

(1) D has not met the burden of the "following competition" defense.

(2) This defense does not allow a defendant simply to follow a competitor in an unlawful pricing scheme.

(3) The Act speaks only of a "lower" price to meet an equally low price of a competitor; the emphasis is on individual competitive situations, not on a general system of competition.

(4) D never attempted to establish its own nondiscriminatory pricing system and then reduce its prices to meet competition when necessary. As a matter of fact, in its market area, D had an advantage over competition since it could have charged a lower freight amount; it never did.

(5) There has not been a "good faith" effort to meet lower prices of competition, at least not where D never attempted to set up a nondiscriminatory pricing system.

(6) The seller who has knowingly discriminated in price must show the existence of facts which would lead a reasonable and prudent person to believe that the granting of a lower price would in fact meet the equally low price of a competitor.

d) **Comments.**

(1) *Staley* probably stands for the proposition that it is the duplication of a competitor's unlawful ***system*** that negates "good faith." Where a firm knows or should know that the system is unlawful, then it probably cannot rely on the "good faith" defense. But it is doubtful that a defendant must look into the facts behind each individual transaction by a competitor to determine if it is lawful before it is able to in "good faith" meet this price. Query the situation where a defendant ***knows*** that the price charged by a competitor in an individual transaction is unlawful. Why shouldn't the defendant be able to meet this competition?

(2) Note that a flexible approach on this defense would allow many firms to lower prices in specific markets or to specific customers on the basis that such lower prices were available to the buyer someplace in the market. This would in one sense add to the competitiveness of the market. On the other hand, if the defense is read more narrowly, narrowing the situations where "good faith following prices of competitors" can be utilized, more rigid price competition will result. This narrower interpretation is the one that seems to be followed; its motivation is to uphold the thrust of the original Robinson-Patman Act against large firms with more financial power coming into local markets and destroying competitors by charging lower prices locally. The point is that the real conflicts in economic policy inherent in the Robinson-Patman Act are only dimly perceived by the courts and the choices between these conflicts are not articulately chosen.

Falls City Industries v. Vanco Beverage

5) **Territorial distinctions--Falls City Industries v. Vanco Beverage,** 460 U.S. 428 (1983).

a) **Facts.** Falls City Industries (D), a brewer, sold beer to Indiana and Kentucky wholesalers. Vanco Beverage (P), the Indiana wholesaler, paid a higher price than the Kentucky wholesalers, even though P was located on the border of Kentucky. As a result, P had to charge its retail customers more than the Kentucky retailer customers paid, and P's customers lost business to the Kentucky customers. P sued, claiming that D's price discrimination was illegal. The district court found for P on the ground that the discrimination resulted from D raising its Indiana price, not from D lowering the Kentucky price. The court of appeals affirmed, and the Supreme Court granted certiorari.

b) **Issue.** May a manufacturer charge different prices to wholesalers in different jurisdictions to meet competition, even if the jurisdictions actually form one market?

c) **Held.** Yes. Judgment reversed.

(1) The price discrimination in this case might have evolved in the two states without collusion, despite the common retail market along the border. This was not like *FTC v. A.E. Staley, supra*, where pricing was set in accordance with an industry-wide practice.

(2) Immunity for the good faith meeting of competition is not limited to situations where a price difference results from subtraction rather than addition.

(3) Territorial pricing may be a perfectly reasonable way to respond to rivals' low prices. D could properly price its goods differently to meet competition in different areas.

D. SUPPLEMENTARY PROVISIONS

1. Buyer's Liability for Inducing or Receiving Discriminations in Price.

a. **Introduction.** Section 2(f) makes it unlawful for any person knowingly to induce or receive a prohibited discrimination in price.

b. **Burden of going forward with the proof--Automatic Canteen Co. of America v. FTC,** 346 U.S. 61 (1953).

Automatic Canteen Co. of America v. FTC

1) **Facts.** Automatic Canteen (D) leases vending machines for candy. As a large wholesaler of candy, D buys large amounts of candy from manufacturers. It put great pressure on the manufacturers to give it discounts and received discounts of as much as 33%; it knew that it was receiving discounts not received by its competitors. D did not inquire into whether these discounts were justified by cost savings, etc. The FTC argued that it had established a prima facie case for a section 2(f) violation when it introduced evidence of the discount with D's knowledge that other competitors were not receiving the same.

2) **Issue.** To prove a violation of section 2(f), must the FTC prove that the buyer knew that the price obtained was discriminatory?

3) **Held.** Yes. The burden of going forward with the proof is on the FTC.

a) The section requires a "knowing" inducement of a prohibited discrimination. It is not prohibited if it is cost justified.

b) It is very difficult to prove cost justification as a defense. Also, the information that would prove this is not in the buyer's hands; to get it, the buyer would have to study the seller's business.

c) D is not liable if the prices it induces are either within one of the seller's defenses or are not known by him to be outside of one of these defenses.

d) The FTC need only prove for a prima facie case that the methods by which D was served and the quantities purchased were the same as other competitors; or, if the methods or quantities differ, that these differences could not give rise to a sufficient savings in cost to justify the price differential, and that the buyer knew that these were the only differences present and could not give rise to sufficient cost savings to justify the price difference.

e) The FTC might want to include the offending seller in these proceedings.

4) **Comment.** In spite of this decision, the FTC has won a number of decisions under section 2(f). The argument that has won these cases has been that the buyer has known that it has received a substantially lower price than its competitors, that its orders and shipments were handled in the same way as its competitors, and that there was therefore probably no cost savings that would justify the price differential. [*See* American Motor Specialties Co. v. FTC, 278 F.2d 225 (2d Cir. 1960), *cert. denied*, 364 U.S. 884 (1960)—auto part jobbers formed a buying corporation to receive volume discounts, although orders and deliveries were made directly to individual firms; Ds knowingly received discounts to which they were not entitled]

Great Atlantic & Pacific Tea Co. v. FTC

c. **Buyer's liability depends on seller's liability--Great Atlantic & Pacific Tea Co. v. FTC,** 440 U.S. 69 (1979).

1) **Facts.** *See* same case, *supra*. In this part of the opinion, the Court considered D's liability.

2) **Issue.** May a buyer be held liable for a Robinson-Patman Act violation if the seller cannot be held liable?

3) **Held.** No. No violation of the Robinson-Patman Act.

a) Section 2(f) provides that a buyer can be liable only if it receives a price discrimination "prohibited by this section." Even though D knew that Borden did not meet, but in fact substantially beat, the competitor's price, D is not liable because Borden has a good faith meeting competition defense. Thus, a buyer who has done no more than accept the lower of two prices competitively offered does not violate section 2(f) if the seller has a meeting competition defense.

2. **Brokerage.**

a. **Section 2(c).** Section 2(c) makes it unlawful for a buyer of goods, or any agent or representative of the buyer, to receive from or be paid by the supplier any brokerage or other commission "except for services rendered in connection with the sale or purchase of goods."

b. **Closed loophole.** This section closed a loophole which buyers had used to set up affiliated agents or brokers who got the same advantage (in effect) as though the buyer received price discriminations.

c. **Per se rule.** No effect on competition need be shown; this is in effect a per se rule.

3. **Advertising Allowances, Services, and Facilities.** Section 2(d) makes it unlawful for a supplier to make any payment to a buyer in consideration of services or facilities provided in promoting the sale of goods, unless similar payments are made available on "proportionally equal terms" to other buyers. Section 2(e) makes it unlawful for the supplier to provide promotional services and facilities to a buyer unless the supplier accords facilities on "proportionally equal terms" to other buyers.

   a. **Purpose.** These sections were aimed at discrimination where a large customer would demand and receive sale-promotional services or special advertising allowances from sellers, but other buyers would not get those allowances. Such an allowance is unjust when (i) the service is not actually rendered, (ii) if rendered the payment is grossly in excess of its value, or (iii) the customer is deriving as much benefit to his own business as the seller is.

   b. **Per se rule.** These are per se rules in the sense that no effect on competition need be shown.

   c. **FTC guidelines.**

      1) **Requirement.** The law requires that customers be treated fairly and without discrimination and that allowances not be disguised discriminatory price discounts.

      2) **When the law applies.** The law applies whenever the buyer furnishes services or facilities in connection with the distribution of the seller's products, or when the seller provides any such services.

      3) **Customers.** A "customer" is someone who buys for resale directly from the seller or from the seller's agent or broker, or buys for resale from or through a wholesaler or other intermediate seller.

      4) **Services or facilities.** Services or facilities include such things as window and floor displays (where the seller pays the buyer for furnishing them), or catalogs, prizes, etc. (where the seller furnishes them to customers).

      5) **A plan.** When such services are provided, they should be furnished in accordance with a written plan.

         a) The services or payments should be available on some proportional basis to all competing customers (*e.g.*, determined by relative volume of sales).

         b) All customers should be informed of the plan.

         c) The seller should take reasonable steps to see that all services are actually performed and that it is not overpaying for them.

FTC v. Simplicity Pattern Co.

d. Injury need not be shown--FTC v. Simplicity Pattern Co., 360 U.S. 55 (1959).

1) **Facts.** Simplicity Pattern Company (D) is the largest manufacturer of dress patterns. It distributed them in two ways: through variety stores and through fabric stores. Prices were uniform, but D provided variety stores with many other types of advantages (*e.g.*, consignment rather than purchase, free catalogs, free display equipment, etc.). The FTC brought a section 2(e) action.

2) **Issue.** Must there be a showing of injury to competition to prove a violation under section 2(e)?

3) **Held.** No. Violation of section 2(e).

a) There is competition between the variety stores and fabric stores in dress patterns.

b) There is a discrimination violating section 2(e).

c) Section 2(e) is a per se rule; no justifications for lack of competitive injury or cost justification are permitted. One reason for this is that these discriminations may be more subtle and harder to detect than price discriminations. Thus, if a supplier wants to make a distinction and can justify it on a cost basis, the supplier must do it through price.

4) **Comment.** The "meeting competition" defense is available. [*See*, *e.g.*, Exquisite Form Brassiere v. FTC, 301 F.2d 499 (D.C. Cir. 1961)]

Vanity Fair Paper Mills v. FTC

e. Availability on proportional terms--Vanity Fair Paper Mills v. FTC, 311 F.2d 480 (2d Cir. 1962).

1) **Facts.** Vanity Fair Paper Mills (D) manufactured household paper products. It had a standard contract whereby it gave its customers advertising and promotional allowances. In addition, on request it entertained proposals for special promotions. In 1958, in one market area it donated money to one store chain for two special promotions; only one other customer requested and received such help. D stated that it was its policy to entertain such special requests; sales personnel were advised of this policy. The FTC brought a section 2(d) action.

2) **Issue.** Must a manufacturer notify all customers of special services it provides upon request?

3) **Held.** Yes. Violation of section 2(d).

a) This section requires that such allowances be made "available" to the customers on a nondiscriminatory basis. Here, it appears that the information that D was willing to participate in special promotions was not uniformly communicated to D's customers.

b) The allowances were not available on a proportional basis; D selected the quantum of services it would support and the degree to which it would support them on an arbitrary basis.

4) **Comment.** This case raises the issue as to how proportionality is tested. Should it be on the basis of proportion of the business that a customer does with the seller, or on the basis of the benefit that the seller is receiving (in which case there would be or could be large differences in the amounts allocated to customers)?

f. **Variable allowances--Lever Brothers Co.,** 50 F.T.C. 494 (1953).

Lever Brothers Co.

1) **Facts.** Lever Brothers Company (D) offered customers two co-op advertising plans under which it would make promotional payments: one was an annual plan of nine promotions, and the other was a single promotion. D paid a differing rate based on the amount of product sold and the type of advertising used by the customers (12¢ to 20¢ per case for newspaper ads, 8¢ to 9¢ for handbill or radio advertising, etc.). The contract read that the newspaper advertising should be included in the advertiser's "regular consumer advertising." The FTC charged a violation under 2(d) on the basis that the newspaper advertising alternative was not made "available" to all customers and, where it was made available, it was not done so on a "proportional" basis. The basis of the complaint was that the volume of some small retailers was such that they could not afford to advertise in newspapers and also that there might be a requirement that such advertising be a part of a "regular advertising program" that included ads on products besides D's.

2) **Issue.** May a seller give variable allowances to customers who provide promotional services as long as the allowances are available to all buyers on proportionately equal terms?

3) **Held.** Yes. No violation of section 2(d).

a) It appears that those who have not been able to afford newspaper advertising due to small volume could advertise in newspapers with circulations limited more to the relevant trade area, or advertise through retailer cooperatives.

b) Also, D has accepted newspaper ads by customers where the ad has been only two or three lines. Thus, it appears that the newspaper advertising program was made "available" to all, even though there may be a few for whom such advertising is not practical.

c) Payment based on volume sold is proportional. Also, a differing rate may be used for different advertising modes since each type varies in cost.

g. **Definition of customers--FTC v. Fred Meyer,** 390 U.S. 341 (1968).

FTC v. Fred Meyer

1) **Facts.** Fred Meyer, Inc. (D) is a large chain of stores in Portland. It has an annual promotion where it sells a book of coupons that offer store products at approximately one-third off. D sells each page in the book as advertising to the supplier of the product offered. These suppliers also

help with the promotion in various ways by reimbursing D. It was shown that two wholesalers that sold to retailers competing with D did not get similar allowances. D claimed that its retail competitors dealt with wholesalers rather than suppliers and so were not entitled to the aid D received from the suppliers. The FTC brought a section 2(d) action.

2) **Issue.** May a retailer who buys through a wholesaler be considered a "customer" of the original supplier?

3) **Held.** Yes. Violation of section 2(d).

   a) Section 2(d) reaches only discrimination between customers competing for resales at the same functional level. Thus, there need not be proportional equality between D and the two wholesalers.

   b) But customers competing with D at the retail level, even though not dealing directly with the suppliers, must be given the same allowances. This may be done through the wholesalers (to pass on to the retailers) and supervised by the suppliers.

4) **Dissent** (Harlan, J.). "Customer" means a party dealing with the supplier directly.

h. **FTC guidelines.** The FTC has issued guidelines for advertising allowances and other merchandising payments and services. [*See* 16 C.F.R. §240 (1980)]

TABLE OF CASES

(Page numbers of briefed cases in bold)

Notes

gilbert LAW SUMMARIES

Property
By Professor Jesse Dukeminier, U.C.L.A.

Possession (including Wild Animals, Bailments, Adverse Possession); Gifts and Sales of Personal Property; Freehold Possessory Estates; Future Interests (including Reversion, Possibility of Reverter, Right of Entry, Executory Interests, Rule Against Perpetuities); Tenancy in Common; Joint Tenancy; Tenancy by the Entirety; Condominiums; Cooperatives; Marital Property; Landlord and Tenant; Easements and Covenants; Nuisance; Rights in Airspace and Water; Right to Support; Zoning; Eminent Domain; Sale of Land (including Mortgage, Deed, Warranties of Title); Methods of Title Assurance (including Recording System, Title Registration, Title Insurance).

ISBN: 0-15-900032-7 Pages: 496 $21.95

Remedies
By Professor John A. Bauman, U.C.L.A., and Professor Kenneth H. York, Pepperdine University

Damages; Equitable Remedies (including Injunctions and Specific Performance); Restitution; Injuries to Tangible Property Interests; Injuries to Business and Commercial Interests (including Business Torts, Inducing Breach of Contract, Patent Infringement, Unfair Competition, Trade Defamation); Injuries to Personal Dignity and Related Interests (including Defamation, Privacy, Religious Status, Civil and Political Rights); Personal Injury and Death; Fraud; Duress, Undue Influence, and Unconscionable Conduct; Mistake; Breach of Contract; Unenforceable Contracts (including Statute of Frauds, Impossibility, Lack of Contractual Capacity, Illegality).

ISBN: 0-15-900325-3 Pages: 375 $20.95

Sale and Lease of Goods
By Professor Douglas J. Whaley, Ohio State University

UCC Article 2; Sales Contract (including Offer and Acceptance, Parol Evidence Rule, Statute of Frauds, Assignment and Delegation, Revision of Contract Terms); Types of Sales (including Cash Sale Transactions, Auctions, "Sale or Return" and "Sale on Approval" Transactions); Warranties (including Express and Implied Warranties, Privity, Disclaimer, Consumer Protection Statutes); Passage of Title; Performance of the Contract; Anticipatory Breach; Demand for Assurance of Performance; Unforeseen Circumstances; Risk of Loss; Remedies; Documents of Title; Lease of Goods; International Sale of Goods.

ISBN: 0-15-900219-2 Pages: 222 $17.95

Secured Transactions
By Professor Douglas J. Whaley, Ohio State University

Coverage of Article 9; Creation of a Security Interest (including Attachment, Security Agreement, Value, Debtor's Rights in the Collateral); Perfection; Filing; Priorities; Bankruptcy Proceedings and Article 9; Default Proceedings; Bulk Transfers.

ISBN: 0-15-900231-1 Pages: 213 $17.95

Securities Regulation
By Professor David H. Barber, and Professor Niels B. Schaumann, William Mitchell College of Law

Jurisdiction and Interstate Commerce; Securities Act of 1933 (including Registration Requirements and Exemptions); Securities Exchange Act of 1934 (including Rule 10b-5, Tender Offers, Proxy Solicitations Regulation, Insider Transactions); Regulation of the Securities Markets; Multinational Transactions; State Regulation of Securities Transactions.

ISBN: 0-15-9000326-1 Pages: 415 $20.95

Torts
By Professor Marc A. Franklin, Stanford University

Intentional Torts; Negligence; Strict Liability; Products Liability; Nuisance; Survival of Tort Actions; Wrongful Death; Immunity; Release and Contribution; Indemnity; Workers' Compensation; No-Fault Auto Insurance; Defamation; Invasion of Privacy; Misrepresentation; Injurious Falsehood; Interference With Economic Relations; Unjustifiable Litigation.

ISBN: 0-15-900220-6 Pages: 439 $19.95

Trusts
By Professor Edward C. Halbach, Jr., U.C. Berkeley

Elements of a Trust; Trust Creation; Transfer of Beneficiary's Interest (including Spendthrift Trusts); Charitable Trusts (including Cy Pres Doctrine); Trustee's Responsibilities, Power, Duties, and Liabilities; Duties and Liabilities of Beneficiaries; Accounting for Income and Principal; Power of Settlor to Modify or Revoke; Powers of Trustee Beneficiaries or Courts to Modify or Terminate; Termination of Trusts by Operation of Law; Resulting Trusts; Purchase Money Resulting Trusts; Constructive Trusts.

ISBN: 0-15-900039-4 Pages: 268 $18.95

Wills
By Professor Stanley M. Johanson, University of Texas

Intestate Succession; Simultaneous Death; Advancements; Disclaimer; Killer of Decedent; Elective Share Statutes; Pretermitted Child Statutes; Homestead; Formal Requisites of a Will; Revocation of Wills; Incorporation by Reference; Pour-Over Gift in Inter Vivos Trust; Joint Wills; Contracts Relating to Wills; Lapsed Gifts; Ademption; Exoneration of Liens; Will Contests; Probate and Estate Administration.

ISBN: 0-15-900040-8 Pages: 310 $19.95

Gilbert Law Summaries FIRST YEAR PROGRAM

Includes Five Gilbert Outlines:

- **Civil Procedure**
  By Professor Thomas D. Rowe, Jr. Duke University Law School, and Professor Richard L. Marcus U.C. Hastings School Of Law
- **Contracts**
  By Professor Melvin A. Eisenberg U.C. Berkeley School Of Law
- **Criminal Law**
  By Professor George E. Dix University Of Texas School Of Law
- **Property**
  By Professor Jesse Dukeminier U.C.L.A. Law School
- **Torts**
  By Professor Marc A. Franklin Stanford University Law School

Plus—

- **Gilbert's Pocket Size Law Dictionary**
  Published By Harcourt Brace
- **The 8 Secrets Of Top Exam Performance In Law School**
  By Professor Charles H. Whitebread USC Law School

All titles are packaged in a convenient carry case with handle. $120 if purchased separately. $95 if purchased as a set. Save $25.

ISBN: 0-15-900254-0 Set $95

Gilbert's Pocket Size Law Dictionary
Gilbert

A dictionary is useless if you don't have it when you need it. If the only law dictionary you own is a thick, bulky one, you'll probably leave it at home most of the time — and if you need to know a definition while you're at school, you're out of luck!

With Gilbert's Pocket Size Law Dictionary, you'll have any definition you need, when you need it. Just pop Gilbert's dictionary into your pocket or purse, and you'll have over 4,000 legal terms and phrases at your fingertips. Gilbert's dictionary also includes a section on law school shorthand, common abbreviations, Latin and French legal terms, periodical abbreviations, and governmental abbreviations.

With Gilbert's Pocket Size Law Dictionary, you'll never be caught at a loss for words!

Available in your choice of 5 colors

- **Brown** ISBN: 0-15-900252-4 $7.95
- **Blue** ISBN: 0-15-900362-3 $7.95
- **Burgundy** ISBN: 0-15-900366-0 $7.95
- **Green** ISBN: 0-15-900365-2 $7.95

Limited Edition: Simulated Alligator Skin Cover

- **Black** ISBN: 0-15-900364-4 $7.95

The Eight Secrets Of Top Exam Performance In Law School
Charles Whitebread

Wouldn't it be great to know exactly what your professor's looking for on your exam? To find out everything that's expected of you, so that you don't waste your time doing anything other than maximizing your grades?

In his easy-to-read, refreshing style, nationally recognized exam expert Professor Charles Whitebread will teach you the eight secrets that will add precious points to every exam answer you write. You'll learn the three keys to handling any essay exam question, and how to add points to your score by making time work for you, not against you. You'll learn flawless issue spotting, and discover how to organize your answer for maximum possible points. You'll find out how the hidden traps in "IRAC" trip up most students… but not you! You'll learn the techniques for digging up the exam questions your professor will ask, before your exam. You'll put your newly-learned skills to the test with sample exam questions, and you can measure your performance against model answers. And there's even a special section that helps you master the skills necessary to crush any exam, not just a typical essay exam — unusual exams like open book, take home, multiple choice, short answer, and policy questions.

"The Eight Secrets of Top Exam Performance in Law School" gives you all the tools you need to maximize your grades — quickly and easily!

ISBN: 0-15-900323-7 $9.95

Call 1-800-787-8717 or visit our web site at http://www.gilbertlaw.com for more information.

Evidence
By Professor Faust F. Rossi
Cornell Law School

TOPICS COVERED: Relevance; Insurance; Remedial Measures; Settlement Offers; Causation; State Of Mind; Rebuttal; Habit; Character Evidence; "MIMIC" Rule; Documentary Evidence; Authentication; Best Evidence Rule; Parol Evidence; Competency; Dead Man Statutes; Examination Of Witnesses; Present Recollection Revived; Past Recollection Recorded; Opinion Testimony; Lay And Expert Witness; Learned Treatises; Impeachment; Collateral Matters; Bias, Interest Or Motive; Rehabilitation; Privileges; Hearsay And Exceptions.
5 Audio Cassettes
ISBN: 0-15-900282-6 $45.95

Family Law
Professor Roger E. Schechter
George Washington University Law School

TOPICS COVERED: National Scope Of Family Law; Marital Relationship; Consequences Of Marriage; Formalities And Solemnization; Common Law Marriage; Impediments; Marriage And Conflict Of Laws; Non-Marital Relationship; Law Of Names; Void And Voidable Marriages; Marital Breakdown; Annulment And Defenses; Divorce — Fault And No-Fault; Separation; Jurisdiction For Divorce; Migratory Divorce; Full Faith And Credit; Temporary Orders; Economic Aspects Of Marital Breakdown; Property Division; Community Property Principles; Equitable Distribution; Marital And Separate Property; Types Of Property Interests; Equitable Reimbursement; Alimony; Modification And Termination Of Alimony; Child Support; Health Insurance; Enforcement Of Orders; Antenuptial And Postnuptial Agreements; Separation And Settlement Agreements; Custody Jurisdiction And Awards; Modification Of Custody; Visitation Rights; Termination Of Parental Rights; Adoption; Illegitimacy; Paternity Actions.
3 Audio Cassettes
ISBN: 0-15-900283-4 $39.95

Federal Courts
Professor John C. Jeffries
University of Virginia School of Law

TOPICS COVERED: History Of The Federal Court System; "Court Or Controversy" And Justiciability; Congressional Power Over Federal Court Jurisdiction; Supreme Court Jurisdiction; District Court Subject Matter Jurisdiction—Federal Question Jurisdiction, Diversity Jurisdiction And Admiralty Jurisdiction; Pendent And Ancillary Jurisdiction; Removal Jurisdiction; Venue; Forum Non Conveniens; Law Applied In The Federal Courts; Federal Law In The State Courts; Collateral Relations Between Federal And State Courts; The Eleventh Amendment And State Sovereign Immunity.
3 Audio Cassettes
ISBN: 0-15-900296-6 $39.95

Federal Income Tax
By Professor Cheryl D. Block
George Washington University Law School

TOPICS COVERED: Administrative Reviews; Tax Formula; Gross Income; Exclusions For Gifts; Inheritances; Personal Injuries; Tax Basis Rules; Divorce Tax Rules; Assignment Of Income; Business Deductions; Investment Deductions; Passive Loss And Interest Limitation Rules; Capital Gains & Losses; Section 1031, 1034, and 121 Deferred/Non Taxable Transactions.
4 Audio Cassettes
ISBN: 0-15-900284-2 $45.95

Future Interests
By Dean Catherine L. Carpenter
Southwestern University Law School

TOPICS COVERED: Rule Against Perpetuities; Class Gifts; Estates In Land; Rule In Shelley's Case; Future Interests In Transferor and Transferee; Life Estates; Defeasible Fees; Doctrine Of Worthier Title; Doctrine Of Merger; Fee Simple Estates; Restraints On Alienation; Power Of Appointment; Rules Of Construction.
2 Audio Cassettes
ISBN: 0-15-900285-0 $24.95

Law School ABC's
By Professor Jennifer S. Kamita
Loyola Marymount Law School, and
Professor Rodney O. Fong
Golden Gate University School of Law

TOPICS COVERED: Introduction; Casebooks; Hornbooks; Selecting Commercial Materials; Briefing; Review; ABC's Of A Lecture; Taking Notes; Lectures & Notes Examples; Study Groups; ABC's Of Outlining; Rules; Outlining Hypothetical; Outlining Assignment And Review; Introduction To Essay Writing; "IRAC"; Call Of The Question Exercise; Issue Spotting Exercise; IRAC Defining & Writing Exercise; Form Tips; ABC's Of Exam Writing; Exam Writing Hypothetical; Practice Exam And Review; Preparation Hints; Exam Diagnostics & Writing Problems.
4 Audio Cassettes
ISBN: 0-15-900286-9 $45.95

Law School Exam Writing
By Professor Charles H. Whitebread
USC School of Law

TOPICS COVERED: With "Law School Exam Writing," you'll learn the secrets of law school test taking . In this fascinating lecture, Professor Whitebread leads you step-by-step through his innovative system, so that you know exactly how to tackle your essay exams without making point draining mistakes. You'll learn how to read questions so you don't miss important issues; how to organize your answer; how to use limited exam time to your maximum advantage; and even how to study for exams.
1 Audio Cassette
ISBN: 0-15-900287-7 $19.95

Professional Responsibility
By Professor Erwin Chemerinsky
USC School of Law

TOPICS COVERED: Regulation of Attorneys; Bar Admission; Unauthorized Practice; Competency; Discipline; Judgment; Lawyer-Client Relationship; Representation; Withdrawal; Conflicts; Disqualification; Clients; Client Interests; Successive And Effective Representation; Integrity; Candor; Confidences; Secrets; Past And Future Crimes; Perjury; Communications; Witnesses; Jurors; The Court; The Press; Trial Tactics; Prosecutors; Market; Solicitation; Advertising; Law Firms; Fees; Client Property; Conduct; Political Activity.
3 Audio Cassettes
ISBN: 0-15-900371-7 $39.95

Real Property
By Professor Paula A. Franzese
Seton Hall Law School

TOPICS COVERED: Estates—Fee Simple; Fee Tail; Life Estate; Co-Tenancy—Joint Tenancy; Tenancy In Common; Tenancy By The Entirety; Landlord-Tenant Relationship; Liability For Condition Of Premises; Assignment & Sublease; Easements; Restrictive Covenants; Adverse Possession; Recording Acts; Conveyancing; Personal Property—Finders; Bailments; Gifts; Future Interests.
4 Audio Cassettes
ISBN: 0-15-900289-3 $45.95

Remedies
By Professor William A. Fletcher
University of California at Berkeley, Boalt Hall School of Law

TOPICS COVERED: Damages; Restitution; Equitable Remedies (including Constructive Trust, Equitable Lien, Injunction, and Specific Performance); Tracing; Rescission and Reformation; Specific topics include Injury and Destruction of Personal Property; Conversion; Injury to Real Property; Trespass; Ouster; Nuisance; Defamation; Trade Libel; Inducing Breach of Contract; Contracts to Purchase Personal Property; Contracts to Purchase Real Property (including Equitable Conversion); Construction Contracts; and Personal Service Contracts.
3 Audio Cassettes
ISBN: 0-15-900353-9 $45.95

Sales & Lease of Goods
By Professor Michael I. Spak
Chicago Kent College of Law

TOPICS COVERED: Goods; Contract Formation; Firm Offers; Statute Of Frauds; Modification; Parol Evidence; Code Methodology; Tender; Payment; Identification; Risk Of Loss; Warranties; Merchantability; Fitness; Disclaimers; Consumer Protection; Remedies; Anticipatory Repudiation; Third Party Rights.
3 Audio Cassettes
ISBN: 0-15-900291-5 $39.95

Secured Transactions
By Professor Michael I. Spak
Chicago Kent College of Law

TOPICS COVERED: Collateral; Inventory; Intangibles; Proceeds; Security Agreements; Attachment; After-Acquired Property; Perfection; Filing; Priorities; Purchase Money Security Interests; Fixtures; Rights Upon Default; Self-Help; Sale; Constitutional Issues.
3 Audio Cassettes
ISBN: 0-15-900292-3 $39.95

Torts
By Professor Richard J. Conviser
Chicago Kent College of Law

TOPICS COVERED: Essay Exam Techniques; Intentional Torts—Assault; Battery; False Imprisonment; Intentional Infliction Of Emotional Distress; Trespass To Land; Trespass To Chattels; Conversion; Defenses: Defamation—Libel; Slander; Defenses; First Amendment Concerns; Invasion Of Right Of Privacy; Misrepresentation; Negligence—Duty; Breach; Actual And Proximate Causation; Damages; Defenses; Strict Liability, Products Liability; Nuisance; General Tort Considerations.
4 Audio Cassettes
ISBN: 0-15-900185-4 $45.95

Wills & Trusts
By Professor Stanley M. Johanson
University of Texas School of Law

TOPICS COVERED: Attested Wills; Holographic Wills; Negligence; Revocation; Changes On Face Of Will; Lapsed Gifts; Negative Bequest Rule; Nonprobate Assets; Intestate Succession; Advancements; Elective Share; Will Contests; Capacity; Undue Influence; Creditors' Rights; Creation Of Trust; Revocable Trusts; Pourover Gifts; Charitable Trusts; Resulting Trusts; Constructive Trusts; Spendthrift Trusts; Self-Dealing; Prudent Investments; Trust Accounting; Termination; Powers Of Appointment.
4 Audio Cassettes
ISBN: 0-15-900294-X $45.95

Law School Legends Series FIRST YEAR PROGRAM

Includes Five Law School Legends Titles:

- **Civil Procedure**
  By Professor Richard D. Freer
  Emory University Law School
- **Contracts**
  By Professor Michael I. Spak
  Chicago Kent College Of Law
- **Criminal Law**
  By Professor Charles H. Whitebread
  USC School of Law
- **Real Property**
  By Professor Paula A. Franzese
  Seton Hall Law School
- **Torts**
  By Professor Richard J. Conviser
  Chicago Kent College of Law

Plus—

- **Law School Exam Writing**
  By Professor Charles H. Whitebread
  USC Law School

All titles are packaged in a convenient carry case. $250 if purchased separately. $195 if purchased as a set. Save $55.

ISBN: 0-15-900306-7 Set $195

NEW!
Call for release dates

Antitrust
ISBN# 0-15-900341-5 $39.95

Estate & Gift Tax
ISBN# 0-15-900354-7 $39.95

Labor Law
ISBN# 0-15-900357-1 $39.95

Product Liability
ISBN# 0-15-900358-X $39.95

Securities Regulation
ISBN# 0-15-900359-8 $39.95

If you accidentally damage a tape within five years from the date of purchase we'll replace it for FREE— No questions asked!

GILBERT LAW AUDIO TAPES · FIVE YEAR · TAPE REPLACEMENT GUARANTEE

Call 1-800-787-8717 or visit our web site at http://www.gilbertlaw.com for more information.

100% Comprehensive, 100% Authoritative, 100% of What You Need

CASEBRIEFS FOR WINDOWS

Casebriefs Interactive Software For Windows

As a law student you can't afford to waste a minute. That's why you need Casebriefs Software. With Casebriefs you simply click on the name of the case you're looking for, and you instantly have an expert brief of it at your fingertips! The facts. The issue. The holding. The rationale. Expert commentary for each and every case. You'll get everything you need, whether you're preparing for class or studying for your final exam!

When you use Casebriefs, you can focus solely on the cases covered in your casebook, or you can use the Case Library, which includes briefs of all of the major cases from every major casebook. The Case Library is ideal for researching cases for writing assignments, Moot Court briefs, Law Review and other periodicals.

With Casebriefs, searching for cases is a breeze. You can search by topic. You can search alphabetically. You can search the cases in the order in which they appear in your casebook. You can even enter the date you'll cover different cases in class, and sort them by those dates. No matter how you want to look for a case, Casebriefs will help you find it instantly!

For each brief, you can add your own notes, or leave it "as is." Whether you customize the briefs or not, you can print them out and take them to class with you. You can even configure Casebriefs to access Lexis/Nexis and Westlaw directly from the Casebriefs screen (with Lexis/Nexis or Westlaw software and account). Whether you want to compare your own briefs to expert briefs, fill in gaps in your class notes, or research cases for your legal writing class, moot court, law review or other periodicals—Casebriefs is the source you'll turn to, over and over again!

- **Administrative Law**
  Includes briefs of all of the major cases from the Breyer, Gellhorn and Schwartz casebooks, many of the major cases from the Bonfield and Mashaw casebooks, plus a Case Library.
  ISBN# 0-15-900190-0 $27.95
- **Civil Procedure**
  Includes briefs of all of the major cases from the Cound, Field, Hazard, Rosenberg and Yeazell casebooks, many of the major cases from the Marcus and Freer casebooks, plus a Case Library.
  ISBN# 0-15-900191-9 $27.95
- **Conflict Of Laws**
  Includes briefs of all of the major cases from the Cramton and Reese casebooks, many of the major cases from the Brilmayer casebook, plus a Case Library.
  ISBN# 0-15-900192-7 $27.95
- **Constitutional Law**
  Includes briefs of all of the major cases from the Brest, Cohen, Lockhart, Rotunda and Stone casebooks, plus a Case Library.
  ISBN# 0-15-900193-5 $27.95
- **Contracts**
  Includes briefs of all of the major cases from the Calamari, Dawson, Farnsworth, Fuller, Kessler and Murphy casebooks, many of the major cases from the Crandall, Hamilton, Knapp, Murray, Rosett and Vernon casebooks, plus a Case Library.
  ISBN# 0-15-900194-3 $27.95
- **Corporations**
  Includes briefs of all of the major cases from the Cary, Choper, Hamilton and Vagts casebooks, many of the major cases from the O'Kelley and Solomon casebooks, plus a Case Library.
  ISBN# 0-15-900195-1 $27.95
- **Criminal Law**
  Includes briefs of all of the major cases from the Boyce, Dix, Johnson, Kadish and La Fave casebooks, many of the major cases from the Dressler, Foote, Kaplan and Weinreb casebooks, plus a Case Library.
  ISBN# 0-15-900196-X $27.95
- **Criminal Procedure**
  Includes briefs of all of the major cases from the Kamisar casebook, many of the major cases from the Allen, Haddad and Saltzburg casebooks, plus a Case Library.
  ISBN# 0-15-900197-8 $27.95
- **Evidence**
  Includes briefs of all of the major cases from the Waltz, Sutton, and Weinstein casebooks, many of the major cases from the Strong, Green, Lempert and Mueller casebooks, plus a Case Library.
  ISBN# 0-15-900198-6 $27.95
- **Family Law**
  Includes briefs of all of the major cases from the Areen casebook, many of the major cases from the Clark, Ellman, Krause and Wadlington casebooks, plus a Case Library.
  ISBN# 0-15-900199-4 $27.95
- **Income Tax**
  Includes briefs of all of the major cases from the Andrews, Freeland and Klein casebooks, many of the major cases from the Graetz casebook, plus a Case Library.
  ISBN# 0-15-900200-1 $27.95
- **Property**
  Includes briefs of all of the major cases from the Browder, Casner, Cribbet, Dukeminier and Rabin casebooks, many of the major cases from the Donahue, Haar and Kurtz casebooks, plus a Case Library.
  ISBN# 0-15-900201-X $27.95
- **Remedies**
  Includes briefs of all of the major cases from the Re and York casebooks, many of the major cases from the Laycock, Leavell and Shoben casebooks, plus a Case Library.
  ISBN# 0-15-900202-8 $27.95
- **Torts**
  Includes briefs of all of the major cases from the Epstein, Franklin, Henderson, Keeton and Prosser casebooks, many of the major cases from the Dobbs and Shulman casebooks, plus a Case Library.
  ISBN# 0-15-900203-6 $27.95
- **Wills, Trusts & Estates**
  Includes briefs of all of the major cases from the Dukeminier casebook plus a Case Library.
  ISBN# 0-15-900204-4 $27.95

Welcome to gilbertlaw.com

- Pre-Law Center
- Bookstore
- Past Exam Library
- Links to Law Sites
- Welcome Center
- Employment Center
- Wanted! Student Marketing Reps
- 1st Year Survival Manual
- Taking the Bar Exam?

GilbertLaw.com is the site that helps law students study smarter. Shop for study aids in the bookstore or get ready for your first year with the 1st Year Survival Manual.

http://www.gilbertlaw.com

Dictionary of Legal Terms

Gilbert's Dictionary Of Legal Terms Software:
Features over 3,500 legal terms and phrases, law school shorthand, common abbreviations, Latin and French legal terms, periodical abbreviations, and governmental abbreviations.
Includes Free Pocket Size Law Dictionary!

ISBN: 0-15-900250-8	**Macintosh**	**$27.95**
ISBN: 0-15-900249-4	**Windows**	**$27.95**

Call 1-800-787-8717 or visit our web site at http://www.gilbertlaw.com for more information.

Employment Guides

A collection of best selling titles that help you identify and reach your career goals.

The National Directory Of Legal Employers
National Association for Law Placement

The National Directory of Legal Employers brings you a universe of vital information about 1,000 of the nation's top legal employers— *in one convenient volume!*

It includes:

- Over 22,000 job openings.
- The names, addresses and phone numbers of hiring partners.
- Listings of firms by state, size, kind and practice area.
- What starting salaries are for full time, part time, and summer associates, plus a detailed description of firm benefits.
- The number of employees by gender and race, as well as the number of employees with disabilities.
- A detailed narrative of each firm, plus much more!

The National Directory Of Legal Employers has been the best kept secret of top legal career search professionals for over a decade. Now, for the first time, it is available in a format specifically designed for law students and new graduates. *Pick up your copy of the Directory today!*

ISBN: 0-15-900248-6 $39.95

Proceed With Caution: A Diary Of The First Year At One Of America's Largest, Most Prestigious Law Firms
William R. Keates

Prestige. Famous clients. High-profile cases. Not to mention a starting salary approaching six figures.

In *Proceed With Caution*, the author takes you behind the scenes, to show you what it's really like to be a junior associate at a huge law firm. After graduating from an Ivy League law school, he took a job as an associate with one of New York's blue-chip law firms.

He also did something not many people do. He kept a diary, where he spilled out his day-to-day life at the firm in graphic detail.

Proceed With Caution excerpts the diary, from his first day at the firm to the day he quit. From the splashy benefits, to the nitty-gritty on the work junior associates do, to the grind of long and unpredictable hours, to the stress that eventually made him leave the firm — he tells story after story that will make you feel as though you're living the life of a new associate.

Whether you're considering a career with a large firm, or you're just curious about what life at the top firms is all about — *Proceed With Caution* is a must read!

ISBN: 0-15-900181-1 $17.95

Guerrilla Tactics for Getting the Legal Job of Your Dreams
Kimm Alayne Walton, J.D.

Whether you're looking for a summer clerkship or your first permanent job after school, this revolutionary book is the key to getting the job of your dreams!

Guerrilla Tactics for Getting the Legal Job of Your Dreams leads you step-by-step through everything you need to do to nail down that perfect job! You'll learn hundreds of simple-to-use strategies that will get you exactly where you want to go. You'll Learn:

- The seven magic opening words in cover letters that ensure you'll get a response.
- The secret to successful interviews every time.
- Killer answers to the toughest interview questions they'll ever ask you.
- Plus Much More!

Guerrilla Tactics features the best strategies from the country's most innovative law school career advisors. The strategies in *Guerrilla Tactics* are so powerful that it even comes with a guarantee: Follow the advice in the book, and within one year of graduation you'll have the job of your dreams… or your money back!

Pick up a copy of *Guerrilla Tactics* today…and you'll be on your way to the job of your dreams!

ISBN: 0-15-900317-2 $24.95

Beyond L.A. Law: Inspiring Stories of People Who've Done Fascinating Things With A Law Degree
National Association for Law Placement

Anyone who watches television knows that being a lawyer means working your way up through a law firm — right?

Wrong!

Beyond L.A. Law gives you a fascinating glimpse into the lives of people who've broken the "lawyer" mold. They come from a variety of backgrounds — some had prior careers, others went straight through college and law school, and yet others have overcome poverty and physical handicaps. They got their degrees from all different kinds of law schools, all over the country. But they have one thing in common: they've all pursued their own, unique vision.

As you read their stories, you'll see how they beat the odds to succeed. You'll learn career tips and strategies that work, from people who've put them to the test. And you'll find fascinating insights that you can apply to your own dream — whether it's a career in law, or anything else!

From Representing Baseball In Australia. To International Finance. To Children's Advocacy. To Directing a Nonprofit Organization. To Entrepreneur.

If You Think Getting A Law Degree Means Joining A Traditional Law Firm — Think Again!.

ISBN: 0-15-900182-X $17.95

America's Greatest Places To Work With A Law Degree
Kimm Alayne Walton, J.D.

"Where do your happiest graduates work?"

That's the question that author Kimm Alayne Walton asked of law school administrators around the country. Their responses revealed the hundreds of wonderful employers profiled in *America's Greatest Places To Work With A Law Degree.*

In this remarkable book, you'll get to know an incredible variety of great places to work, including:

- Glamorous sports and entertainment employers – the jobs that sound as though they would be great, and they are!
- The 250 best law firms to work for between 20 and 600 attorneys.
- Companies where law school graduates love to work and not just as in-house counsel.
- Wonderful public interest employers – the "white knight" jobs that are so incredibly satisfying.
- Court-related positions, where lawyers entertain fascinating issues, tremendous variety, and an enjoyable lifestyle.
- Outstanding government jobs, at the federal, state and local level.

Beyond learning about incredible employers, you'll discover:

- The ten traits that define a wonderful place to work…the sometimes surprising qualities that outstanding employers share.
- How to handle law school debt, when your dream job pays less than you think you need to make.
- How to find – and get! – great jobs at firms with fewer than 20 attorneys.

And no matter where you work, you'll learn expert tips for making the most of your job. You'll learn the specific strategies that distinguish people headed for the top…how to position yourself for the most interesting, high-profile work…how to handle difficult personalities… how to negotiate for more money…and what to do now to help you get your next great job!

ISBN: 0-15-900180-3 $24.95

Presented by The National Law Journal

The Job Goddess column is a weekly feature of the *National Law Journal's Law Journal Extra*, and is written by Kimm Alayne Walton, author of the national best seller *Guerrilla Tactics For Getting The Legal Job Of Your Dreams.* View recent columns or e-mail the Job Goddess with your job search questions on the Internet at www.gilbertlaw.com

Call 1-800-787-8717 or visit our web site at http://www.gilbertlaw.com for more information.